HAND PSYCHOLOGY

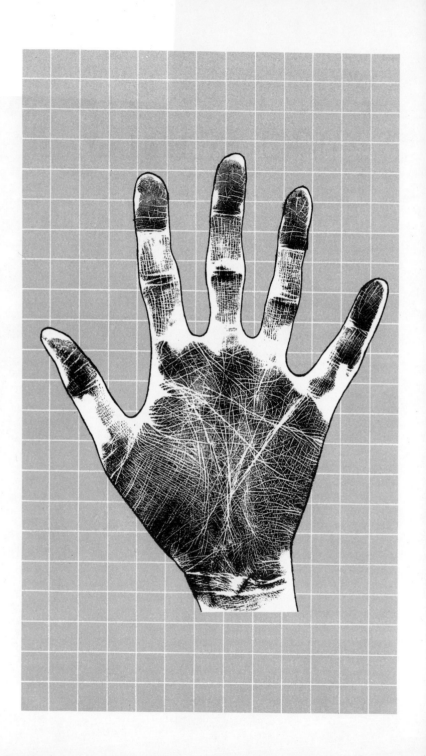

A NEW INSIGHT INTO SOLVING YOUR PROBLEMS

HAND PSYCHOLOGY

ANDREW FITZHERBERT

ANGUS
& ROBERTSON
PUBLISHERS

To the fellows and members of the Society
for the Study of Physiological Patterns
and my friends and co-workers
in the British Astrological and Psychic Society

ANGUS & ROBERTSON PUBLISHERS

Unit 4, Eden Park, 31 Waterloo Road,
North Ryde, NSW, Australia 2113, and
16 Golden Square, London W1R 4BN,
United Kingdom

First published in Australia
by Angus & Robertson Publishers in 1986
First published in the United Kingdom
by Angus & Robertson (UK) Ltd in 1986
Reprinted 1987

Copyright © Andrew Fitzherbert 1986

National Library of Australia
Cataloguing-in-publication data.

Fitzherbert, Andrew, 1949-   .
   Hand psychology.

   Bibliography.
   ISBN 0 207 15131 8.

   1. Palmistry. 2. Self-actualization (Psychology). I. Title.
133.6

Designed by April Briscoe
Typeset in 10pt Trump Mediaeval
by Setrite Typesetters
Printed in Singapore

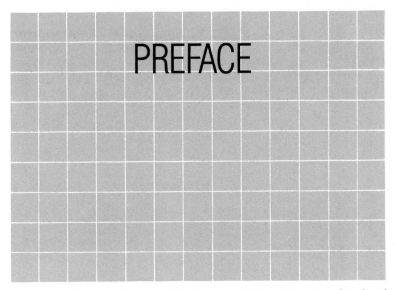

PREFACE

Experienced palmists may find some of the ideas in this book quite new. They will also notice that many traditional ideas are not mentioned, particularly the Seven Hand Types and also the mounts of the hand. This is intentional. I have omitted much that my experience has shown to be misleading or simply untrue.

Few of the new ideas are completely original. The great emphasis I place on the index and little fingers is derived from the work of the German palmist, Julius Spier, and Mr Fred Gettings. Mr Gettings is also responsible for the fourfold classification system. The information on dermatoglyphics comes from the Society for the Study of Physiological Patterns, as presented in Beryl Hutchinson's book, *Your Life in Your Hands*.

During the 22 years that I have been studying hands, I have collected nearly every book on palmistry ever published in English (over 300), as well as many in French, German and Spanish. A lot of palmistry books are just a rehash of earlier writers. Others put forward theories that do not hold up in practice. I have tested them all and selected everything that works. In addition, I have read thousands of hands in five countries and have corresponded with palmists around the world. I should be pleased to hear from other palmists at any time for the further exchange of information and data.

Doctors and psychologists may wonder whether there is any scientific research in support of hand psychology. About 20 papers have been published in reputable journals. There are also university theses from France, Israel, England, America and Australia. All this research is assessed and described in Geoff

Dean's forthcoming book, *Recent Advances in Palmistry*, listed in the bibliography. If any doctor or psychologist would like to carry out further research, both Dr Dean and I would be happy to give advice on such things as research methodology and information on the work that has already been done.

CONTENTS

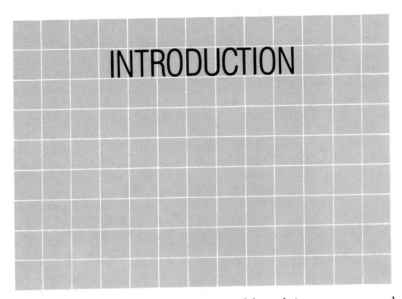

INTRODUCTION

Hand psychology is a new, effective tool for solving your personal problems. The answers to many nagging difficulties which crop up day to day are, quite literally, right there in your hands. Half the problems which send people racing to psychologists, counsellors and other high-priced experts can be solved by a study of the human hand.

Your hands reveal a vast amount of psychological information about you. By interpreting and applying this information, you can help straighten out not only your own life but also the lives of family and friends. Your home, work, leisure interests and personal relationships can all benefit from hand psychology.

The traditional name for the study of hands is palmistry. But palmistry has earned a bad name in North America due to its association with gypsies and con artists. In England, palmistry is more highly respected. "Scientific palmistry" is a term often used to distinguish the real study of the hand from the nonsensical babble of the gypsy fortune-teller.

The term "scientific palmistry" means exactly what it says: the scientific study of the hand. Scientists and laymen in many countries have devoted years to this work. In laboratories and research institutes in England, India, Australia and the United States, endless experiments and tests have been carried out to establish the validity of this science. Now at last, there is a book which will tell you how to apply it.

How does your hand come to reveal so much information? The answers are quite complex. Much of your character is genetic, that is, inherited from your ancestors. These inherited traits are reflected in your finger prints and in the other skin ridge patterns of your palm. Other aspects of your character are determined by your body itself, particularly by your hormones. These natural chemicals have a major influence over your behaviour and they also affect the shape of your hands. Such things as the length of each finger and the shape of your palm are largely determined by body chemicals.

A third way in which the hands reflect character is through the close link between the hand and the brain. Your hands are controlled by a larger area of the brain cortex than any other part of the body. The lines of your palm are not created by folding, but by the nervous system itself. Your hand is the direct servant of the mind, or as one expert put it, ''The hand is the visible part of the brain.'' Through the nervous system, the hand takes on a direct symbolic relationship with the mind.

Most books on scientific palmistry to date have been neither clear nor interesting. This book has been especially designed in the most interesting way possible. It is in two sections.

1. Chapters I to VIII, the first section, deal with problem solving through hand psychology. Chapter I is introductory while the others take up specific areas of human life to show how your hands can help deal with them. Each chapter of this section can be read separately and without any prior knowledge of scientific palmistry.

2. Chapter IX forms the second section and is composed of a set of lessons. It is for those who want to go further. It is a ''teach yourself'' program, complete with questions and answers, examples and step-by-step instructions. If you read this section last, you should find it very easy to assimilate because you will have encountered many of the ideas in the section on problem solving.

There is a certain amount of repetition in this book, and it has been done intentionally, to help you learn. Hand psychology, or scientific palmistry, is the most exciting and personal of all self-discovery systems. You can apply it both to yourself and to others. With the aid of this book, you can learn more about a person in a few minutes' study of their hands than by hours of questioning. The value of this knowledge can hardly be overestimated.

C H A P T E R   I

AN OUTLINE AND HISTORY OF HAND PSYCHOLOGY

Hold up your hands and take a good look at them. What do you see? "That's easy," you say. "Four fingers, a thumb and lines all over my palm."

Good. Now close your eyes. Without looking, see whether you can tell me if your third finger is longer or shorter than your index finger. Bet you can't. Still with your eyes closed, tell me whether the shape of the tip of your little finger is the same as that of your ring finger. If you can, congratulations. Only about one person in a thousand is well acquainted with his or her own hands.

"What are you, a palmist?" you ask, rather annoyed. "Can you tell me how long I'm going to live and when I will get married?" You may be holding your palm out at this point. "What about my Head Line? Am I intelligent?"

Yes, I am a palmist, also known as a hand analyst. Believe it or not, those lines in your palm are not that important for my analysis. I study every single part of your hand. The shape of your thumb and the length of each finger give me vital clues about the real you. It may shock you to know that your Life Line and Fate Line do not give away as much about you as your fingerprints do. These amazing patterns on the tips of your fingers are your genetic inheritance.

Look carefully at the fingerprint on your index finger. Compare it with the patterns on your other fingers and you will almost certainly discover that they are not the same. Some fingerprints are made up of concentric circles while others are more of a loop shape. Still other fingerprints resemble a bridge or arch. Very few people have the same sort of print on all fingers.

1

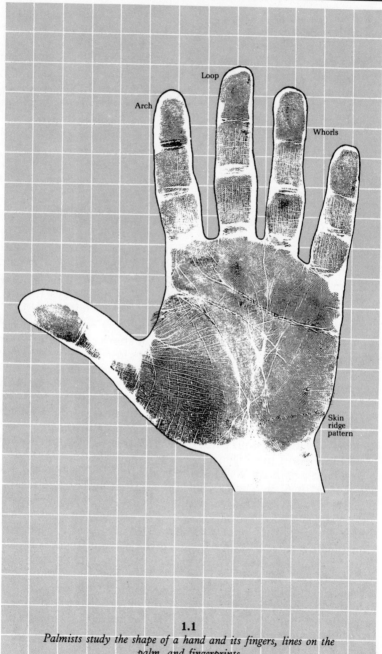

1.1
Palmists study the shape of a hand and its fingers, lines on the palm, and fingerprints

In diagram 1.1 the first three fingerprints are an arch, a loop and a whorl respectively. If you look carefully at the lower, outer corner of the palm, you will also see the skin ridges forming a distinct pattern. The Heart Line (just under the fingers), the Head Line (across the middle of the palm) and the Life Line (around the thumb) are all quite clear. The Fate Line, running upwards through the palm, is not so clear-cut. It is made up of two irregular pieces.

There are three aspects of the hand which a hand analyst must study to get a full picture of the owner.

1. The shape of the hand and the fingers.
2. The lines on the palm.
3. The fingerprints.

Check out your fingerprints in a good light (sunlight is best) and you will notice that they are actually composed of tiny furrows in the skin. These are known as skin ridges and they cover the whole of your palms and the soles of your feet. Yet they are found nowhere else on the body. On the fingertips and sometimes in the palm of the hand, these ridges form distinct patterns. The study of these patterns is called ''dermatoglyphics'' and it can give us such diverse information about someone as whether he keeps secrets, is a born cynic or has a talent for playing stringed instruments. Imagine being able to give a complete stranger intimate details about himself and you will understand the great fascination of dermatoglyphics.

All of the aspects of your hands that I have mentioned reveal a wealth of information about yourself. Talents and abilities, strengths and weaknesses of character, are all revealed by your hands. The way you behave, your attitude to sex, work and recreation — all of these are right there in your hands. ''But what about my future?'' you ask. ''When am I getting married again?''

I can offer something much more useful than predicting the date of your next marriage. From your hands, I can tell you why the last marriage went wrong and what you need to know to make the next one work better. I can tell you what sort of person you are likely to marry and what sort of relationship it is likely to be. The study of your hands can help you to understand yourself and others.

Isn't that more useful than making vague predictions about the future? With predictions, you must wait to find out if they are true, so they are seldom useful to you. With the psychology of the hand and the knowledge it gives, you can *make* your life go the way you want it to. You will also acquire insight into other people simply by looking at their hands.

In my professional work as a hand analyst, I have seen

thousands of people with problems — work problems, romantic problems, financial problems, health problems, the list is endless. In virtually every case, by studying the hands, I can tell what the problem is and how it should be dealt with. Often, I can make predictions based entirely on the psychological patterns that I see. I have told a housewife that she should write novels and her books are in shops today. I told another that her children would become doctors and lawyers and they did. I advised an army sergeant that he would quit the forces and open his own business. He visited me two years later to tell me all about it. I have predicted travel, fame, wealth, sickness, accidents and countless other things all by assessing the psychological information in the hands. And unlike predictions based on glimpses into the future, these psychologically-based predictions are almost always right.

The lines in your palm certainly do contain signs relating to specific events in your past and future. The Life Line and Fate Line in particular often reveal precise dates of things that have happened or are yet to happen in your life. But that is subject matter for another book I have yet to write, dealing with the divinatory side of palmistry. In it I will set out all the rules about determining past and future events. Sure, it's fascinating stuff. But the contents of this book are far more intriguing since they help you to shape your own future.

Where did hand psychology come from? Its roots go back thousands of years, to when humans searched for clues about their future. These early fortune-tellers peered at the stars, inspected the intestines of slaughtered animals and drew omens from the weather. In India, some three thousand years ago, certain sages looked at the palms of the hand and saw patterns of lines. These too, they reasoned, must contain indications of the future. Using their imagination, they made up all sorts of fanciful rules. "If the lines in your palm form the shape of an elephant, you will be a powerful leader. If they form a bow, you will be a warrior." The fact that most people have enough lines to form any shape you care to name never occurred to them. They called their system "Samudrika", which is Sanskrit for "lucky marks and lines."

From ancient India, this superstitious practice spread to China when the first Buddhist missionary arrived. The Chinese noticed that the hands of rich or cultured people looked different from the hands of peasants. Accordingly, they worked out their own system of palmistry based on the Indian superstitions, with some personal observations tossed in.

In time, the Arab civilisation made contact with India too,

resulting in the great Moghul Empires of Northern India which adhered to the religion of Islam. The idea of palmistry was passed on to the Arab nations where the study of hands became associated with the religious and mystical beliefs of the people. The hand was seen to be an important religious symbol which could be used to remind the people about the nature of God.

In the late Middle Ages, Europe launched the Crusades to liberate Palestine from Arab control. The Crusades led to the ending of the so-called Dark Ages when the European invaders came into contact with Arab knowledge. Medicine, science, mathematics and other subjects were brought to Europe with the return of the Crusaders. Palmistry came too.

European scholars of the 11th century jotted down a few notes on palmistry based on Arabic ideas. Before long, astrologers and students of the occult sciences took up the subject, adding their own ideas. By the year 1600, astrology hit the heights of popularity across Europe. Palmistry and other forms of divination were popular as well. Unfortunately, the palmistry books contained little more than the superstitions started in India two thousand years before. Such outrageous nonsense as, "If you have a cross marked on your thumb, you will be hanged for murder," could be found in their pages. Not surprisingly, few people took it seriously.

Within the next century, the dawn of modern science took place. People learned to investigate, to experiment and to test the traditions of the past. Astrology, palmistry and similar subjects were forgotten. The Age of Enlightenment had arrived. Only the wandering gypsies maintained a tradition of fortune-telling. "Cross my palm with silver," the gypsy woman would whisper to an unsuspecting maid, "and I will tell you your husband and how many children you will have." While she made up stories, the gypsy male was busy extracting cutlery from the kitchen or escaping with a chicken under his arm.

Early in the 19th century, a young French army officer had a run-in with a gypsy in Spain. He was Captain Casimir D'Arpentigny of Napoleon's army and he was destined to change the history of palmistry. When the gypsy flattered him by reading his hand, he wondered if there might be something in it.

Years later, after retirement, he carried out some investigations. It happened that he lived near a rich landowner who had married a young woman with different interests from his own. The gentleman was intrigued by science while his wife loved the arts. Once a week, she invited friends over, a lively group of artists, painters and musicians. Also weekly, but on a different day, the husband had his own friends round, the scientists, engineers and

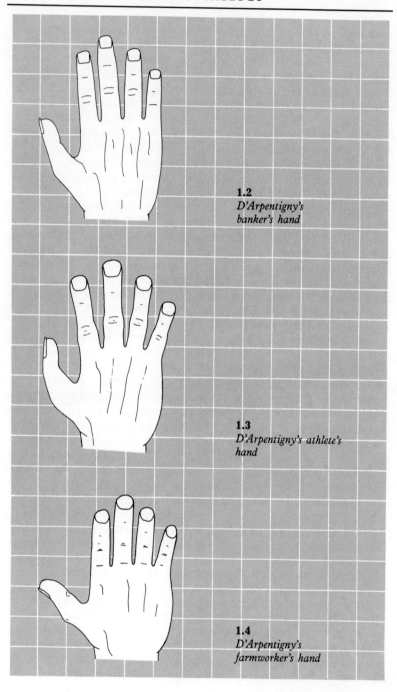

1.2
D'Arpentigny's banker's hand

1.3
D'Arpentigny's athlete's hand

1.4
D'Arpentigny's farmworker's hand

philosophers. Casimir D'Arpentigny went to both sets of parties and he noticed an interesting thing. All the artistically inclined people had smooth fingers while the scientific types had bony fingers with bumpy joints. D'Arpentigny called these "knotty fingers" and deduced that they must indicate a scientific turn of mind. The "smooth fingers" on the others showed an intuitive mentality.

For a long time, he continued to study hands. He concluded that if you were a banker, or a stockbroker, you probably had a hand something like that in diagram 1.2.

And if you were a sportsperson or an athlete, your hand would most probably look like that in diagram 1.3.

If you were a farm worker, your hand would look like that in diagram 1.4.

Altogether he listed six different kinds of hands. Any hand which did not fit into these classifications, he called a "mixed hand" which made up the seventh type. It was all terribly clever and he wrote a little book about it in 1843 called *La Cheirognomy* which means "the study of hand shapes". D'Arpentigny was a witty, sarcastic fellow and his book took off like a rocket. Some people read it because it was new and interesting, others because it was entertaining and clever. Suddenly, everybody was looking at hands. D'Arpentigny's book was translated into German and then into English as *The Science of the Hand* in 1885.

There was another man in France who had been looking at hands while D'Arpentigny was doing his research. He was Adolphe Desbarrolles, a portrait painter. By a strange coincidence, he too had gone to Spain on a painting trip and had his hand read by a gypsy. Back in France, he got to know a famous occultist, Eliphas Levi, who taught him the Cabala — the mystical tradition of the Jews. One day Mr Levi said to him, "You know, you ought to look into the subject of palmistry. It used to be very popular a hundred years ago. Maybe you could bring it up to date." So Desbarrolles entered the nearest library and dug up some of the centuries-old palmistry books. He believed they were full of nonsense, but he set himself the task of going through to see if any of it made sense.

Unlike D'Arpentigny, who looked at the shapes of hands, Desbarrolles looked at the lines. He began to read hands professionally and, before long, he believed that the lines of the palm really did reveal details of a person's destiny. He also discovered interesting things like the shape of the Head Line corresponded to a person's intelligence while the Heart Line had a lot to do with a person's romantic and sexual nature. His book came out only a few years after that of D'Arpentigny and was

called *The Mysteries of the Hand*. Following so soon after the
sensation caused by the former book, this volume led to a whole
new interest in the subject of palmistry. All over Europe,
palmistry became more and more popular. In England, particularly, a palmistry society was set up and a palmistry magazine
was launched. By 1900, nearly one hundred new palmistry books
had appeared.

Yet even this wave of enthusiasm did not prove to be
permanent. All the enthusiasts for palmistry had failed to
convince the scientific community. Although famous palmists
like Cheiro (Count Louis Hamon) made a fortune out of reading
hands and travelled the world giving demonstrations, no
reputable scientist ever bothered to investigate this popular
subject. By 1930, the boom was over.

Finally, the modern science of hand psychology began to take
shape. In 1924, an American psychology student, Elizabeth
Wilson, carried out a statistical comparison of the hands of
schizophrenic patients, mentally retarded patients and ordinary
people. A statistician in India compared the hands of 200 students
to those of 200 manual labourers. A few years later, Dr Charlotte
Wolff, a resident of France and then England, carried out
extensive research into the hands of delinquent boys in
institutions. In the 1960s, Dr Eugene Scheimann, a respected
American doctor, studied the palms of alcoholic men, people
with sexual problems and others whom he had seen in his
medical practice. And Fred Gettings, a lecturer in Art at an
English Technical College, produced four magnificent books in
which he included graphs based on line frequencies from
thousands of handprints in support of his views on palmistry.

It was also in the 1930s that the first study of fingerprints
began. Since the turn of the century, police had been collecting
fingerprints. It was left to an English palmist, Noel Jaquin, to
prove that fingerprints have psychological significance. Jaquin
helped found the Society for the Study of Physiological Patterns
and that society eventually published the results of very
extensive investigations into the meanings of the papillary
patterns (dermatoglyphics) of the palm.

It is these dermatoglyphic patterns which have received the
most scientific research in the last two decades. Starting in 1967,
some American doctors concluded that the study of skin-ridge
patterns could reveal invaluable medical information about such
things as congenital heart defects and genetic disturbances. Since
then, more than 200 scientific papers have been published on this
topic and several books devoted to it.

Today, the modern scientific palmist has an invaluable fund of information from which to work. There are the traditions first established by Desbarrolles and D'Arpentigny. There are the refinements and further discoveries made by the palmists in the early years of this century. And there are the exciting modern scientific confirmations made by several psychologists, doctors and other scientific men.

Let's look at a hand and see the sort of features that hand psychology deals with. First, there are the fingers. Your index finger represents your self-confidence. A long, straight index shows a bossy, confident person. A short or bent index means that you are unsure of yourself. Your index is the finger you point with, the one you shake at people when telling them off. It represents your self-assertiveness.

The second (or middle) finger shows stability and seriousness. The longer and heavier it is, the more stable and materialistic you will be. Physiologically, the second finger is the straightest and strongest of the digits. It represents the solid, dependable side of your nature.

The ring finger shows artistic and creative tendencies. A well-developed ring finger is the sign of an artist.

The little finger relates to the most personal side of your nature, the sexual, emotional side. It is also linked to intelligence and your ability to express yourself in words. It is the smallest and least noticeable of the digits. It is tied to your innermost psychological drives.

Thumbs show your willpower. Powerful, domineering people have big thumbs. Mild-mannered folk have small ones.

The actual shape of your fingertips is important. Squared-off tips show a precise, tidy mind. People with round-tipped fingers are much more easy-going. Athletes and sportspeople invariably have swollen fingertips, known as ''spatulate''. These indicate an abundance of physical energy.

The proportions between the finger lengths and the lengths of the palm can be extremely revealing. In general, the longer your fingers, the more careful and finicky you will be. Short fingers belong to the quick and impulsive among us.

There is a special system of determining the four types of hands by comparing finger and palm lengths. You will learn a great deal more about these four types and what they mean later on.

Short, square palm + short fingers = Earth Hand.
Short, square palm + long fingers = Air Hand.
Long, narrow palm + short fingers = Fire Hand.
Long, narrow palm + long fingers = Water Hand.

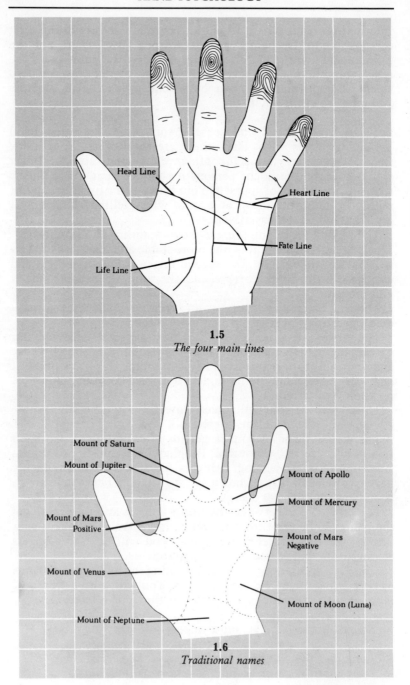

1.5
The four main lines

Head Line

Heart Line

Fate Line

Life Line

1.6
Traditional names

Mount of Saturn

Mount of Jupiter

Mount of Apollo

Mount of Mercury

Mount of Mars Positive

Mount of Mars Negative

Mount of Venus

Mount of Moon (Luna)

Mount of Neptune

You have already had a look at some fingerprints and dermatoglyphics in the handprint on page 2. There is an immense amount to be learned from these tiny furrows. They are always worth close attention when looking at a hand.

The normal human hand has four main lines (diag.1.5) and several minor ones. A few hands are missing the Fate Line but just about every other hand has the other three main lines. Children often don't develop a Fate Line until 10 or 12 years of age, so don't be concerned if your youngster hasn't got one. The more nervous and sensitive a person, the more lines will be found in the hands. Calm people have few lines. Men tend to have fewer lines in their hands than do women.

The Heart Line is linked with your sexual nature. It reveals what you look for in a relationship and how you behave in a love affair.

The Head Line is linked to your mental powers but, oddly enough, not to your intelligence. It shows whether you are imaginative or realistic, clear-thinking or muddle-headed, a quick thinker or a mental slowpoke. You can learn a great deal about a person's thinking from looking at his Head Line with the sole exception of his actual IQ.

The Life Line is basically a line of physical vitality. It has more to do with the strength of your body than your personality.

The Fate Line is a line of stability. Erratic, changeable people have broken or fragmentary Fate Lines. Dull, plodding folk have unusually strong ones. The Fate Line often indicates what sort of work you are most suited for.

You may be wondering about the difference between the left hand and the right hand. Hand psychologists examine the hand which you use the most. If you are right-handed, they study your right hand and vice versa. It is your active hand (the one you write with) which is the most relevant, reflecting your current personality .

The passive hand (the one you don't use so much) is not to be completely ignored. This hand contains a mixture of information, mainly your hereditary characteristics and childhood personality. A lot of what is in your passive hand is no longer relevant to the person you are today.

There are traditional names for certain parts of the hand which have been in use for centuries. We could invent new, modern names for them but this seems hardly worthwhile. Palmists prefer to use the standard names, depicted in diagram 1.6.

So there you have it. Turn to the next chapter and you are now ready to plunge into the mysteries of the hand.

CHAPTER 11

PALMISTRY AND YOUR LOVE LIFE

A few years ago, a 73-year-old lady drove her car almost 500 kilometres to my office to have her hands read. Can you guess what had brought her? It was a romantic problem, the same thing that brings so many people to see a palmist.

She was a small, bright-eyed lady whose active mind and alert expression showed that her age had hardly slowed her down. She lost no time in getting to the point of her problem.

"I've been a worker all my life, and now that I'm getting on I've decided to prepare for my old age by buying a little farm. It's only small, and I can manage it quite well on my own. A few months ago, an old suitor of mine started paying me attention and now he has asked me to marry him.

"I like Ted, but what I want to know is this: does he really love me or is he just trying to get his hands on my farm?" Seventy-three years old and still wondering about romance! Is there anyone who has no interest in this most fascinating of subjects? If so, I've yet to meet them. I've seen dozens of older folk, male and female, with new romances in their lives. And a girl of 17 entered my office with her two young children to ask whether she should stay with the man who fathered one of them or leave him in search of someone better.

Will I get married? Will I be divorced? Will I marry again? How often does the man or woman who asks the first question ask the second and then the third, before reaching the age of 30!

One famous palmist, Cheiro, commented that men want to know about their business life and women about their love life. Not a bit of it! From the hoary old misogynist who asks about

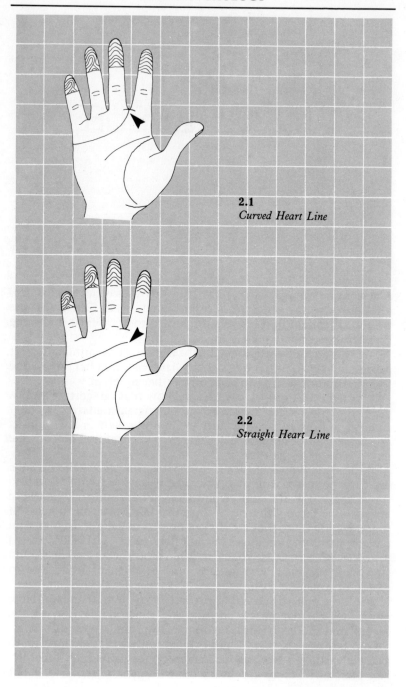

2.1
Curved Heart Line

2.2
Straight Heart Line

marriage for the pleasure of hearing the palmist answer "no", to the eager teenager who desperately prays that the answer will be "yes", everyone, male and female, wants to know about their love life.

Contrary to popular opinion, palmistry is not simply a way of telling what will happen. It is a method of finding out why things occur. It can tell you what sort of husband or wife or lover will suit you best. It can tell you why you behave as you do, why you are compatible with one person and yet have no chance at all with someone else. A palmist can make an excellent guess as to whether you'll marry and whether you'll divorce . . . purely by studying your psychological make-up through your hands without once looking at your Life Line or your Line of Fate.

Which is more valuable: to be told what is going to happen to you or to learn how to make your life go the way you want it to? If you have read this far, you should be in no doubt about the answer to this question.

To assess all aspects of a relationship, very detailed studies of the hands need to be made. But the key to understanding most matters of love and sex lies in the Heart Line. This is the line which reveals your emotional make-up, your likes and dislikes, your needs, your hopes, your expectations in all affairs of the heart. It is, indeed, a most important line.

There are two basic forms of the line, each of which has some subclassifications. These two basic forms are the curved line (diag. 2.1) which represents the warm, emotional approach to love and the straight line (diag. 2.2) representing the cool, thoughtful approach.

Imagine two Heart Lines (as illustrated in diagrams 2.1 and 2.2), each of which extends from the edge of the hand below the little finger to a point between the first and second fingers. The first line runs in a deep curve while the second line is a much straighter one. Both these lines represent a good interest in romantic matters, but in two very different ways. The curved-lined person is *active*, the straight-lined person is *passive*. The curved-lined person is aggressive in love, the straight-lined person is receptive. The curved-lined person is demonstrative about affection while the straight-lined person talks and thinks about it!

Let us look at some examples of how people with curved Heart Lines and those with straight Heart Lines behave. Imagine two young men in love; Tom has a curved line while Joe has a straight line. Tom is going round with a flushed face, a happy smile and snappy walk. He telephones his girlfriend twice a day, when he isn't actually taking her out. When they are together, he either has her hand in his or his arm around her shoulder. He has told all his mates how wonderful she is and has asked her to come and live with him within a week of meeting her.

Joe, with his straight Heart Line, doesn't look much different from how he normally does, except that his mind isn't on the job. It seems to be miles away and his friends are smiling to themselves about his distracted appearance. He has enquired of his girlfriend what sort of shows she likes and what sort of food she prefers and he is planning where he is going to take her on the next three dates. When Joe and his girlfriend are together, they spend a lot of time laughing and talking. Joe is thinking about discussing marriage soon.

The way that Tom and Joe met their girlfriends is also revealing. Tom met Jennifer when she called in as a customer at the place where he works. The first time she called, he got talking to her. The second time, he asked her for a date and she said yes.

Joe actually met Mary at a dance, a friend's wedding reception. Mary was sitting at the same table as Joe, which was how they got talking. By the end of the evening, they had discovered several common interests and Mary had agreed to accompany Joe to a party the following week.

Now let us imagine what might happen in six months' time if Mary and Jennifer both decide to break off their relationships. Tom with his curved Heart Line would be badly upset. The chances are that he would either wreck his car or angrily seek some way of venting his fury on someone else. All his friends would tactfully avoid him. But within a week or two he would be his normal self again and there is a good chance that he would find another girlfriend before long.

Joe would also be badly upset but with his straight Heart Line he would show it quite differently. He would become depressed and moody. He would sleep poorly at night, lying awake worrying about his romantic problems. His friends would be sympathetic and listen as he discussed what went wrong. A year later, the chances are that he would still be thinking about Mary. If Joe visits a palmist, he may ask if there is a chance of getting Mary back again, long after Tom has forgotten all about Jennifer.

In these two cases, we have all of the known characteristics of the two Heart Lines.

The curved-lined person
1. Starts new relationships rather than waiting for them to begin.
2. Looks for warmth, affection, love and sex.
3. Shows his or her feelings clearly and demonstratively.

4. Takes the lead in a relationship.

The straight-lined person
1. Finds that relationships develop by themselves.
2. Looks for compatibility, affection, companionship and sex.
3. Is thoughtful rather than demonstrative.
4. Prefers to share responsibility in a relationship rather than being the dominant partner.

The palmist who first examined the sexual indications in hands was Noel Jaquin. He wrote several books and innumerable articles on hand analysis, most of them dealing in part or in full with his theory of sex. He believed that a curved line indicated a ''masculine'' or physical approach to sex, while the straight line showed a ''feminine''or mental attitude. This theory is a simplification of the true facts — human nature is never simple — but it does contain a degree of truth.

For the curved-Heart-Lined person, the physical side of love is more important than it is for the straight-Heart-Lined person. This does not mean that straight-lined people are not physically orientated, but for them physical matters are not so important. For example, Mr or Ms Curved Line might well be attracted to somebody simply because that person is good-looking. A curved-lined person rarely dates someone who is plain-looking. But a straight-lined person would certainly consider it if the person had other worthwhile qualities. Both curved- and straight-lined people may want to touch and hold the person they love, but the curved-lined person will do so more frequently and more ostentatiously. Curved lines belong to people who do the courting and the seduction, whether male or female, whereas straight lines are found on those who are courted and seduced.

There are innumerable men with straight lines and innumerable women with curved lines. To speak of the lines as ''masculine'' or ''feminine'' is therefore incorrect. Nevertheless, the curved line is a little more common on male hands and the straight line is more common on the hands of females. It is also generally true that the aggressive and dominant lesbian has curved lines whereas the gentle, sensitive male homosexual invariably has straight Heart Lines.

With this information, you are now in a position to start applying your knowledge. For example, if you are a woman going out with a man whose Heart Line runs straight, don't expect him to shower you with hugs and kisses in public. Snuggle up to him in private and you'll get your hugs and kisses, particularly if he

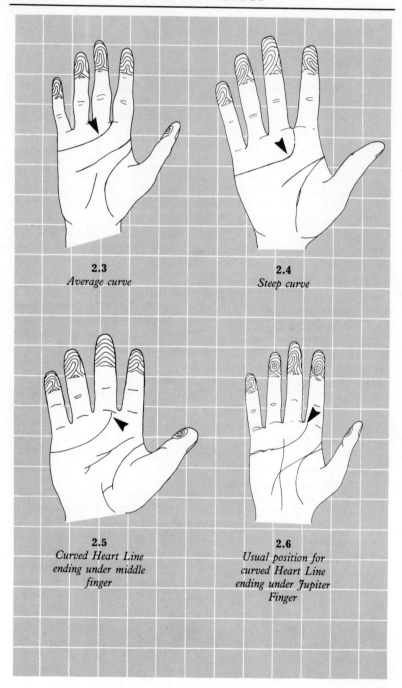

2.3
Average curve

2.4
Steep curve

2.5
*Curved Heart Line
ending under middle
finger*

2.6
*Usual position for
curved Heart Line
ending under Jupiter
Finger*

knows you are interested in him as a person. On the other hand, if your new boyfriend has a deeply curved line, don't be surprised if he is more blatant about sex than a straight-Heart-Lined person. The fact that sex is on his mind does not mean that it's the only thing he's interested in, though it may appear to be uppermost!

Remember that there is more to this than just the physical/mental question. A person with a deeply curved line is always more demonstrative than one with a straight line. If you are a man going out with a woman whose Heart Line curves, you can expect to get your face slapped if she catches you cheating on her. She will also expect a good deal of attention. Phoning her up once a week is not good enough. She will phone you up when she's lonely without waiting for you to ring her. With her curved lines, she has a real need for a demonstrative romance.

I have studied the hands of a great many married couples and found that, in most cases where the relationship is a particularly strong or long-lasting one, the Heart Lines are strikingly similar. It is certainly possible for people whose emotional natures differ to enjoy a worthwhile relationship, but in the majority of cases, men and women eventually settle with someone whose emotional and sexual nature is basically similar to their own.

When two people whose Heart Lines differ live together, they have to be particularly understanding of each other's emotional needs. Differing Heart Lines are not usually the cause of a couple splitting up, simply because such people rarely get together anyway. However, if you encounter a couple who are experiencing difficulty in their relationship, their Heart Lines are the first thing you should examine.

Once, at a party, I commented how well-matched a middle-aged man and his wife were. Instantly, a dozen hands were thrust forward for my inspection as several young and not-so-young persons demanded to know whether they were compatible with their partners. A young male friend of mine who was accompanied by a new girlfriend, a striking young woman, showed their hands first. Her Heart Line was strongly curved, while his was quite straight. I made a mental note that their friendship wouldn't last and subsequently learned from my friend that she had been "unavailable" when he tried to call her for a second date. I didn't tell him that she was undoubtedly disappointed by what she would have considered to be his "unexciting" personality!

Both types of Heart Line come in a number of varieties. Taking the curved line for a start, note that the deeper the curve, the more dramatic the emotional reactions will be. The average curved Heart Line usually looks like that in diagram 2.3.

Occasionally, one finds a much more pronounced curve (diag. 2.4) which goes with a particularly strong emotional and sexual drive.

In most cases, the line ends between the first two fingers. It is very rare indeed for the curved line to end under the middle finger, the finger of Saturn, but when it does this brings about the strongest manifestations of the curved pattern (diag. 2.5). The need for physical and romantic satisfaction is so strong in such a person that the whole life becomes dominated by the need. I have encountered this pattern among prostitutes, where the woman has turned to this form of employment to satisfy her own demand for sex. The majority of prostitutes, however, have little interest in sex at all and their Heart Lines are poorly developed.

It is more common for the curved line to end under the first finger if not in its usual place between the first and second digits. When this occurs, the tip of the line is usually only just to one side (diag. 2.6), never under the actual centre of the Jupiter finger (diag. 2.7).

This is a very interesting form of the line. Assuming that 50 per cent of men and women have curved lines, I would think that about one in six of these has the line straying towards the Jupiter mount. Because the line is curved, there is a strong emotional/sexual drive in such people, but they are more choosy and idealistic about their romantic partners! Anyone with such a line will be most particular about whom they have for friends. Most single people are happy to go out with any suitable member of the opposite sex, but the man or woman with this mark is much more fussy. A woman with this line will survey six attractive men who have successively asked her for a date and coolly turn them all down in favour of a seventh who happens to suit her fancy. A man with the line may flirt with lots of girls but if he asks one of them out she can be sure that he has a special reason for picking her rather than one of the others.

The other side of this characteristic is that the owner tends to idealise the loved one. People with these lines see their friends as being much better than they actually are. They also expect the very best from these friends and can be bitterly disappointed when they turn out to be only human after all!

The pattern also occurs more frequently with women than with men, possibly because a woman's emotional make-up is generally more complex than that of the male sex. I always regret finding this mark in the hands of a female client because all too often it leads to difficulties in her love life.

Present-day Western society is still not ready for self-assertive young women who select their partners instead of waiting to be selected themselves. The fault lies in society, not in the women, but nevertheless such women generally find that they are not as easily accepted as their more accommodating sisters.

I have repeatedly met young women in their mid-20s who have this mark and who are becoming a little worried because all their friends are getting married while they remain single. Their question is usually phrased like this: "I don't really want to get married right now, but I would like to one day. Can you tell me when it will be?" To those who ask this question, I reply encouragingly.

"The reason you haven't married so far is not for lack of opportunity, but because you are unwilling to settle with anyone who isn't exactly right for you. Other people can settle for second best, but you can't. In my experience, women of your type seldom marry before the end of their 20s and sometimes not until after 30. So there is still plenty of time ahead of you. With your psychological make-up, it would be disastrous for you to attempt a marriage with someone not quite right. I advise you to wait patiently, have as much fun as you can while you are single and don't worry about getting married for the moment. When you do marry, you have the capability of making an outstanding success of it."

Women with this mark really are capable of making excellent matches, and not simply because of their choosiness. They possess initiative and usually intelligence as well as "character". With all this going for them, plus the warmth and affection which always go with a curved Heart Line, it is no wonder that their marriages so often turn out well.

When such a woman marries young, there is a danger that she will come to regret her early commitment. If she has chosen wisely, all will be well, but all too often a spouse chosen when one is 18 or 20 is not an ideal life partner. A less demanding woman might live happily for years with an adequate husband. A woman with this Heart Line will not accept adequacy, she wants perfection! There is another danger associated with the mark, and this is that a person with it may expect too much from his or her partner. Here is an example.

A female client of mine once got into the habit of sending me handprints of her successive boyfriends. As she is both good-looking and unwise in her choice of men, a good number of prints began arriving through my mailbox. One day, some prints arrived which interested me greatly. They were obviously the prints of a successful businessman, secure, stable, intelligent and very involved with his career. An outstanding feature of both hands was a Heart Line which swung well up onto the Mount of Jupiter,

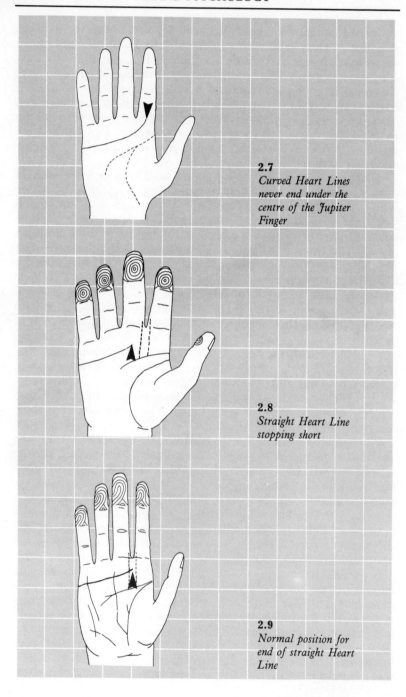

2.7
*Curved Heart Lines
never end under the
centre of the Jupiter
Finger*

2.8
*Straight Heart Line
stopping short*

2.9
*Normal position for
end of straight Heart
Line*

the idealistic pattern. I wrote to my client and told her that the man was a fine person, but that he would undoubtedly require a great deal of her, probably more than she was prepared to give. Several months later, I received this reply:

"You were right about him! He was absolutely devoted to me, but gradually I discovered that he expected me to be the ideal companion for him. When at a business lunch, he would phone me up and expect me to come right over, impeccably dressed and charming, to impress *his* colleagues. He actually shouted at me one day when I wore a dress he didn't approve of. Our weekends were supposed to be idylls of perfect bliss . . . in fact, the pressure of keeping everything perfect all the time drove me away from him. I am relieved to be rid of him."

To anyone, male or female, who comes to me complaining of marital problems and who exhibits this mark in the hand, I say: "Are you sure that you are not demanding too much from your partner?" Sometimes, if such people can learn to moderate their expectations and not be unreasonable in what they require from a partner, the marriage can be saved.

Let us now consider the straight Heart Line and its subdivisions, starting with the line which stops short under the second finger (diag. 2.8). The normal position, as you know, is more or less directly underneath the point where the two fingers join at the top of the palm (diag. 2.9). Stopping a little on either side is of no consequence but if the line runs only halfway underneath the second finger, it can be classified as short. This formation is never a good one. In view of what has been said about straight Heart Lines, it may surprise you to hear that this formation is often associated with a strong sex drive, particularly if the hand is a crude and heavy one. It also goes with a lack of feeling and warmth.

When the line is curved, there is warmth and demonstrativeness. When it is straight, there is thoughtfulness and consideration. When the line is *straight and short*, neither of these sets of qualities is present, and all that is left is the crude sex drive, unaccompanied either by emotional warmth or thoughtful consideration. I have found this line on men who showed the greatest interest in sex but whose idea of sex consisted of spending a few minutes with any available female as often as possible. They could hardly be classified as great lovers, in spite of their sexual activity. To be fair, I have found the line on men who were quite decent people, but never on a man who was in any degree sensitive or complex.

Whether the pattern ever occurs on female hands, I do not know. I do not recall having encountered it. In fact, men with such lines are not prone to visiting palmists and it may be more common than I have experienced among people who do not come near my office at all.

There are some hands with very few lines and those lines are all short and simple, including the Heart Line. With such a hand (diag. 2.10), one needs to assess factors such as the quality of the skin, skin ridges and the structure of the thumb to decide whether this is a crude, unpleasant character or merely a simple, uncomplicated one.

Just as the straight Heart Line may end under Saturn, so too it may reach out right onto the Mount of Jupiter (diag. 2.11). When this occurs, the end of the line usually reaches dramatically out past the middle of the mount, even towards the actual edge of the mount. Very distinctive personality traits go with this formation. It is the mark of the humanitarian, the person who is not simply caring and thoughtful about one partner, but about the whole of mankind.

Most people seek someone special to love. Not so the person with the long, straight Heart Line. He or she reaches out to everyone. An excellent example of this line exists on the hands of a well-known psychic healer. He married in his 20s and divorced a few years later, since which time he has helped untold thousands of people who have come to him for healing of mind and body. He is a counsellor specialising in helping with emotional and employment problems. He practises massage, herbalism and other healing arts. He runs seminars on these topics for the public, besides teaching private courses for those who wish to learn. His whole life has been devoted to helping others.

In Chapter VII, I have touched on the fact that such people often wind up in missionary or church groups. There is no need to go into this further here, but it is worth noting that groups and societies often attract people with this Heart Line formation.

One lady I know is the secretary of three different organisations, in all of which she plays a leading role. One of the groups is a religious one, while the other two are welfare societies. In her late 40s, this woman has never married although she has been engaged more than once. She is universally popular, largely because of the helpful interest she shows in the lives of all those she meets. Her Heart Line is the long, straight type. For some years now, she has enjoyed an excellent relationship with a straight-Heart-Lined man who does not have the length of Heart Line that she does. He readily admits that her ability to befriend anyone and everybody is stronger than his own! They are planning to marry in a few years' time (how unlike the

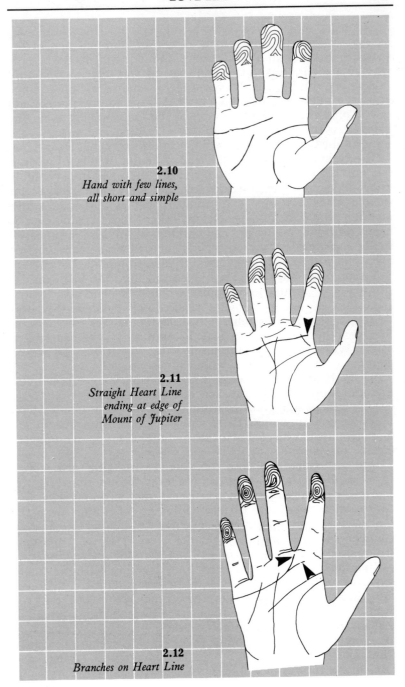

2.10
*Hand with few lines,
all short and simple*

2.11
*Straight Heart Line
ending at edge of
Mount of Jupiter*

2.12
Branches on Heart Line

impetuosity of a curved-Heart-Lined person). The relationship between these two individuals developed through one of the societies to which they both belong, and it commenced when the woman made it clear to the man that she was interested in him!

Here is a third case: a 20-year-old girl entered my office some years ago and when she placed her hands out for my inspection I saw at once that her Heart Line was the long, straight type. She listened with interest to the whole reading and when I had finished she began to talk about my comments on her Heart Line.

"Everything you have said is true and quite right and I want to tell you that I can confirm what you told me about my love life. I know all about my own nature and I do believe that I was meant to live in an extended community, such as a village. I love meeting people, helping people and I don't think I could ever be happy with just a husband and children of my own. I suppose I shall marry one day, but when I do I hope it's to an understanding man who will let me have lots of friends around us."

A year or so later I had a letter from her. She had joined a commune, a farming community which had plans of eventual expansion to take in perhaps hundreds of members. She was writing to say that she felt she had now found her true place in life. This then was the "extended community" she had spoken about. With her Heart Line formed the way it was, I have no doubt that such a situation would suit her ideally.

All the Heart Line patterns so far mentioned are simple ones. Anyone whose line falls into one of these classes has a relatively easy-to-understand emotional make-up. A good many Heart Lines are not simple like these, however, but instead run in two or more branches instead of just the one. These types require very careful analysis.

Two or more branches on the Heart Line indicate a corresponding number of different sides to the emotional nature. The most common pattern consists of just two branches: one curves up between the fingers while the other runs onto the Mount of Jupiter (diag. 2.12). People like this remind me of a two-cylinder motor bike: they require two types of emotional stimulation to keep them going. They have the active, romantic inclinations of the well-curved line, together with the more sensitive, introspective qualities of the straighter pattern. Unlike the purely straight Heart Line, the bottom branch of the forked Heart Line is usually curved upward a little, adding a touch of realism to the already complex emotional range. This is an excellent pattern. In fact, branches of any sort seem to be a good thing on the Heart Line. Branches increase the range and intensity of the emotional responses.

It is very rare to find someone with this pattern getting a divorce. The combination of qualities ensures that the person will give a lot of attention to the spouse, which is probably the best method of keeping a relationship together. Happy is the man or woman who winds up with a partner like this.

There is a tradition in palmistry that the ideal Heart Line should end in a trident: three distinctive branches. Traditional palmistry sees three-pronged forks on the end of most lines as a fortunate symbol, a sort of good luck mark. The reason is that three clear branches usually indicate all the best qualities of a line, which is naturally inclined to make a person successful and thus in the eyes of the world, "fortunate". When the Heart Line takes this form (diag. 2.13), the third branch (B) comes between the two forks previously described.

I usually tell clients with this marking that it indicates a need for "physical, mental and emotional" satisfaction in romance. Sexual involvement, emotional warmth and mental compatibility are all strongly developed. It is not a common pattern and when found is usually in a hand with many strong, clear lines, indicating overall enthusiasm for most aspects of life. It is possible for a Heart Line to be even more complex than this (diag. 2.14). This Heart Line could, for example, belong to a man who becomes obsessively involved with the women in his life, to the point where many of his female friends have been unable to cope with his constant devotion. One can have too much of a good thing, and multiple-branches like this one on the end of the Heart Line definitely indicate an overdevelopment of the romantic nature.

Sometimes a branch of the Heart Line sweeps downwards, to touch or cut the Line of Life (diag. 2.15). This has a twofold interpretation. In the first place, it shows that the owner is capable of being very easily hurt in love. Many of us are quite thick-skinned when it comes to breaking off a relationship or dealing with a hurt or a slight inflicted on us by someone we love. This downward branch line indicates the opposite quality, a sort of "thin-skinned" nature which reacts very poorly to emotional hurts. The distraught lover who throws himself off the local cliff probably has a branch like this on his Heart Line.

Any adult with this mark will have been badly hurt by a loved one at least once in his or her past. There will have been a jilted engagement, a case of trust betrayed or some similar incident. The actual date of such an event can be determined from the Life Line, but regardless of exactly what event or events may have taken place, the psychological quality of being susceptible to such hurts is what is at the root of it.

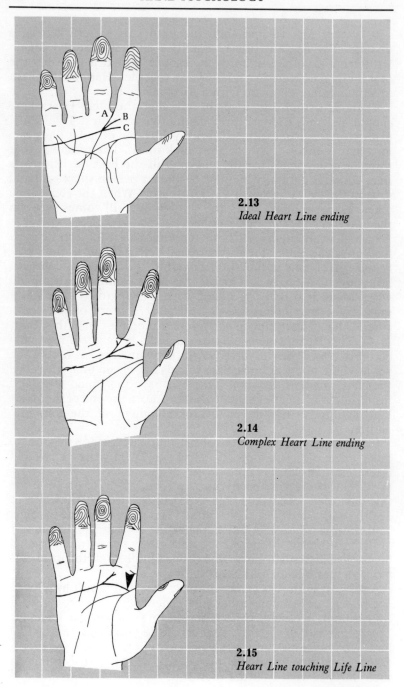

2.13
Ideal Heart Line ending

2.14
Complex Heart Line ending

2.15
Heart Line touching Life Line

The second implication of the mark springs from the fact that anyone sensitive enough to be hurt will also be capable of learning from the experience. These folk are noted for their ability to be considerate and understanding about other people's feelings. If you get into a relationship with someone who has this pattern, you can be sure of comfort when you are upset and a sympathetic ear when you want to talk about your troubles. It is also very unlikely that he or she will ever do anything that could hurt you. Having experienced hurt, he or she will be doubly careful to avoid hurting another.

This chapter has covered a good deal which may seem confusing at first reading. In fact, these interpretations are all quite plain and reliable, so that once you understand each of the Heart Line patterns, you should have no difficulty in interpreting them in your own hands and the hands of your friends. You do not need to study all the other points in the hands in order to read the Heart Line. Certainly, the whole hand must be considered in judging how one person will react with another, but the emotional parts of that reaction can be studied from this one line.

There are many ways you can use this knowledge. Why not start by examining your own hands and deciding how well what you see there applies to your own past romantic experiences? Self-understanding is one of the most priceless gifts anyone can have. You can also investigate the hands of any couple who are having difficulties in their relationship. Careful and tactful discussion of the emotional nature of each party can help tremendously in overcoming problems.

You can tell in advance what to expect from a new friend or lover, what to do and what not to do when getting to know this person who has just entered your life. When you have gained experience with palmistry, you can even tell right from the start whether you are compatible with someone new. You can offer advice to your friends about what to do in their romantic situations. Couples who are armed in advance with knowledge of the potential strengths and weaknesses of their relationship are in an excellent position to make the best of things.

An interesting exercise is to take the prints of couples you know who have been together happily for many years. The majority of such couples show remarkable similarities in many parts of their hands, not just in the Heart Lines! There are couples with major differences, generally qualities present in one but not in the other, who complement each other. Each makes up for what the other lacks. For this reason, never predict dogmatically that two people are bound to be incompatible, or alternatively, that they are sure to be well-suited. Content yourself with pointing out the positive and negative traits, advantages and disadvantages in each case. By all means offer advice, but be as constructive as you can.

The hands of young people are particularly prone to change and the Heart Line often changes shape during the teenage years. For this reason, readings for adolescents should be regarded as conditional: true at the time but capable of being modified as the years go by.

CHAPTER III

RELATIONSHIP PROBLEMS AND THE LITTLE FINGER

If you are a parent having difficulties with your children, or a lover having trouble with your loved one, or if you are one of those people who find it hard to keep friends for any length of time — the reason may be found in your little finger. Traditionally, this digit is known as the Finger of Mercury. It is associated with, among other things, emotional and sexual attitudes.

The three problems associated with this finger are as follows.

1. A too-short finger (diag. 3.1).
2. A low-set finger (diag. 3.2).
3. A finger held wide apart from the rest (diag. 3.3).

Short little finger
The average little finger reaches to the first joint line that marks the top phalanx of the ring finger. If it is a little shorter than this, there will be some of the problems described, but if it is markedly short, the problems will be acute. (Check to make sure the finger really is short and not simply a normal length finger which is low set.)

Low-set little finger
Note that nearly all Mercury fingers are set a little low. To be classed as low, it must be really noticeable, especially when the fingers are spread a bit. A low-set finger usually does not reach to the top joint line of the ring finger because of its low start, but it is not really short.

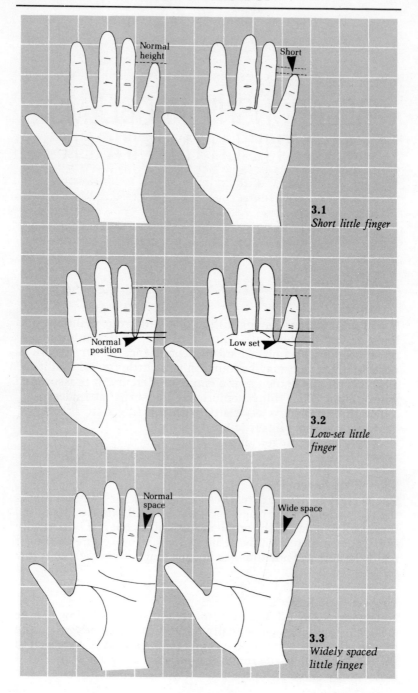

3.1
Short little finger

3.2
Low-set little finger

3.3
Widely spaced little finger

Widely spaced little finger

If the space between the ring finger and little finger is more than twice as great as the space between the other fingers, it is classed as wide. Less than twice as wide as the others is not important enough to take notice of.

The most common of these formations is the too-short little finger. Instead of behaving like a mature adult, the person with this formation behaves like an immature youngster, generally getting into all sorts of bother as a result. This immaturity can take various forms, all of them more or less troublesome.

One pattern consists of getting into romantic situations which turn out to be unstable. For example, are you someone whose romances and friendships tend to be short and not necessarily sweet? If so, you may have a short little finger like the following case histories.

Trevor was a good-looking, 30-year-old entertainer from New Zealand. A member of the Maori race, he had the easy-going charm and good-natured personality common to his people. In his early 20s he married a lovely girl with whom he had fallen in love and for several years they enjoyed an excellent relationship.

Trevor's work as a musician and singer took him to night clubs and cabarets across the country and overseas. Again and again in his travels, he came across girls who found him attractive and he had notched up more than a score of casual affairs. Throughout this time, he continued to love his wife. Indeed, he commented when he came to have his hands read that she was the only woman he had ever really loved. But Trevor's wife was understandably annoyed with him and eventually she left, taking their two young children with her.

Poor Trevor ran from one fortune-teller to another, trying to discover if he would ever get his wife back. Eventually, he called in to see a palmist. His usually happy face wore a serious expression as he explained his case. "I love my wife, but I can't seem to resist all the other girls. I can't stop having affairs because my work is constantly bringing me into contact with them; but I love my wife and want her back. What can I do?" On both his hands, Trevor possessed short little fingers.

The 37-year-old woman who called in at my office appeared to be a strikingly pretty 20 year old! As I read her hands, the complicated story of her love life unfolded.

She had married at 18, but had left her husband two years later.

In the following year, she had three short affairs before moving in to live with a young man with whom she stayed for a year. After that, she went from relationship to relationship, some lasting for months, others lasting less than a week. Unlike many people who experience lots of affairs, this woman genuinely fell in love with each of her men, the only trouble being that she fell out of love as quickly as she fell into it. Her habit was to meet a new man, fall for him and establish a new relationship. Sooner or later, she invariably came to wonder what on earth had attracted her to him in the first place. In the most hectic week she had ever experienced, she actually fell in love three times with different men, none of the affairs lasting more than two days.

At the time she came to see me, she had been living with a man for nearly 12 months and was anxious to know whether the relationship would be permanent. Looking at her hands, I could see that both her little fingers were shorter than average.

Belinda is a lady who once had a short affair with a friend of mine. She was then an attractive woman just past 40, a widow whose husband had died 10 years before. Like the woman just described, she looked many years younger than her actual age. When her husband died, he left her a house, a sizeable income and so the freedom to spend her life as she chose. Belinda was a person with a wide circle of friends, active socially and so before long she had a good number of admirers. Although she was not actually looking for a husband, Belinda was not averse to marrying again if she could find a suitable man.

In fact, Belinda found several suitable men. She was intelligent, wealthy and beautiful, just the type to attract the most eligible bachelors in town. Unfortunately, Belinda had a problem. She was jealous of her men friends, becoming indignant if they so much as looked at another woman. She was also easily upset. Any minor criticism or disagreement caused her to fly off the handle. One by one, her gentlemen friends discovered that while she was excellent for a casual friendship or an occasional social outing, she was not at all suitable for a close relationship.

Several of her acquaintances thought that her behaviour might be caused by the tragic loss of her husband, though this was now 10 years in the past. As a palmist, I examined her hands and found, as I had suspected, that both her little fingers were shorter than they should be.

What can be done for people like this? What is the real problem facing people who have these short little fingers? And what can they do about it? A short little finger tends to indicate immaturity. The owners of these fingers seem to age less than other folk. Two of the cases I have quoted show physical signs of this as it is not uncommon for those with this hand feature to remain younger-looking than their actual age throughout their lives. This immaturity is partly physical and partly mental. Besides the youthful appearance, such people often have a youthful enthusiasm for life. They have more fun and lead a more varied, interesting life than more mature folk. A 70 year old with a short little finger may behave in a more youthful manner than most 40 year olds!

In Trevor's case, his own immaturity prevented him from grasping the simple fact that he could not maintain a string of lovers and a wife at the same time. Like a child who greedily wants to have all, Trevor could not resist the temptation of so many available females. The woman who kept falling in love was showing another aspect of this immaturity. Falling in love is a syndrome of adolescence, which with her had persisted throughout her life. She had never learned that relationships need to be based on compatibility, common interest and a mutual regard between parties, not on sudden bursts of emotion. She thought that the moment her passion decreased was the time to abandon the relationship.

Belinda showed perhaps the most common symptom of immaturity, the inability to control negative emotions. Most children cry and throw tantrums whenever something goes wrong until they learn that it is simply not possible to keep doing this. Although most adults can take a small criticism or disagreement quite lightly, for Belinda any such irritation was a source of great distress. Because of this, her relationships seldom lasted.

In these cases, the palmist cannot change the personality of the man or woman who has the defective finger, but he can explain carefully exactly what this finger type means and what behaviour it induces. If a palmist points out the advantages and disadvantages of this immaturity or youthfulness to the person concerned, he can help the person towards self-understanding. A person who knows his or her own characteristics and who understands exactly why relationships run the way they do, is in a position to try to conquer the more negative characteristics of the short little finger.

With each of the three people I have described, I counselled them to spend an hour or two seriously thinking about their past relationships, trying to see how their own tendency towards immaturity was the cause of the problem. I also advised them to keep a careful watch on their own behaviour, to note any immature behaviour that might occur. It is important when talking with such people to reassure them that there are advantages to their youthful tendencies. It is also important for them to know that, as short little fingers are not rare, they are not alone. If a person with a short little finger tries to control the less desirable traits, it is usually possible to lead a more satisfactory life. Dealing with problems is not easy, but once the problem is understood, any effort to overcome it will be rewarded.

The immaturity of a person with a short little finger can also take other forms. A common problem is difficulty between parents and children. If you find there is often friction between you and your offspring, you may be like one of the following cases:

A heavily built, middle-aged housewife who came to have her hands read was interested to hear how people with short little fingers often overreact to any hurt or irritation. She herself had a pair of such fingers on hands otherwise indicating a good level of commonsense and a basically stable personality.

"I know exactly what you mean," she volunteered. "And a year or two ago I realised myself what was going on. I wish I'd come to see you when I was a girl. It's taken me 50 years to discover what you just told me by looking at my hands. I've got five kids and I realise they have to live their own lives, but every time they want to go out or want to be independent, I feel really hurt. We used to have the most fearful rows. Every time we had a disagreement I would get so upset over it. A few years ago I realised that it was all just me, that I was overreacting. Nowadays I still feel hurt inside when one of my sons says something thoughtless or one of my girls does what I've never done, but I've learned to bite my tongue and not fly off the handle. As a result, we get on really well now, but if I hadn't woken up to the fact that it was me at fault, we'd still be fighting and miserable."

By contrast, a working man who once visited my office showed a complete lack of self-understanding. He too had a large family, but he expressed a deep disapproval of both his wife and his children. According to him, his wife was disobedient and most disrespectful, his children a crew of thankless, inconsiderate, thoroughly undesirable brats. His hands were of the simple type known as Earth Hands, but unlike the typical Earth Hand, his little fingers were quite diminutive. The Earth Hand is normally found in farming communities and among labouring classes and indicates a simple, basic approach to life. Usually such people have very stable family lives, but such a hand with small little fingers indicates a complete, childlike inability to adjust to normal relationships.

There may be many causes of discord in a family, but if you are a parent who has trouble with your children it would be a good idea to check your hands and the size of your little fingers. If you find that they are short or even that the little finger on your active hand (right hand for a right-hander, left hand if you are left-handed) is shorter than on the other hand, you should start to consider carefully whether the discord is partly because you are reacting too strongly to the small irritations that come up in any family.

When you compare your two hands, if one of the fingers is short and the other is long, the explanation is probably that you have not had the symptoms all through your life. If you are a right-hander, a short little finger on your left hand will only show that there was a problem in the earlier years of life, perhaps as late as the end of the teenage period, but that it no longer affects you today. If you are left-handed, the reverse rules apply.

You should also remember that a person who comes under sudden stress, especially in an emergency, will often react in an instinctive way according to the indications in his or her passive hand. In normal circumstances, the active hand holds sway.

Here is one final example of immaturity in human relationships due to a small little finger. Immaturity can take many forms, some more common than others. Here is an example of a rare form.

The elderly lady who came to have her hands read was tall, stern-looking and had a faintly forbidding expression on her unlined and unsmiling face. She gave me her birthdate and I calculated that she was 74 years old. People of this age seldom come to see a palmist unless they have some pressing problem, or because they have a strong interest in occult matters.

In her case, it was the latter. She was a spiritualist, a keen member of a local church and in her younger days she'd been an active clairvoyant. At the end of her reading, she spent some 20 minutes talking about her interests, discussing her plans to visit other churches overseas and showing me a document which was supposed to have been written by a spirit, all about love and human kindness.

Both her hands showed short little fingers and while I was talking to her about the associated characteristics, I was mentally noting that she had the fine skin and well-preserved body I would expect to find as traits of people with these short digits.

Spiritualism emphasises the need for love and understanding between people. Keen spiritualists, like most sincerely religious people, are usually very kindly disposed towards their fellow human being. Not so this woman! She started by telling me how ill-mannered all the other spiritualist churches were. There are several other churches in her town and she despised every one of them, telling me none of the other congregations were worth knowing. She accused them of being intolerant, selfish and antagonistic towards one another. Next, she described the members of her own church. They too, it seemed, were a nasty lot, selfish and narrow-minded. The minister and the organist in particular were always arguing with her. She had worked as a clairvoyant tea cup reader in several local tea rooms where fortune-telling was offered free to customers. Nowadays, she said, none of the cup readers were any good at all and even when she was working there, none was as good as she had been. They were an ill-educated, selfish and motley crew who were jealous of her superior powers.

She had come to see me in company with two other people from her own religion, a small woman of 65 and a genial old man of 80 who seemed to be the leader of the group. I had read his hands before she came in, and she confided to me as she left that although she tolerated him, she found him very annoying at times as he frequently disagreed with her over all sorts of things. And so she left, firmly convinced that she, as a spiritualist, was a helpful, kindly, understanding person.

So far, we have dealt mainly with the troubled side of the short little finger and it is important to remember that there is a lighter side. As stated before, these folk have a youthful freshness about them, besides a pleasantly youthful appearance. It is also a fact that they are almost never dull. They can be charming, quick-witted, attractive and sometimes amusing. Don't forget to stress these points if you are counselling someone who has this hand formation.

The second type of Mercury finger abnormality occurs when the finger is low-set (see diag. 3.2, p. 32). A short little finger can easily be confused with one which is simply low-set, but the problems shown by these two formations are quite different. In the majority of hands, the base of the first, second and third fingers are all set in a line, while the base of the little finger is set a little lower than the other three. In a small percentage of hands however, the little finger is set so low as to be down beneath the others. The top of the finger will not reach up to the crease line that marks the top joint of the ring finger. At first glance, this may appear to be a short finger, but a moment's examination will show you that it is actually low-set.

This low-set formation reveals that the person concerned had a severe problem with one or both parents during childhood. The low-set pattern develops in the early years when something is astray between the parents and their offspring. When the child grows to adulthood, a further psychological problem invariably arises. Often the person is not aware that the problem exists and the palmist can help this person to understand what is wrong and why it came about by explaining the meaning of the low-set little finger.

When one parent has a disturbed personality, it is very likely to cause psychological damage to the child. Astonishingly, when the child grows up, he or she is likely to marry someone who has the same problem which the disturbed parent had! People with an alcoholic parent are themselves likely to marry alcoholics. Children who were raised by nervous, worrying parents in turn marry nervous, worrying people. There are endless cases of this senseless repetition, occurring through innumerable, varied patterns and all leading to great unhappiness for the people concerned. Palmistry provides a method of understanding the psychological principles involved here.

One of the most dramatic cases of a mother complex I have ever encountered concerned a youthful 40-year-old woman. At the time I knew her, she had long since divorced her husband and was enjoying an active social life.

I first met Joanna at the home of a friend. When I came to examine her hands, I found both her little fingers so low-set that her hands almost appeared to be deformed. I thought that there must be quite a story behind this case, and indeed there was. Joanna's mother, I quickly discovered, had played a disastrously influential part in the woman's life. She had been a living incarnation of snobbery, dictating to young Joanna about clothes, manners, speech, behaviour, friendships and everything else, crushing the girl's spirit and forcing her to live according to her mother's bigoted ideas of social convention. Joanna's father was a mild-mannered little man totally dominated by his wife. Among the mother's traits were hypocrisy, egotism and acute hypochondria. She was, as she still is, a remarkably unpleasant woman.

Joanna married at 17, "to escape", as she now puts it. She gave birth to several children in quick succession. Mother pronounced it a good match and made much of Joanna's "duty" to raise a family. Privately, Joanna thought that any situation was preferable to living at home with mother.

Today, Joanna indulges in many interesting pursuits which her mother would deem unacceptable, mixes with a variety of lively friends from all social levels and is busy building a new profession with the aid of a recently won university degree.

She retains one obvious symptom of her mother's powerful influence: in any conversation, she brings up her mother within the first 10 minutes. Joanna still visits her mother every month. But though the stay is brief, she cannot refrain from bringing details of it into every ensuing conversation, regardless of the original subject matter! The talk is generously laced with her parent's latest outrageous behaviour toward her daughter. Joanna herself is unaware of how much her mother still dominates her thoughts. But her friends, listening to her, are only too aware of the enduring influence!

Two interesting points arise from this story: the first is that the marriage was to a quiet, inoffensive man very similar to Joanna's father. Secondly, her later years of rebellion and adventure are an obvious direct reversal of the earlier, formative years. Thus, both the early behaviour and the later behaviour have their origin in her mother's influence.

Here is another case, less dramatic but still informative. Sue is a 28-year-old secretary working for a large government department. She is small and pretty and popular, loves going out and has dated just about every eligible bachelor in the building where she works. Sue has been at her job for 12 years. In that time, she has built up a large bank balance for she lives with her mother, doesn't travel and is careful with her money. For years, she has dreamed of going abroad, seeing new places and meeting new people. But she has never dared to do so. Nine years back, her dad died. Today her mum makes it very clear that she depends on Sue for everything. As the youngest child, and the only one at home at the time of her father's death, Sue felt totally responsible for her mother. But now, at the age of 28, she is feeling left out of life.

When Sue came to see me, the first thing I noticed about her hands were the low-set Mercury fingers. Unlike Joanna, Sue has an excellent relationship with her mother, but her life is just as dominated by the parental need. In her case, the influence is simply a restrictive one. By a study of her Life Line, I told Sue that she was due to make an overseas trip which she later admitted she was already planning. I reassured her that once this trip was completed she would be able to break away from home. She had booked a tour of Europe and during this time her mother would be forced to cope with her own life at last. Sue's delight at being told this was typical of many clients whose readings provide reassurance and guidance. She was able to plan her travel now with confidence and to disregard her mother's negative reactions to the impending departure.

When Joanna married at 17, she chose a man similar to her father. In many cases, women whose fathers have a particular personality defect find themselves attracted to men with the identical defect. One of the saddest forms of this situation occurs *when a girl has an alcoholic father. Very frequently, such a girl grows up and marries an alcoholic man, or has a series of relationships with men who have this problem. Senseless as this behaviour appears to be, it occurs with monotonous regularity. Often a woman who has had half-a-dozen alcoholic boyfriends will quite fail to realise what they all had in common or that this problem feature stemmed from her father.*

In Chapter VII, you can read the story of Simon, an army man with Simian Lines in his hands. Simian-Lined people are often dogmatic, forceful, strong-minded characters. Two of Simon's daughters grew up with low-set little fingers and both married men who were dominant, dogmatic and forceful! Both of them also had various relationships with men who pushed them around just as Simon had done when they were children.

The low-set little finger can occur in male hands as well as in those of women. However, males are less frequently dominated by a single parent. Among men, the low-set little finger seems to be most common when both parents were discontent with the marriage, generally divorcing before the children were grown. Boys who grow up in an atmosphere of parental quarrelling may show no obvious signs of a parent complex, but all too often their own marriage degenerates into fights and arguments. I have seen cases of men with the low-set little finger who divorced at exactly the point in their marriage at which their parents had broken up.

It may seem a sexist remark to claim that parent complexes as shown by the little finger are more common with women than with men. Perhaps as society changes, this phenomenon may change as well, but at present it appears to be a general rule. Of course, there are men who have a preoccupation with one parent, including the well-known example of men who wish to marry "someone just like mum". Men who make this sort of statement often wind up marrying a woman who actually looks like their mother, regardless of whether she otherwise acts like his mother.

Whenever you find a person who has the little finger low-set, you may be sure that some sort of parental fixation exists. Remember that most little fingers are set a little lower than the ring finger and that to be sure the interpretation applies the finger must be set much lower than normal. If you know a person who has this feature, you should counsel him or her to take a serious look at his or her own relationships or marriage. A single person who has the pattern will usually find that a consideration of the last few romances will come up with a common feature. Once it has been identified, the person is in a much better position to control his or her own life, instead of being subjected to the unconscious influence of the early childhood conditioning. A married person with this pattern may benefit from discussing the subject even if the marriage is a stable and happy one, more so if it is not.

Low-set little fingers can be passed down through a family and recur through the generations. At first glance, it may seem that this would not indicate a psychological problem since a problem cannot be inherited the way that eye colour is passed on. In fact, the problem is indeed passed from parent to child, not through genetic inheritance but rather through behavioural conditioning.

The shape of the hand is determined mainly during the first few years of life. A baby is born with hands lacking any definite shape. In the first years, the child's environment determines the position the little finger will take. On page 259 you will find a remarkable case of a parent complex found in the hand of a child who is less than three years old. This little boy lost his parents at 14 months and went through emotional turbulence for the next few years. The handprints show that he exhibits a preoccupation with security as well as being markedly anxious. Now that he has settled with a caring guardian it is to be hoped that these problems will resolve themselves.

The third type of disturbance shown by the little finger is different from the other two in that it can change when the problem is gone. This pattern consists simply of having the finger widely separated from all the others (see diagram 3.3, p. 32). It is common to have a space between the fourth and fifth fingers when the hand is at rest but if this space becomes exaggerated, you may be sure that there is something wrong. This outward-jutting finger is a sign that some emotional or sexual problem is worrying the owner. If it is clearly evident, the interpretation is almost infallible. People going through a divorce commonly carry the little finger in this position. Lovers suffering through a troubled romance also have this formation as do individuals with sexual problems.

It is a completely unconscious gesture which disappears if the problem is resolved but which increases if the problem worsens. It can even increase or diminish according to whether the person is thinking about the problem or not.

Before giving some examples of this interesting phenomenon, I must dispose of an ancient misapprehension concerning the outward-jutting little finger. All the earlier text books claim that spaces between the fingers indicate independence and that a wide space between the last two fingers shows "independence of action". This is not true! It shows a sexual or emotional problem.

It is true that spaces go with independent thinking but this particular misapprehension about the little finger arose in

Victorian times when sexual matters simply were not discussed. The Victorian palmists, noticing that people with outward-thrust little fingers were often associated with divorces, promiscuity and sexual deviance, tactfully declared that these folks were "independent in their actions". It took a few 20th century palmists to discover the truth of the matter. Yet even today, many palmists who have absorbed the traditional teachings will cling to this "independence of action" theory, unaware that the veil has been lifted. This interpretation does have a certain degree of truth to it since wide spaces always show an independent turn of mind. But a more accurate assessment would be "temporary emotional or sexual difficulties".

If you notice that someone's little finger is thrust out, check first to see if it is present on both hands. If not, the interpretation may or may not be reliable. But if both hands show the pattern, there can be no doubt about it. To make doubly sure, wait until the person changes the position of his or her hands and then check to see whether the fingers are still thrust out.

In my professional work, I find that most people who come with a marital problem possess this pattern. Before I even look at the events marked along the Life Line, I can be sure that it is an emotional problem which has brought this client along. In cases like this, I study the Heart Line and related features to see what sort of emotional make-up my client possesses. Nine times out of 10 it is possible to guess exactly what is wrong and what sort of emotional behaviour the client has. Different sorts of behaviour are associated with different types of emotional problems. Chapter II explains all this in detail. If the hand shows a well-balanced emotional make-up, but the little finger is jutting out, the problem may be an unusual one. The only thing that is certain is that some sort of relationship difficulty exists.

One interesting case was an intelligent young woman who had married an engineer with whom she enjoyed an excellent relationship. At the time I saw her, her husband had given up his work in order to join a commune. He found that community living suited him admirably. His wife, who loved him dearly, hated commune life! The result was that she became very unhappy and her little finger was stuck out. This was certainly an "emotional relationship" problem but an unusual one.

When a husband or wife dies, the surviving partner may have the little finger held outwards for months or even years afterward, depending upon how long the emotional shock lasts. Not all of those who lose a partner have this hand pattern. It seems that everyone experiencing the loss of a loved one goes through a period of distress but only a few maintain the sense of loss long after the actual death. It is these few who continue missing their dead partner who exhibit the outward-thrust little finger.

Some people visit the palmist determined to reveal nothing in order to see how much the palmist will discover. In cases where such a person has an emotional problem, the outward-spreading little finger will not show itself for the first few minutes. But after a while, when the consultation has commenced, that little finger will start to creep out, until eventually both hands show a wide space between the last two digits. Consciously, the client may hide the problem but then unconsciously it becomes revealed.

An amateur palmist once argued with me about the meaning of this pattern. He claimed that a great many people carry their little fingers out and that they cannot all have emotional problems. This palmist was in the process of divorcing his wife and had recently sent me prints of himself and his partner. I produced the two sets of prints for his inspection, pointing out that all four little fingers were projecting. Yet a set of his prints taken two years previously, during more tranquil domestic times, showed no such pattern.

When you are counselling someone who has a problem of this type, the most important thing you can do is to study the rest of the hand. Chapter II is particularly helpful. People with problems want to know what's going to happen. The palmist's job is not to predict an unalterable future, but to advise the client how to make the best of things. As always, understanding the problem is the key.

Speaking of unconscious hand gestures brings to mind a curious one common in the late 19th and early 20th centuries. It was fashionable at the time for ladies drinking cups of tea or coffee to project the little finger. This was done quite deliberately as a social convention. No-one had the slightest idea where this gesture had originated. In fact, it was the first period of female emancipation, where for the first time women were beginning to assert themselves and to look for independence. It was a time of social tensions when the male exchanged the stability of centuries for the uncertainty of modern times. No wonder the "liberated" woman of 1905 had her little finger stuck out! Even today, one can still meet elderly ladies who carefully crook this appendage while drinking tea, a relic of a long-gone social convention.

There is a tendency for some writers on these subjects to class all emotional and relationship problems as "sexual problems". In one sense, this is quite correct. One could indeed say that an outward-thrust little finger indicates a sexual problem, but it would have to be called "sexual" in the widest sense. Only in a minority of cases will the problem be sex itself as distinct from emotional or romantic problems.

Many male homosexuals and lesbians show this pattern. Homosexuality as such does not cause the finger to project, but far too often a homosexual person experiences difficulties in his or her love life which in turn affect the finger. I do not propose to say much about homosexuality here for the good reason that there are no positive formations in the hand which indicate this pattern. There are certainly features which occur in homosexual hands more frequently than in the hands of heterosexual men or women, but these are never reliable enough to "prove" that someone is homosexual. When the outward-thrust little finger occurs on the hand of a homosexual you may deal with the case exactly as you would for a non-homosexual person.

Of course, both short little fingers and low-set ones are often found to be jutting out as well. This is only to be expected since both these patterns indicate qualities which are likely to create difficulties in the emotional life.

In this chapter we have dealt with the three major patterns to do with the little finger: the finger that is too short, the one that is low-set and the one found jutting outwards. Occasionally, you may find an oddity in this digit, notably the absence or extreme shortness of one of the finger joints. These oddities are covered in Chapter VI.

When you find any of the three major patterns, you would do well to study the rest of the hand. Emotional problems are often tied up with the whole of a person's personality, not just the love life. However, with the information in this chapter you should be in a position to offer a good deal of help and "problem solving" to anyone whose little finger appears to be out of the ordinary.

THE SMOKING HABIT AND HOW PALMISTRY CAN BEAT IT

Cigarette smoking is the second most common form of legal drug abuse in the world. The first, of course, is alcohol. Cigarette smoking at the rate of three or four a day is virtually harmless and a quiet pipe by the fireside in the evening can be one of life's little luxuries. Yet who among modern-day smokers uses tobacco as moderately as this? The average smoker is in the grip of an addictive habit and, according to the degree to which he or she smokes, the body is being destroyed at a corresponding rate. There is no escape as long as the habit persists.

Smoking is not just linked with lung cancer. It is now known to be associated with half-a-dozen other lung complaints, many types of heart trouble, cancer in a dozen parts of the body (not just the lungs) and a host of other illnesses. One smoker out of four dies as a direct result of illness related to smoking, while three out of four lifetime smokers develop symptoms of smoking-related complaints before their lives draw to a close.

Like all addictions, cigarette smoking is hard to beat. Fortunately, it is not impossible. The social acceptance of smoking and drinking is the main reason for their widespread abuse. A study of smokers' hands shows that they fall into certain definite personality groups: conformist, egotistical, oddball, nervous, insecure. In most cases a smoker can be helped by learning from the palmist exactly why he has fallen into the habit. Part of cigarette addiction is psychological rather than physical, so it follows that psychological help can be a major factor in overcoming the problem.

Below you will find an account of the major types of smokers, as classified by their hands. Of course, there is some overlap between one type and the next, but by and large the types are quite distinct.

TYPE A —
THE CONFORMIST

4.1
Conformist smoker

The most common smoker is simply a conformist who smokes because others around him or her do so. Generally, this person began smoking at school and continues it throughout his life. The largest single group of chronic conformist smokers appears to be the nursing profession, followed closely by the armed forces and then by "big business" people. It is particularly ironic that nurses should fit so strongly into the conformist smokers' group since their training should make them especially aware of the medical dangers of their habit.

The majority of conformist smokers have closely spaced fingers (diag. 4.1). As explained elsewhere, fingers which lie close together at the base always show a conventional, non-independent mind, unless there are other strong factors in the hand for compensation. This closeness of the fingers affects the personality in two ways: it makes the owner conform to the behaviour and ideas of his or her peer group and it makes him or her a creature of habit who will seldom alter any aspect of behaviour once it is established.

If you wish to help a smoker of this type, you should start by pointing out and describing these conformist traits. You can point out the solidarity and social acceptability that the closed fingers bring along with the conformity and resistance to change. Advise the person that his or her very nature will always make it hard to change any habit, but stress that this is no reason not to make the effort. A person with closed fingers who once gets into the habit of not smoking is unlikely ever to revert. You should dwell upon this point in order to give encouragement.

Conformist smokers always smoke more heavily at parties and social gatherings, since this is where the pressure to conform is greatest. Try to get them to make a specific mental affirmation whenever they go to a party not to fall under this social pressure to smoke. Get them to make mental notes of the times and circumstances when they find themselves automatically reaching for a cigarette. One reformed smoker reported that he noticed the reaction most strongly when he changed a flat tyre on his car. The instinct to reach for a cigarette was automatic, even though the rational part of his mind told him that there was no possible way that a cigarette could make it easier to change a wheel!

You should present the medical evidence of the harm smoking causes. Remember that people with closed fingers need to be motivated before they will change, so it is up to you to provide the motivation. The stronger the case you make, the more chance you will have of convincing a closed-fingered person.

If a conformist smoker wants to give up the habit, you can suggest ways of modifying her behaviour, such as making a point of smoking only at certain times or places rather than all the time, or the pausing to think every time a cigarette is taken out of the packet. If the smoker makes a habit of asking, "Do I really need this?" whenever she touches a cigarette, this habit will help to break the usual automatic action of lighting up. You should stress that this question must be consciously adopted as a habit, however, as the method will never work if it is not made habitual.

TYPE B —
THE EGOTIST

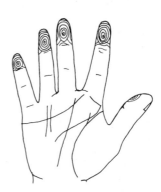

4.2
Egotist smoker

The most difficult smoker to influence is the one with a long index finger (diag. 4.2), indicative of a strongly developed ego. Oddly, such people do usually give up smoking eventually, but they invariably do this when they are ready, not when they are told! Having the long index, they feel that they must always make their own decisions about their lives.

A person with a long first finger is quite immune to threats. He will greet with quiet indifference your statement that he is wrecking his health. A child smoker with this long first finger will ignore beatings, bribery and tearful pleadings, so strong is the desire to be in control of his own life. Of course, the long index itself does not predispose its owner to smoke, but when a person with such a finger takes up smoking, nothing is going to make him give it up except his own will to do so.

Nevertheless, smokers of this type usually quit in the end because they also possess a high level of self-respect. Sooner or later the realisation comes that the habit is damaging, and then the person with the long first finger takes action accordingly. The rare exceptions are those whose egos are actually over-inflated, usually shown in the finger being thick as well as long, or by strong developments on the mount under the finger. With these people, self-assurance is so marked that they convince themselves that smoking couldn't do them harm. Other people may suffer, yes, but not them. These characters can be found puffing a cigarette in the cancer ward of the hospital.

TYPE C —
THE ODDBALL

4.3
Oddball smoker

A good proportion of the more unusual members of society smoke. There are people who stand out from the crowd by virtue of their odd personalities and strange ways, some of them being definitely disturbed mentally while others are merely eccentric. When one of these people smokes, you are likely to see unusual tobaccos, pipes and apparatus, imported cigars or roll-your-own cigarettes dangling from the mouth. Naturally, there are many odd characters who don't smoke at all. It is interesting to note that original thinkers who come from poorer backgrounds or working-class parents generally stick to cigarettes, while original thinkers from other spheres take to pipes and cigars.

Your chances of getting an original thinker to stop smoking are slim, as these people are in no sense conformist. Often they actually like tobacco, unlike other smokers for whom smoking is a habit rather than a genuine source of pleasure. If you persuade one of these people to stop smoking, the chances are that she will take it up again when her mood next changes.

There are two useful plans you might like to try. The first is to present your case, placing great emphasis on how logical it is to stop and how illogical to keep smoking. Many original thinkers pride themselves on being logical and sensible, unlike the bulk of humanity whom they consider to be slaves of habit and instinct. Knotty fingers (diag. 4.3) are an infallible sign of a person who responds to logic and reason, so if you see this formation you will know that you are on the right track. If you stress that you are appealing to his sense of reason rather than his emotions, this can sometimes win him over, the same way that the long-index-fingered person responds to your acknowledgement of his need to control his own affairs. Most people listen more to someone who understands them.

The other possible plan works for those odd people who believe in conspiracies and hidden forces in society. A good proportion of original thinkers fit into this class. They generally get involved in such things as food fads, flying saucer societies and mental-training groups. With the right persuasion, they may be talked into realising how harmful and destructive the smoking habit is. Talk about the money tobacco firms spend on advertising their harmful product. Talk about the unwillingness of governments to take action because of the enormous revenue they make from tobacco. Mention the way society is manipulated to accept smoking in spite of the medical evidence against it. A few words about the secret influence of big business companies and the possibility of governments and business interests working together against the real good of the people never go astray when you are talking with one of these unconventional people.

The indications of an original thinker are varied, for the good reason that no two of them are ever quite the same. If two or more of the fingers are of unusual lengths, this may be a clue, and if three fingers on a hand are out of proportion it is almost certain that the owner will be unusual. Long, knotty fingers or fingers which are extremely knotty, are other possibilities. A Head Line which slopes down deeply in the palm or a Head Line which takes a curvy path in the palm rather than the usual straight or curved form, probably indicates unconventional ideas. Perhaps the most important rule is that the real eccentric should have several signs of oddity in the hands, rather than one, and usually has signs of an active mind: whorl fingerprints, strong complex lines or interestingly shaped thumbs.

TYPE D —
THE NERVOUS TYPE

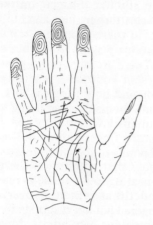

4.4
Nervous smoker

There are many people who smoke cigarettes in a desperate attempt to keep themselves calm. For them, cigarettes are a crutch. Sadly, cigarettes make the problem of nervous tension worse rather than better, so the nervous smoker is in need of help in breaking the habit both for psychological reasons and the usual health considerations.

The nervous hand can be distinguished by its multitude of fine lines (diag. 4.4). The most amateur palmist will notice that some hands have few lines while others have many. The nervous hand does not simply have many lines, it is covered with a spider-web of fine lines running in all directions, overlapping, crossing, doubling up in a confused tangle. The hand is usually long and slim, with a thin or weak thumb, but a tangle of innumerable lines is a sure sign of a highly strung temperament, whatever the hand shape may be.

Characteristically, such people are described by friends as "highly strung". They are always on the go, thinking and acting in a quick, jerky manner. Worries and problems abound in their lives. Owners of these hands think that life is full of difficulties and indeed it is. It is not the difficulties, however, which have caused the nervous tension, but the nervy personality which brings on one disaster after another!

With a person of this type, your approach must be different from what you would use in other cases. There is no point in trying to scare a nervous person, since although you will undoubtedly succeed, this will not incline her to give up the habit. Indeed, she will reach for a cigarette to calm herself when you graphically describe the symptoms of the illnesses that smoking can cause. What you must do is to sympathetically offer the smoker other, more productive ways of dealing with tension than smoking cigarettes.

However, there is one point that you should always raise with a nervous smoker and this is that smoking does not aid relaxation. When a person who smokes lights up a cigarette, it is true that this is a soothing experience, but the effects of nicotine on the nervous system mean that that person is always more tense than normal simply because of the smoking. The smoker who relaxes with a cigarette is merely temporarily reducing his tension to the point it would be if he had never taken up smoking in the first place. Regular use of cigarettes will keep a naturally tense person in a constant state of nervousness. By abandoning the habit, the nervousness will abate a little, usually between six weeks to four months after quitting smoking.

You should explain this point at least twice to the nervous type of smoker. It is a new thought to most people which takes a while to absorb. Nervous people require everything to be explained carefully, soothingly and sympathetically. I have never met a person who denied the argument in spite of the fact that smokers never seem to realise this illusionary nature of the supposed relaxation they gain from cigarettes until it is pointed out to them.

Here are some direct instructions to give to a nervous smoker.

1. "You can make yourself a lot calmer if you practise relaxation regularly every day. Sit down quietly and relax every muscle in your body, starting from your feet and working up to your head. Then just sit for 10 minutes keeping your mind quiet and your body totally relaxed. But you must do this regularly. It doesn't matter how long you spend relaxing each day. Ten minutes is enough providing it is done every day without fail. If you do this, you will find that it helps to keep you more relaxed throughout the day.

2. "If you want, you could go to a reputable hypnotist, not to stop smoking but to learn to relax. Any good hypnotist will be happy to teach you relaxation techniques if you ask him. You could also take up meditation if you want, though this is not really necessary. Any of the groups which teach meditation would help although this will cost you money. There is a simple form of meditation which is as good as any other and you can teach yourself.

Just sit down and relax completely. Close your eyes and just listen to your own breathing for 10 minutes without thinking about anything else. Every time you breathe out, say the word 'one' to yourself. If you do this for 10 minutes every day, it will work wonders. But remember once again, that it must be every day. Just thinking about relaxing won't do it. You've actually got to do it and do it regularly and then it will work.

3. "You could also practise being calm during the day. For example, watch your speech and your arm and hand movements. You will notice that you speak fast and wave your hands about a lot. Practise speaking slowly. You'll find this helps to calm you down. Also, practise letting your hands remain still. Don't force them, but just make a conscious effort to let them remain still and relaxed.

4. "Finally, make an effort to be indifferent to things. In other words, practise not letting things annoy or bother you. Say to yourself: 'This doesn't matter. I'm not going to worry about it.' You mustn't force yourself, or try to put troubles out of your mind, as that will just make you more tense, but try to practise genuinely not caring about them. It's the difference between holding back a wall of water or just letting it flow around you. You can do it if you try. If you meditate, spend 10 minutes before you start, quietly thinking about the events of the day and mentally standing back from them, realising that they are not things to worry about. Like meditation, this helps if you do it regularly.

"If you carry out these things I will guarantee that you can get rid of a lot of your tension and give up smoking. But you've got to try. It will only work if you practise. Those cigarettes are killing you: why not use these other methods of helping yourself and then you won't need to smoke any more."

A pep talk like this will sometimes work wonders with a nervous smoker, but most people lack the strength to carry out this sort of program by themselves. It will help if you write this out, or make copies of it, or if you put it on a cassette tape. If you can, get the person to join any of the groups or societies which teach meditation or yoga, although you need to know whether the groups in your local area are reputable. Unfortunately, there are some high-cost teaching societies which are little short of con games designed to extort money from the unhappy people who come to them seeking help. Never send a nervous person off to a dubious society. The unscrupulous prey upon just such people.

TYPE E —
THE INSECURE TYPE

4.5
Insecure smoker

Closely allied with the nervous smoker is the smoker with an inferiority complex. This, of course, is revealed by a short index finger (diag. 4.5). One odd point is that smokers with this formation often have a badly nicotine-stained index finger. Why this should be so is an intriguing puzzle: my own view is that insecure people tend to grip the cigarette tightly and to draw on it in a close, hard manner thus increasing the amount of nicotine left on their fingers.

The techniques for helping a smoker with the short index finger are the same as those used for a conformist smoker. However, it is worth pointing out to the client that for her smoking is a way of dealing with insecurity and that she undoubtedly smokes more when worried, when nervous, when in strange or new circumstances, and whenever an effort of any sort has to be made. Her own mind tends to cast doubts upon her chances of succeeding at anything she does. Elsewhere in this book, you will find a discussion of the short index finger, in which it is pointed out that you can help such a person by boosting her ego. If you can make it abundantly clear to a smoker that smoking is just a prop, related to her own feelings of inferiority, there is some chance that she will see the silliness of continuing to smoke. If you then give her suggestions for counteracting her insecurity, plus the usual presentation of hard evidence against smoking, she may be persuaded to kick the habit.

Unlike the nervous smoker, the smoker with a short index will not become upset if you paint a graphic picture of the horrors of the physical illness of the smoker.

As stated at the beginning of this chapter, the various types of smokers overlap and, although you will find clear examples of the above-mentioned types, there are of course smokers who do not fit into any of the categories.

The human hand often gives clear warnings about the health of its owner, which may be very useful in underlining the dangers of smoking. Medical palmistry is a complete branch of hand analysis with a literature all of its own. However, let me sound a warning here — medical palmistry is a very specialised area which is not suitable for the amateur to dabble in.

In the first place, many medical indications in the hand are hints only, not absolutely infallible diagnostic clues. Most of them can be invaluable when used in conjunction with proper medical tests, but it is obviously ridiculous to diagnose, say, high blood pressure from the hand without checking the blood pressure to discover if the diagnosis is correct. Secondly, most medical indications are fairly subtle things which cannot be identified without a good deal of practice. Thirdly, medicine is most definitely a practice which should only be attempted by those with proper medical training. While it is true that there are many incompetent doctors, many competent healers who are not doctors and many forms of treatment not used by the medical profession, it is equally true that no-one should practise healing unless they have an excellent understanding of the workings of the human body. There are so-called "fringe practitioners" who achieve excellent results, but there are also some who are a positive menace to society. Therefore, tread most carefully if you wish to investigate the medical aspects of hand reading.

One final warning: there is a great deal of conflict in the various theories of medical signs in the hand. Half-a-dozen practitioners are likely to give you half-a-dozen different interpretations. Use your commonsense to the utmost if you want to look into this area.

MEDICAL INDICATIONS

I claim that there are four major indications in the hand which are relevant to the smoking problem: lung trouble, heart trouble, afflictions of the nervous system, and nicotine poisoning.

There is also a Mark of Cancer, which is in a different class from these four.

These are all discussed in detail below.

LUNG AFFLICTIONS

"Clubbing" of the fingertips is recognised by the medical profession as being very common in heart and lung disease. There is a particular type of curving of the fingernails which is particularly related to trouble with the lungs, and this formation

4.6
Normal fingernail

4.7
Curved fingernail

is extremely common with chronic smokers while it is extremely rare with non-smokers.

The formation consists of a curving of the nail into a hooked formation from the nail bed to its tip. The normal nail is shaped much like the nail in diagram 4.6, while in chronic smokers it often starts to take on the shape of the nail in diagram 4.7. This pattern invariably commences with the index finger of the left hand, followed by the index finger of the right hand. It spreads in time to the middle fingers of both hands and over decades of smoking it will continue until all the nails have this form.

The fingernails may occasionally all have this form in a person who is not a smoker. It is the progressive development from the first to the fifth finger that distinguishes the developing lung damage. Interestingly, Hippocrates, the father of medicine, identified a related type of nail disturbance to tuberculosis and this symptom is still recognised by doctors today. Further confirmation of the fact that these nail changes reflect lung damage is provided by the fact that you will not find them in smokers who have indulged only for a year or two in smoking.

When you find all the nails curved, there is likely to be a history of colds, flu and possibly bronchitis, regardless of whether the person is a smoker or not. However, a few females have naturally curved nails and no obvious lung weakness. (This is quite different from a set of progressively curved nails.) Such nails are never found on males and may be related to the female hormones. For this reason, a diagnosis made from naturally curved nails is not as certain as one made from nails which curve progressively from first to fifth fingers.

When you find this smoker's syndrome in a hand, you may be sure that the person has a chronic cough (which they will usually assure you is just a current thing caused by a recent cold!), probably gets colds regularly in winter and, if the formation is extremely pronounced, probably suffers from shortness of breath. If the person stops smoking, the nails will return to normal within months. Even in the worst cases, two years' abstinence from smoking is usually enough to bring the nails back to normal.

Telling the person about these medical signs and pointing out the contrast between the curved first and second fingernails on the left hand and the relatively flat ones on the little finger is one of the most convincing ways to get through to smokers. In most cases where index nails are curved, you will be able to point out that the left is worse than the right.

You will occasionally find a person with lung trouble who does not show this syndrome and you will even sometimes find heavy smokers with a bad cough who do not show it. However, such exceptions to the rule are uncommon and simply reinforce the basic rule of palmistry: "Absence of a marking does not prove that a quality is *not* present, but the presence of a marking always proves that the quality is present."

A clear island in the Life Line, under the first finger (diag. 4.8) is often a record of past attacks of bronchitis, particularly when the person has suffered from this disease in childhood.

AFFLICTIONS OF THE HEART

Smokers are much more susceptible to heart trouble than non-smokers. This rule also applies to other disturbances to blood circulation besides heart complaints, e.g. among women who use the contraceptive pill and who smoke as well, blood clots are far more frequent than for women who use the pill but do not smoke. It is also worth noting that being overweight also increases the chances of heart complaints so that an overweight person who smokes is in even more danger than a slim person who smokes.

There is no sign of heart trouble in the hands which can be directly related to smoking, but there are signs of heart trouble which may come about for varying reasons. If you find these signs in the hands of a smoker, you can be fairly certain that the person is running a severe risk of heart failure well before he reaches the normal limits of longevity.

Short nails (diag. 4.9) are commonly found among sufferers from high blood pressure and those who have a history of heart complaints. They are also common among people with a family history of death from heart attacks. Note that the word "short" refers to the length of the nail from the cuticle to the tip of the finger, since the length which overlaps the fingertip is quite irrelevant. The short nail is always defined as having a length

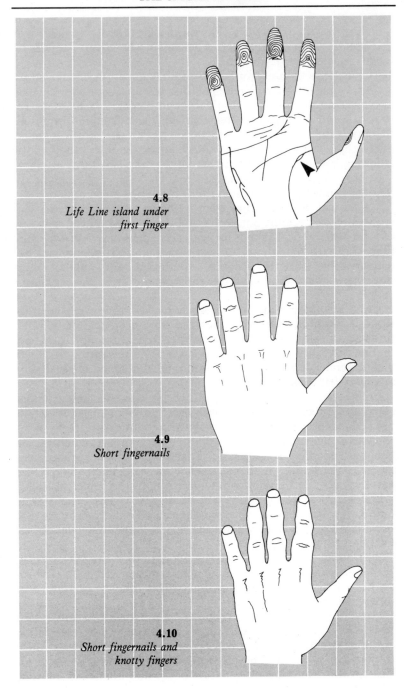

4.8
*Life Line island under
first finger*

4.9
Short fingernails

4.10
*Short fingernails and
knotty fingers*

which is less than its width. There is a type of nail which is short and square. Such a nail is not to be considered "short" unless its length is less than its width.

I have some grounds for believing that nails can change shape and that a person with a predisposition towards heart trouble who also smokes may find his nails alter imperceptibly in shape till they take on this typical, short, broad, heart-trouble formation. At any rate, a person with these nails who smokes or is overweight is in danger of eventual heart trouble, whether the smoking has actually caused the nail to take this form or not.

These short, broad nails always go with a psychological tendency to be critical. This is infallible. The person undoubtedly has a critical mind, so that even if she is a gentle type she will still be quick to point out faults and flaws in whatever she sees. On the other hand, if she is an aggressive person you may be sure that she will be sharp in her manner and cranky in her conversation. Knotty fingers, combined with these short fingernails (diag. 4.10) are found on argumentative, cantankerous people.

It is an interesting question, whether the predisposition towards heart conditions makes the person critical or whether this type of mind predisposes its owner to heart complaints! I am inclined to believe that it is the latter. The relaxation exercises recommended for the nervous smoker should be suggested to anyone with these fingernails.

Arch type fingerprints (diag. 4.11) are also associated with a congenital predisposition towards heart problems, particularly to high blood pressure. A person with arch fingerprints is in no danger if he remains slim, doesn't smoke and indulges in moderate exercise all of his life. There are also some pronounced signs in the hand which are associated with heart defects but these are rare. A thickening and swelling of the fingertips (diag. 4.12) occurs in some serious heart diseases. Also, the Simian Line (a bar line across the hand instead of a normal Head Line and Heart Line) is closely associated with congenital weakness of the heart (diag. 4.13).

Both arch fingerprints and the Simian Line are often found with a high axial tri-radius in the palmar skin patterns. If all three of these signs occur together (diag. 4.14) there is certain to be some weakness of the heart.

Most medical palmists agree that the end of the Heart Line under the little finger reveals much about the physical condition of the heart. But this is one of those matters about which there are varying opinions. There seems to be no doubt that the basic idea is valid, but the precise nature of the disturbance found with

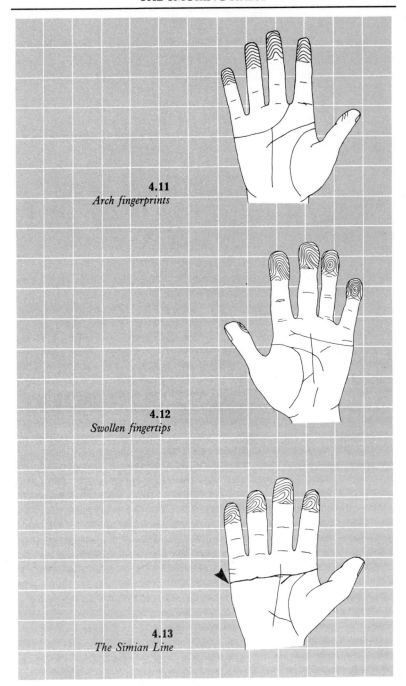

4.11
Arch fingerprints

4.12
Swollen fingertips

4.13
The Simian Line

each type of heart complaint is variable. The normal Heart Line is somewhat chained under the little finger (diag. 4.15). If it is totally unchained and appears as a thin, bare line you may suspect something is wrong. If the chaining is unusually pronounced and continues up the line past the ring finger, this also suggests a physical disturbance to the heart (diag. 4.16). A complete breaking up and fragmenting of the line at its end (diag. 4.17) often occurs in a person with a history of heart troubles before a final heart attack. Because of the uncertainty of these matters, I would advise readers never to make a judgment from the Heart Line alone, unless they have considerable experience in medical palmistry. The investigation of these markings could be a very worthwhile area for further research by anyone with access to complete medical records of heart sufferers *and* with the medical knowledge to know what they are dealing with!

AFFLICTIONS OF THE NERVOUS SYSTEM

In some people there is a tendency towards problems which may loosely be termed complaints of the nervous system. These include headache, some back and neck pains, eyestrain, skin complaints such as reddening and cracking of the skin on the hands as well as a host of major skin diseases. Nervous tics and tremors fit into this category. I distinguish these complaints from psychosomatic ones because they are not simply caused by mental conditions. Usually, there is a mental component in these illnesses, but there is also a physical component, generally some irritant in the diet or even the atmosphere, or some insufficiency in the diet such as a mineral imbalance.

In making these observations, I am lumping together in an informal manner complaints which orthodox medicine may consider quite unrelated. I do this because there is a type of fingernail which, when found, will be associated with one or even several of the complaints. Although the nail is rare, when found it is usually in the hands of a smoker. The nail may be any shape, but it is characterised by a whitish tinge which, carried to extremes, makes the whole nail almost dead white. Most nails show either a healthy pink or the deeper purple-blue colour, the latter indicating poor circulation in the extremities (hands, feet, nose, ears). If the nail has neither of these colours it will generally be so pale or colourless as to be almost white and this is the nail of which I speak. (This nail is not to be confused with the white specks that sometimes occur in fingernails.)

If you encounter a person who has the whitish nails, who is also a smoker, tell him to stop smoking and he will lose either the whole or the greater part of his symptoms. Medical and cosmetic

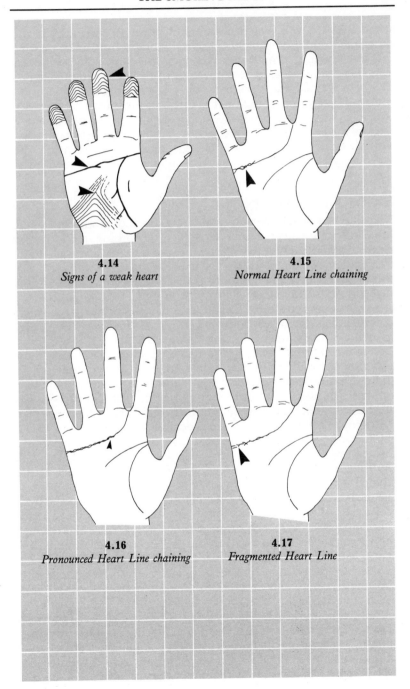

4.14
Signs of a weak heart

4.15
Normal Heart Line chaining

4.16
Pronounced Heart Line chaining

4.17
Fragmented Heart Line

authorities are well aware that smoking promotes wrinkles in the skin, and people who have these nails and who smoke may be able to achieve reformation if you emphasise this point. Sufferers from head and back pain who have these nails should have it clearly explained that smoking is only aggravating their condition and perhaps even causing it! It is difficult for most people to see how cigarettes could possibly play a part in back pain and, certainly, in most cases, they do not. Yet with these uncommon, whitish nails, the smoking habit seems to be affecting the nervous system rather than causing more common lung or heart troubles.

NICOTINE POISONING
Nicotine is a deadly poison, and a few drops of it injected under the skin can cause death. However, absorbing this drug in cigarette smoke obviously does not cause instantaneous death for the smoker. Taken in this way, it has a much slower and more subtle effect. It is my contention that some people are far more susceptible to the effect of nicotine in cigarette smoke than are others. For such people, the smoking habit is prone to causing a general poisoning of the body and thus leads to a very wide range of medical complaints.

It has been proved that cancer of many parts of the body is more common in smokers than in non-smokers. Recent studies have shown that nicotine is present in the breasts of any female who smokes. Illnesses of the kidneys and of the various parts of the digestive system can also be related to smoking.

It is not possible to tell a great deal about these matters from the hands — although medical palmists have found many interesting clues. However, in certain hands you will find that the fingernails are discoloured by nicotine, not because it has stained the finger in the way that roll-your-owns do, but because the growing nail itself is stained before it emerges from the flesh of the nail bed! What is happening in these cases is that nicotine is actually being excreted through the hair, the nails and through the whole of the skin as well as the more obvious channels. One example of this little-recognised fact is the odour, literally exhaled by the skin, which can be created by a particular diet. Chronic smokers may smell of tobacco no matter how hard they scrub their hands!

Nails which show nicotine stains while the rest of the finger does not are a sure sign that the body is saturated with this drug. Although you cannot draw definite conclusions from this, it should be pointed out to the owner of the hands concerned and followed by a discussion of the effect that nicotine is known to have on the human body. The fact that people can see this stain in their nails usually comes as a shock to them when you point it out.

CANCER

4.18
*Clearly formed island
at bottom of Life Line*

Medical palmists claim that there can be signs of cancer in the hands. Most of these signs occur in some cases of cancer but not in others and therefore have limited value. There is just one clear marking which can be easily recognised, and I shall deal with this later. First, here are some essential points to be noted.

This marking is not an infallible indication of cancer, nor is it a forecast that cancer will occur. It is, at most, an indication that cancer is a possibility. I have found it in people who have lost close relatives from cancer. I have found it in cancer sufferers. I have found it in chronic smokers and in fair-skinned people who have indulged in excessive sunbathing. I have seldom, if ever, found it in a person who did not fulfil one of these conditions. There are people, on the other hand, who have died from cancer and whose hands showed no mark of this kind.

I would advise you to proceed with great care if you find this mark. First, check whether the person is a smoker or habitual sun-seeker (this latter point applies more in tropic regions than in colder climates). If so, proceed to remind them of the dangers, then point out the mark and advise her that although it is not a prediction that cancer *will* occur, it is an obvious *warning* sign that she cannot afford to ignore. Advise strongly that she should no longer take any risks with her health. Enquire if there is any family history of cancer. If the answer is in the affirmative, stress that she has excellent prospects of avoiding any trace of the disease providing she takes stringent precautions with her health. Suggest that she obtain from the government health department a leaflet on the warning signs of cancer and that she familiarise herself with these. Stress again that this is a sensible pre-cautionary measure rather than an implication that cancer is to be expected.

The marking is an egg-shaped island at the bottom of the Life Line, as shown (diag. 4.18). Note well that it is necessary for the mark to be *clearly formed*. A large island or poorly formed island is not the mark.

The Cancer Island is invariably clear and obvious. One peculiarity of the mark is that it is generally clearer on the hand itself than on a print, unlike the majority of lines which appear more clearly on an inked print than they do on the hand. The reason for this is that the lines which make it up are often deep, and depth of lines does not reproduce on paper.

Like all lines, this marking may grow, fade or change completely. If you find it in the hands of a smoker you are justified in drawing it to his attention and making the appropriate recommendations. Remember always to speak with care. One young student of mine, on learning about this mark, proceeded to examine the hands of a young woman and announced: "Oh, you're going to die of cancer. You've got the cancer mark." For sheer stupidity and a total misuse of the science of palmistry, this would be hard to beat.

In concluding these comments on smoking and health, remember that if you are in any doubt you should recommend that expert medical advice be sought. You may annoy your local doctor if he starts getting patients who demand a checkup for a complaint that you have diagnosed, but it is better to get confirmation of a palmist's medical opinion than to ignore medical signs in the hands completely. With the hands of smokers, however, the more evidence you can raise on the destructive effect of this addiction on their bodies, the better your chances of encouraging them to break the habit.

CHAPTER V

HOW YOUR HANDS CAN SOLVE YOUR EMPLOYMENT PROBLEMS

Your love life and your job — the two subjects everyone wants to know about. We are entering an age where many jobs are becoming obsolete, so there is a chance that 20 years from now you'll be asking: "Will I ever have a job?" rather than: "What sort of job should I have?" Nevertheless, employment today is one of the biggest causes of dissatisfaction for people, and palmistry offers an excellent way to solve the dilemma and find what you are suited to.

By studying the hands of people in all types of work, I have found that certain sorts of work require people who have particular markings in their hands. With most of my clients I can say, "You are most suited for such-and-such a job," and in many of these cases the instant reply is, "That's exactly what I'm doing." People do gravitate to the type of employment that they feel happiest with, often after unsuccessful attempts at other work. If they had consulted the palmist in the first place, what a lot of time could have been saved.

The palmist can look at the hands of a teenager and pick the best possible field for his or her future employment. The palmist can advise the discontented worker on what jobs he would prefer to his present occupation. In some cases, the palmist can tell a specialist worker how to get the most out of her profession or how to avoid particular tensions in the work which may be causing aggravation. However, not everyone is ideally suited to one particular job, nor does every job require one particular type of worker. For this reason, palmistry is not a magical way of slotting every individual into the only suitable occupation.

There has been a good deal of nonsense talked about "vocational guidance through palmistry" by some of the earlier palmists. Many writers have produced books based entirely on theory, containing no practical evidence whatsoever. Just as palmists in Victorian times used to discourse learnedly on the hands of different nationalities without ever having examined a Russian or an Asian hand, so too they listed all the features in the hands of every occupation from chief cook to banking official. Little if any of it was accurate. Palmists who had seen the hand of a local doctor felt qualified to lecture about the hands of surgeons, general practitioners and specialists in tropical diseases, with complete but spurious authority.

In this book you will find nothing which is not backed up by hard evidence. But the most important discovery made from studying the hands of workers is this: *If someone is determined to succeed in a particular profession, he or she may do so no matter how unsuited the hands may seem to that work.* Ninety per cent of sportspeople have similar hands but I have seen the hands of a top footballer whose palm showed he would have made an excellent poet. I have seen a forest ranger who would have made a first class accountant.

Such cases prove that you can succeed in a job against all odds, providing your will to do so is strong enough. But these cases are the determined few. Following is an outline of hand patterns commonly associated with specific vocations.

OUTDOOR EMPLOYMENT

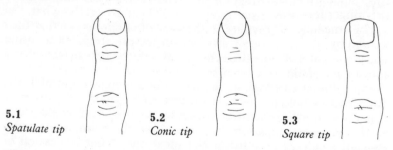

5.1
Spatulate tip

5.2
Conic tip

5.3
Square tip

There is a whole range of jobs which involve being out-of-doors, such as a construction worker, transport worker, agriculturalist, postman, park ranger, and so on. Of course, this covers an enormous range of specific skills. Nevertheless, there is one simple hand feature which marks the person who does not like to work indoors and is therefore commonly found in these occupations. That feature is spatulate fingertips (diag. 5.1). Most fingertips are relatively rounded (diag. 5.2), technically called conic tips. Very rarely they may even be pointed. A good number of tips are relatively square (diag. 5.3), but spatulate tips are found on the outdoors people.

Diagram 5.4 shows a full set of these fingers. Note that the first and smallest fingers are less swollen than the two central ones. Many people have a slight spatulate tendency in the ring finger which is of no real significance. The outstanding characteristic associated with the spatulate tips is activity. People with them like the freedom to move about and they have a corresponding dislike of sitting still. They like to walk, run, and indulge in active sports such as hockey, cycling or squash.

Not everyone with these fingers gravitates to an outdoor job although a high proportion of them do. The remainder invariably confine their love of activity to their leisure time if the working environment does not provide it. One spatulate-tipped friend of mine is an electrician by trade who has extensive part-time involvement in professional archery, canoeing and hunting. Another is a farmer who, in his middle years, has opened a successful occult bookstore. Whether the outdoor instincts are expressed through full-time or part-time activity they will always play a big part in the lives of those who have this hand feature

There is a second quality associated with the spatulate tips and that is inventiveness. There is no apparent reason for this and yet it is generally so. Inventors, and those who show a knack for inventive suggestion, often have these tips. Professionals of the Edison variety need to possess other qualities besides spatulate tips, but the inventive tendency will be present in anyone with this finger formation.

The medical profession recognises a phenomenon called "clubbing of the fingers", which is an exaggerated form of the spatulate pattern. All the fingertips take on a very swollen appearance (diag. 5.5). This is caused by serious heart defects. I suspect that the energy of a spatulate-tipped person comes from an enlarged or strongly beating heart and I would therefore advise anyone with this pattern not to risk heart strain: don't smoke, minimise the intake of red meat, reduce salt and sugar consumption and concentrate on eating fresh fruit and vegetables. Moderate exercise should be kept up all through the years and retirement should not be a time of inactivity.

There is a major feature of the hands of an outdoors person which is reflected by a particular shape of the hand itself. As explained in Chapter I, I use a system of classifying hands into

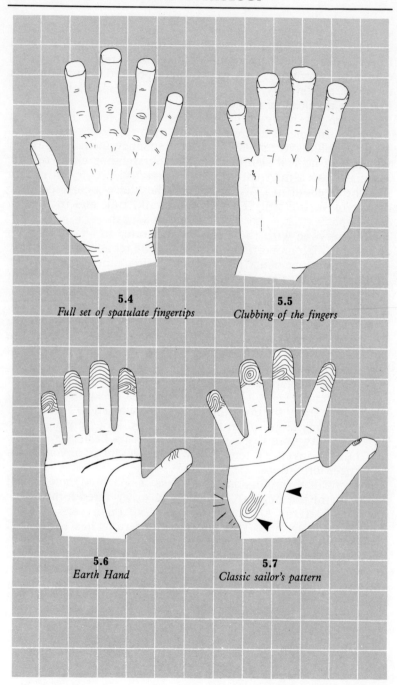

5.4
Full set of spatulate fingertips

5.5
Clubbing of the fingers

5.6
Earth Hand

5.7
Classic sailor's pattern

four main types: Earth Hands, Fire Hands, Water Hands and Air Hands. The Earth Hand is a simple hand. People with such a hand tend to get out into the countryside. City life and indoor jobs rarely appeal to Earth-Handed people (diag. 5.6).

In farming communities, every second person you meet will be an Earth-Hand type, from the person who runs the local store to the small-town mayor. Farmers themselves almost all have Earth Hands. There is a very important principle at work here. It is not just the simplicity of working on the land which appeals to Earth-Handed folk, but an actual affinity with nature. Occasionally, you will meet one of these people in an urban job, perhaps a factory worker, and invariably if you get into conversation with him you will hear of his dream to buy a piece of land. Open spaces, vegetation, sunshine, these things have a deep attraction for the Earth-Handed individual. He may even be in an outdoor job, but he would be happier if he worked at that same job in a small town rather than in a large city.

The Earth-Handed person enjoys repetitive, rhythmic work. The flow of the seasons is in her blood and if her work has seasonal fluctuations, so much the better. She is also a hard worker. There is nothing lazy about her. Two problems may arise with these folk. The first occurs when such a person is in a non-rural job and accordingly feels discontent. I once encountered an Earth-Handed bank manager who was planning to retire to a farm. To any such person I would say, by all means stay in your present occupation, but see if you can move to a smaller town or one of the outer suburbs of the city. This simple step is generally all that is required to improve the level of contentment.

The second problem concerns change. Earth-Handed folk are stable and dislike altering their lifestyles. Occasionally, I am approached by such a person who has come to a crisis in his life and is worried by the impending changes. All that is required in such a case is encouragement, the reassurance from someone that he can handle the change. The stability of these people prevents them from becoming nervy, and as much as they hate upheaval they do manage to cope with it.

The hands of outdoor workers are usually strong, simple ones with deep lines, no matter what actual shape the hand may be. Very energetic outdoor types may show a profusion of deep lines rather than just a few, but this is uncommon.

There is one final formation found with these folk and that is a development of the Mount of Luna, a pattern often found on sailors. Here again we are dealing with something which is not easy to explain. Just as the attraction of rural life seems to operate almost on a spiritual or psychic level with Earth-Handed people, so the attraction to water is present in all those whose Mount of Luna is strongly developed. Often there will also be a wide-sweeping Life Line which is a sign of vitality. A great many sailors possess both these marks plus the skin-ridge pattern shown here (diag. 5.7). But of the three points, the development of the Mount of Luna is the classic sailor's pattern.

BUSINESS SKILLS

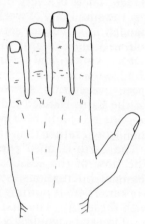

5.8
A full set of square fingertips indicates an orderly, methodical mind

To be a clerk may not seem a very high achievement to some, but there are certain clerical skills which are both profitable and fairly high-status: accountancy, bookkeeping, banking and senior positions within government all require a special type of mind, which is revealed by a particular shape of the fingertips.

The finger shape required is the square tip (diag. 5.8), one of the major shapes. It is the sign of an orderly, regular, methodical mind. Someone with fingers of this shape is virtually certain to be neat. If she works with tools, every one will be put back into place the moment she has finished with it. If she works at a desk, every pen and pencil is in its precise position. Documents, letters, bills, receipts are all dealt with in regular order and filed into place when no longer needed. If there is any figure work to be done, the columns of numbers are totalled up with scrupulous accuracy.

Usually, these tips are found on the hands of intelligent folk and so nearly all of them wind up in the fields already listed. But I have sometimes found these tips on outdoors people or certain musicians. But these tips are so universal in the banking, clerical and accounting trades that they can be considered the real mark of these occupations.

Accountants typically have smooth fingers with square tips and the fingers themselves are rather long. Here we have a point which was quite misunderstood by some earlier palmists who assumed that since knotty fingers go with a reasoning, logical mind then accountants should have long knotty fingers. In fact, out of the hundreds of accountants whose hands I have studied, I have never encountered one whose fingers were not absolutely smooth, most with the tips squared. Often these hands have the fingers close together, the sign of a conservative nature. Commonly the fingerprints will be loops, which go with a sensible way of dealing with things. Whatever other features may be found, the square fingertips show a mind suited to this type of work.

These people take work problems in their stride. When one of them consults a palmist, it is rarely because there is any particular worry. Why do they come to me? Among my clients, square-tipped people come in when one of their relatives or friends has visited me. They have a respect for quality and efficiency and when they hear of a palmist turning out high-quality work, they are not averse to coming to investigate for themselves. Then, too, these professions are often high-tension positions and while the banker usually feels confident to cope, he carries within himself a sort of keyed-up alertness for possible trouble ahead. He is not worried, but he is always watchful for danger. A visit to a good palmist gives him useful facts or ideas which assure him that things will continue to run smoothly.

Troubles in their personal lives do occur, but generally it is those people around the square-tipped person who have the problem. Believing that there is one right way to do things, Ms Square Tips does not see eye-to-eye with those whose ideas may be different. Accordingly, some people find square-tipped folk hard to get on with. The typical bohemian is so alien to the square-tipped person that the two types could never understand each other.

Business and professional people of all types commonly have a distinctive skin-ridge pattern. It indicates a serious turn of mind. Most people have one or other of the skin-ridge patterns known as "the Loop of Seriousness" and "the Loop of Humour" (diags 5.9 and 5.10). The former loop is also known as "the Business Loop". Obviously, not everyone with this loop goes into business. Some have other interests, some lack the intelligence or the opportunity to follow a business career. Nevertheless, among business and professional people the Loop of Seriousness is twice as common as it is among the general population.

Neither loop indicates any special ability. Instead, they reveal the fundamental *attitude* of their owners. The Humour Loop goes with a light-hearted approach to life. These people smile, make

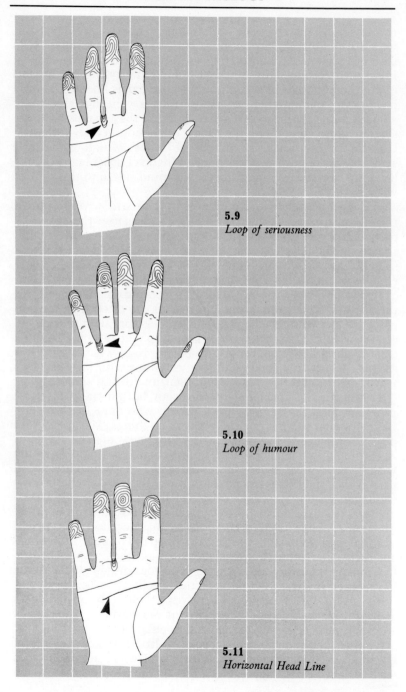

5.9
Loop of seriousness

5.10
Loop of humour

5.11
Horizontal Head Line

jokes, love to party and can relax without feeling guilty about it. The person with a Loop of Seriousness, on the other hand, believes in getting ahead, doing something worthwhile in life. As a result, a person with this marking usually makes money and attains success in whatever business or career is undertaken.

Here is a sexist comment: women with the Serious Loop tend to become nurses and teachers. There is no reason why more should not be stockbrokers, lawyers and business managers as well, but the depressing fact is that the nursing and teaching professions absorb a high proportion of career-minded young women. As more women break into once male-dominated business spheres, however, they may well bring different results to palmists researching a decade from now.

People with Humour Loops can and do succeed in professional and business careers but they are certainly in the minority. There are people with Serious Loops who are quite unsuited to such a career, but they too would be in the minority. By and large, the presence of the Serious Loop in the active hand (right hand for a right-hander, left hand for a left-hander) is a strong indication of a successful business or professional career.

Three minor rules conclude this survey of business hands.

1. Head Lines which run more or less horizontally across the palm, with little slope or curve, go with a calculative turn of mind (diag. 5.11). They have been called "business Head Lines" because their owners show a definite business acumen. I personally regard this name as inaccurate since business men and women can have almost any sort of Head Line and this horizontal line is no more common on business hands than on others. What it does do, however, is to give the owner an eye for a bargain and a good business sense. All too often they are not very nice people.

2. A long, straight Fate Line running most of the length of the palm (diag. 5.12) is a sure sign of someone who easily gets into a rut. As a result, such people seldom change their direction in life or their ways. Instead, they spend years with the same life-style only rarely breaking out to make a change. Because of this, there long ago arose the theory that a long, straight Fate Line indicates a success-ful career. But remember that the term "successful career" is a relative one.

The Fate Line has little to do with fate, but a lot to do with psychological attitudes. The influence of destiny does show in the hands, primarily in the Life Line and to a lesser extent in the Fate Line. Primarily, the Fate Line

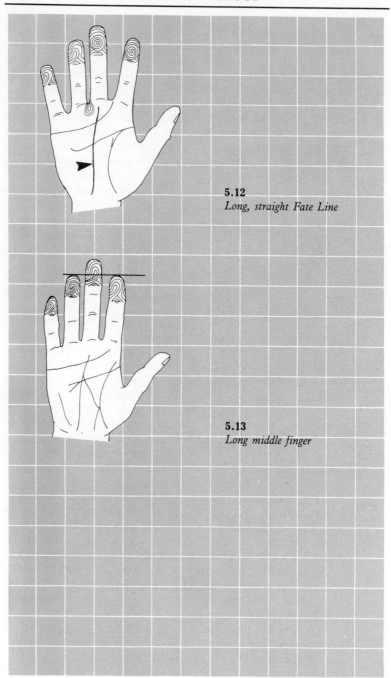

5.12
Long, straight Fate Line

5.13
Long middle finger

reveals our attitude to employment, the sort of work patterns that suit us best. Because the long Fate Line indicates an attitude only, it is unwise to predict with certainty that its owner will follow just one path through life. Psychologically, he is prone to doing so, but circumstances may interfere which cause him to change his employment even though he would prefer not to.

3.   An unusually long middle finger (diag. 5.13) is a rarity but when found it has much the same meaning as the Loop of Seriousness. You will recall that this finger relates to our working life. On most hands, the index finger and the ring finger reach about two-thirds of the way up the top joint of the middle finger. If this Saturn finger projects much further than this, you may conclude that the owner has a serious turn of mind. A Loop of Seriousness usually accompanies this rare long middle finger.

ADMINISTRATION

5.14
*Hand of the head of a
department. The index finger
provides clues to
administrative ability*

Would you like to be a leader? Do you have a secret desire to take over the boss's job? Perhaps you are the boss after all! Does the idea of being self-employed appeal to you? Would you like to have your own business? Would you make a good salesperson? A palmist looking at your hands can answer all these questions quite as well as you can answer them yourself, maybe better. All of these points are clearly reflected in your hands.

To make a good leader, many qualities are needed: knowledge, skill, wisdom, the ability to handle people. Yet there are some who have all these attributes and yet have no desire to lead or to boss others around. You must study the whole hand to get at these features. To learn about a person's desire to get ahead, you need look no further than the index finger. This interesting digit

provides two major clues to self-confidence in its length and its
position. Remember that the position of the fingers must be
judged when the hand is relaxed and at rest.

A wide space between the first and second fingers (diag. 5.14),
not the outward-thrust index finger (diag. 5.15), indicates a talent
for making decisions. Nine times out of 10 you will find this
pattern on the hands of someone whose job requires her to be a
decision-maker. You will rarely find it on the hands of someone
who has a natural gift for decision-making, the difference being
subtle but all-important. For this space between the fingers
develops in people who undertake decision-making jobs or
lifestyles (e.g. a personnel officer in a job agency or the single
parent who must now take the place of two parents). I have often
found this pattern in those who are not officially at the top of a
business but who manage to do most of the running of that
business. The department head will show this formation more
often than the chairperson of the board. Strictly speaking, this is
not a sign of leadership but rather one of initiative; the ability to
decide what to do and when to do it.

People whose hands show this pattern thrive on situations
where decision-making is necessary. Whether the job brings out
this quality in a worker, so that his hands become like this, or
whether the worker with this pattern gravitates to a job where the
ability can be utilised, both his personal life and his employment
are virtually certain to display this characteristic trait.

The true mark of leadership is the long index finger, the sign of
self-confidence and self-awareness (diag. 5.16). If this long index
is found on a hand which shows business ability then the owner
will certainly rise to the top of whatever profession she has
chosen. It is an interesting fact that workers with this pattern are
sometimes picked for promotion when they themselves have
little desire to get to the top. Their natural self-assurance is noted
by those around them, including the boss, even though they may
not be aware of this quality in themselves.

Occasionally, you will meet a long-index-fingered person who
claims to have plenty of self-doubt. Don't believe it! Many long-
indexed people pay great attention to every step they take,
carefully making sure they do and say everything properly. They
imagine that this carefulness means that they are doubtful about
themselves, but if you challenge them on any issue at all, you
will find resolute confidence in their own point of view! This is
not self-doubt, it is simply a preoccupation with one's own self-
image.

The most amazing case of such a person that I have
encountered was a middle-aged lady who visited me with an

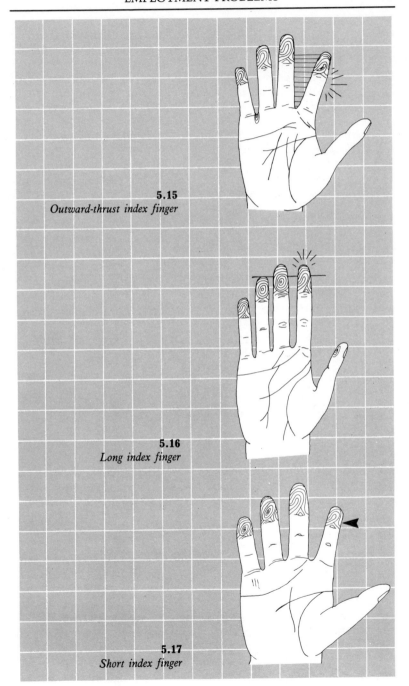

5.15
Outward-thrust index finger

5.16
Long index finger

5.17
Short index finger

*elderly friend. Let's call her Ms Smith. This client entered my
office with her friend in tow. "Come on in, Myrtle. I've found the
place," she announced loudly and then proceeded to introduce
her friend to me as if she had known me all her life instead of
having just laid eyes on me. "Now, Myrtle, you run along and
have a nice cup of tea while Mr Fitzherbert reads my hands," she
went on.*

*When we were seated, she raised her hands in the air with a
flourish, then dramatically laid them down for my inspection.
Her index finger was exactly the length of the middle finger! I
proceeded to read her hands, a difficult task as she interrupted me
continually. My comments on her massive egotism excited her
considerably. "Oh, Mr Fitzherbert, it's not true! I'm the shyest
person in the whole world. I don't know why you say that about
me. I am terribly timid really." At the end of the interview,
Ms Smith went out to her friend in the waiting room and I heard
her say, "Now you go right on in, Myrtle, and don't be shy. You
go straight in and sit down." Myrtle came in, a thin lady of 70,
and gave me a smile. "Ms Smith is a lovely person," she
whispered, "but rather bossy, don't you think?" I heartily agreed
with her.*

*Several weeks later a letter arrived for me from Ms Smith. I
opened it with considerable curiosity. It read:*

> *Dear Mr Fitzherbert,*
>
> *I feel I must write to tell you my feelings about what you
> said. I don't think I'm as egotistical as you say I am, but I
> suppose I may see myself differently to the way all my friends
> see me. I really want to thank you for an excellent reading of
> my character and I will try to make myself less outspoken in
> the future. I will try to take your advice and I will let you
> know how I am doing. I have told all my friends about you and
> am sending them along for readings as well.*
>
> *Yours sincerely,*
> *Mary Smith*

*Her signature was doubly underlined. When I took a pencil and
circled all the "my", "I" and "me"'s in her letter, I counted 19
of them!*

You may be surprised to learn that the short-index-fingered
person can also make a leader, though not nearly as frequently as
the long-index fingered person. The short-index-fingered person
is plagued by self-doubt and uncertainty and occasionally this can
act as a spur to drive the owner on to high achievement. Such a
person is never satisfied, must push himself higher and higher in

a continual attempt to prove that he is a success. Idi Amin, former ruler of Uganda, is a good example. Napoleon Bonaparte also possessed a short index and rose from being an undersized army corporal with a Corsican accent to being Emperor of France.

The majority of short-index-fingered people do not end up like this. With them, the poor self-image holds them back and makes them unwilling to engage in any sort of competition. Accordingly, they remain in subordinate positions, timidly avoiding any strife or any responsibility. A great many short-index-fingered people become self-employed. If a man or woman with this finger pattern has any ability or talent at all, he or she is very likely to use it in self-employment (e.g. freelance writer, photographer, artist, etc.).

In normal employment, there are pressures from the employer and pressures from fellow employees. To a basically shy person, these can be quite painful. Working for oneself is an obvious solution to this dilemma. If you meet someone with a short index finger, and she has the spacing between the first and second fingers described previously, there is little doubt that this is a self-employed person. A hand which reveals some manual skill plus a short index probably belongs to a self-employed tradesperson, for example a builder or plumber.

Outward-thrust index fingers always indicate a person who is strenuously trying to make the most of himself and to make an impression on other people. Often such a finger is also short, indicating a person with poor self-confidence who is compensating for the defect. The classic salesperson's hand has a short index finger thrust out like a flag (diag. 5.17). A high proportion of salespeople are in fact insecure people who hide this insecurity under a cloak of loud-mouthed, aggressive sales talk. This pattern is so common that it is hard to find a salesperson whose hand does not reveal it. Sales work is basically a form of self-employment for, although employed by a company, the salesperson is largely his or her own boss. The highly aggressive nature of the work means that only someone who is able to project herself can succeed. The combination of these two factors means this work is highly suitable for anyone with an outward-thrust, short index finger.

To anyone who has a short index finger, I would suggest self-employment if at all possible. Any form of quiet, non-competitive work which also offers good prospects for success or security through hard work or applied skill is also suitable. "Rat-race" occupations are not beneficial to these folk except those individuals whose short index juts way out.

The most important piece of advice for anyone with this finger formation, the short index, is to consider carefully the whole subject of self-doubt. Self-doubt is a sort of trick played by one's own mind and a person who suffers from it can learn to deal with the affliction. Next time you feel yourself coming unglued, unsure of your decision or your position, stop and remind yourself emphatically that this is unnecessary. Tell yourself that these feelings of self-doubt are harmful, destructive and that you must not allow them to take control. Don't say, "I'm not afraid," when you feel fear, but instead say, "I am afraid, but I will not let that fear stop me from going ahead. I know that the self-doubt is only a trick of my own mind."

In most cases, a short index finger results either from innate sensitivity or from some actual defect such as being clumsy, plain-looking, less brilliant than one's brothers and sisters or otherwise feeling inferior. Why should just one weakness like this saddle a person with an inferiority complex throughout the rest of life? A short-index-fingered person can benefit from making a list of his good points and bad points. All too often, such a person tends to dwell on the defects and fails to think about the talents and merits of his character. He might even belittle these good points. Making a list to carry around can help to redress the balance.

Most people have an index finger of normal length, reaching two-thirds of the way up the top joint of the middle finger. Occasionally, they may become salespeople, work for themselves, or take the lead in an office or business. In most cases, the special qualities required by these types of work ensure, however, that those with the appropriate index fingers eventually fill the position.

MANUAL SKILLS

The skilled worker is undoubtedly the most important person in society. We can get by without lawyers, politicians, accountants and poets, but we cannot make do without the butcher or the farmer unless we become butchers or farmers ourselves. The person who unplugs your drains or puts windows in your walls is ultimately more useful than the psychologist who charges 100 dollars an hour to solve your "problems".

There are no general rules about manual workers' hands but there are two specific rules for special types of work. Jobs that require special skill with the hands usually attract people with arch fingerprints (diag. 5.18). An electrician or a plumber might

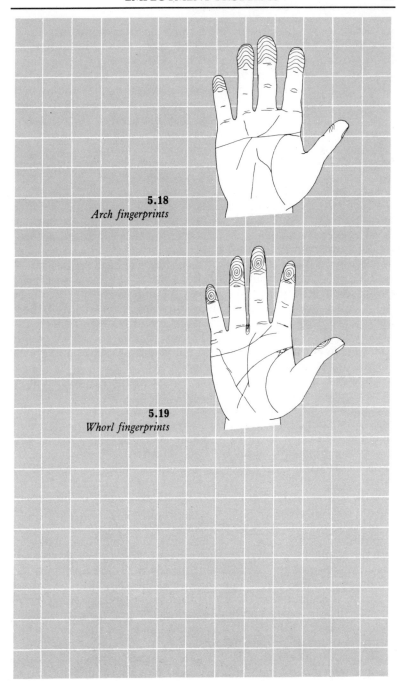

5.18
Arch fingerprints

5.19
Whorl fingerprints

have any sort of fingerprint but a cabinetmaker or gunsmith will usually have at least one arched print, often three, four or five per hand. In fact, any type of hand may indulge in skilled manual work, but an arched fingerprint hand will nearly always do so. There is something about these prints which makes the owners itch to touch and handle things, preferably in a constructive way by making or mending. This urge may manifest itself in a hobby or it may become a lifetime profession.

Whorl fingerprints (diag. 5.19) often show manual skill as well, but usually in some artistic or creative field. The whorl is the sign of a concentrated, thoughtful, self-contained person who generally does well at anything attempted seriously.

People with very large hands have an affinity for fine, detailed work with the result that dentists, jewellers and watchmakers all possess enormous hands. A very small number of these professionals may be an exception. This association of large hands with detailed work has been known since the time of the very earliest writers on scientific palmistry. It is one of the most surprising things about hands, that the largest specimens are capable of the most delicate manipulation. Not only are the owners of these hands capable of such work, they are actually attracted to it and often take it up at an early age. The fact that large-handed people like to concentrate their attention on small problems and small-scale work is an extension of this.

On my last visit to my dentist, I commented to him that he appeared to be the exception to this rule since his hands were not particularly large. He laughed at my remark, and replied that I was mistaken since his hands were indeed much larger than average. Only that week he had been speaking with a client who was a boxer boasting of his big fists. The dentist had wrapped his own hands around the boxer's pair and completely covered them. My mistake with my dentist was based on the fact that he is a big man and, at a casual glance, his large hands seemed in proportion to his overall size. In fact, like most dentists, his hands were much bigger than his body build warranted.

Small-handed people like to do things on a big scale. They are often organisers, good at getting a large group of people to work together. A painter with small hands will specialise in big landscapes. An army officer with small hands is more likely to become a general than to remain a captain, other things being equal. People with big hands definitely gravitate to skilled, detailed work while those with small hands get themselves into all sorts of different occupations.

Manual workers' hands are often rather simple, but many people who are not manual workers also have simple hands so no rule can be drawn from this. Certainly, it is rare to find a sensitive, complex hand on a manual worker.

ENTERTAINERS AND PERFORMERS

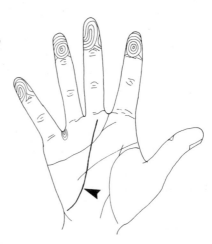

5.20
*A Fate Line rising
from Mount of Luna
is common to all
types of performers*

There is a typical actor's hand, a typical musician's hand and a typical artist's hand. More important, however, are some patterns which encompass all the rest. We could call them "public characters" since those who have them always end up in the public eye in one way or another.

The simplest of these and the easiest to identify is the Fate Line which rises from the Mount of Luna (diag. 5.20). The simple rule with this line is that the owner will deal extensively with the public. This line is very common with all types of performers, from acrobats to symphony orchestra musicians. Since it does *not* indicate the presence of talent, there are some people whose outstanding talent brings them to public fame *without* this Fate Line formation. Thus you must not assume that everyone on stage has this line but you may rest assured that many of them will have it. Anyone with the line will be in the public eye whether this means on stage or not. Certain professions are closely linked with this pattern. Teaching (which certainly puts a person "on-stage" in front of a critical audience), modelling, waiting on tables, and hairdressing all attract those with the Luna Fate Line. Politics, of course, must be included in this list. In Alice Denton Jennings's book, *Your Hand Tells All*, you will see the print of American President Theodore Roosevelt who had a magnificent example of this line.

Palmists have debated exactly what the reason may be for these particular people getting into public positions. One theory is that

they have a gift for getting on well with other folk. Another
theory is that they like to depend on others rather than on
themselves. Whatever the reason may be, there is no doubt that
this Fate Line is the mark of a public person.

The second general feature found on many performers and
communicators is the Air Hand shape (diag. 5.21), that is the
square palm with the long fingers. Strictly speaking, this hand
belongs to those who seek to communicate with others either
through writing, talking or acting. It also crops up amongst
musicians and painters, but not so often. Amateur palmists often
find it difficult to recognise this hand shape. Examine the palm
carefully and measure whether the length, from top to bottom, is
greater than the width. If it is, the palm is rectangular. If,
however, both measurements are about the same then the palm is
square. With this square palm, and with fingers as long or longer
than the palm length, you have an Air Hand.

Three features stand out about Air-Handed people.
1. They are curious about things.
2. They like to express themselves.
3. They like to see how things fit together.

One could summarise these points under two headings, *Understanding* and *Communication*. In my contacts with the press,
radio and television, I have found Air Hands very common
indeed. Yet among the general public, and the clients in my
office, they are quite rare. It appears that this hand shape is an
uncommon one but that those who have it flock to a few specific
fields of employment.

Air-Handed people are always communicators. You will find
them standing on soap boxes, hosting discos, writing endless
letters, books, articles and talking with others or interviewing
them for the media. Certainly they sometimes turn up in
mundane jobs, but when they do, you can be sure that their spare
time is filled with the sorts of activities just listed. Any parent of
a child with a hand like this should guide the youngster into one
of the communication fields: radio, television, the press, public
relations etc. If there is a specific talent, whether dancing, acting
or musical ability, the youngster could well make a career out of
this.

Now let us consider some specific ''performers'' hands. The
artist — artistic talent is a very difficult one to identify with
certainty. Some famous artists show it clearly, other equally
talented ones have none of the typical patterns in their hands.
The classic artistic indication is a long third finger, the Finger of
Apollo, with a whorl fingerprint on it (diag. 5.22). This whorl
shows a basic ability to draw or paint while the finger being long

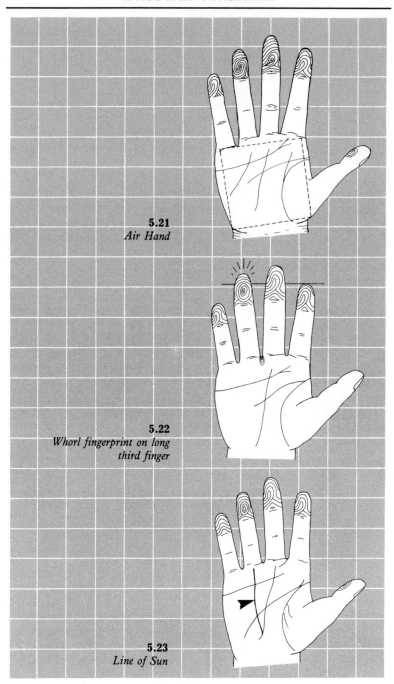

5.21
Air Hand

5.22
*Whorl fingerprint on long
third finger*

5.23
Line of Sun

shows an interest in things artistic. This combination of length
with the specific print is a strong clue to artistic talent.

A clear Line of Sun (diag. 5.23) is traditionally found with
artists but you must never assume that there is talent from this
alone. It must be backed up with other features. Smooth fingers
are almost universal among artists, knotty fingers being virtually
unknown. Short Head Lines are rare on the artist, with long or
curving ones predominating. Only if you have found all of these
things on an Air Hand could you feel sure that the owner is an
artist.

Earlier books on palmistry mentioned a special type of hand,
known as the Conic or Artistic Hand (diag. 5.24). The hand is
distinguished by an all-over roundness and smoothness, with
soft, velvety skin, and pure specimens of this type are quite rare.
If you ever find such a hand, however, there is a good chance that
the owner will have artistic ability. If there are little droplets, or
pads, on the fingertips (diag. 5.25) this will increase the
probability of an artistic bent since such droplets indicate
sensitivity to beauty in all its forms. Nevertheless, artistic talent,
as previously stated, is almost impossible to determine accurately.

The musician — musical hands nearly always have a pronounced development of the "angles" at the side of the thumb
(diag. 5.26). This development is sufficient to determine musical
ability, or a sense of musical rhythm (dancers often have this
pattern).

There is a very rare musical talent, the gift of "perfect pitch",
found on a small number of hands. It is a development of the
Mount of Venus, at the base of the thumb. In most hands, the pad
is shaped in a rounded curve (diag. 5.27). A man or woman with
perfect pitch possesses an angular pad (diag. 5.28), a rather
strange formation.

Keyboard musicians (pianists and organists) usually have
square fingertips (diag. 5.29), a sign of regular, methodical
thinking. Drummers commonly have very strong, simple hands
with a massive Mount of Venus and the "angles" of the thumb
very marked indeed (diag. 5.30).

Finally, there are two skin-ridge patterns which show a strong
affinity with certain types of music. Note carefully that these
patterns do not indicate musical talent, merely a strong interest
in and appreciation of music. In practice, many of the people with
"the bee" (diag. 5.31), the sign of a love of stringed-instrument
music, do take up playing the guitar. A loop pattern (diag. 5.32)
shows a general love of music, though the specimen marked A is
more likely to favour brass music than the B form.

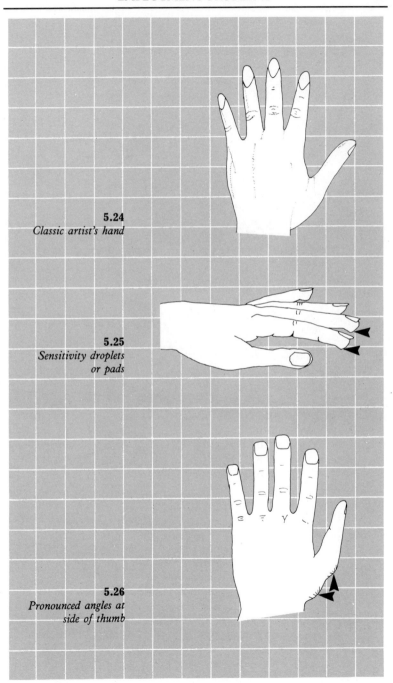

5.24
Classic artist's hand

5.25
*Sensitivity droplets
or pads*

5.26
*Pronounced angles at
side of thumb*

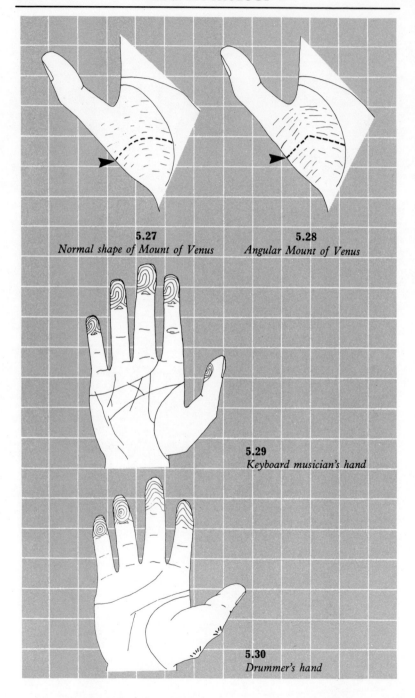

5.27
Normal shape of Mount of Venus

5.28
Angular Mount of Venus

5.29
Keyboard musician's hand

5.30
Drummer's hand

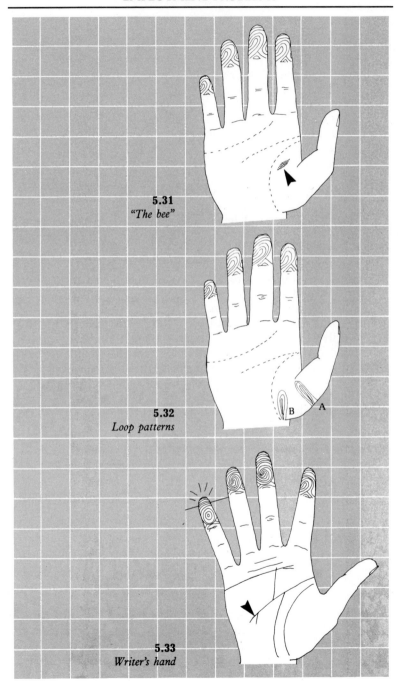

5.31
"The bee"

5.32
Loop patterns

B   A

5.33
Writer's hand

The teacher — teachers come in all types, but long index fingers, long little fingers and the so-called "teacher's square" on the Mount of Jupiter (see page 93) are common patterns.

The actor — every actor's hand I have seen has had unusual features: strange line patterns, weird finger lengths, etc. There is no way of pinning this down since the patterns vary so much from actor to actor, from actress to actress. But if you find an Air Hand with highly unusual markings, it could well belong to an actress. Unusual little fingers, i.e. long, short, twisted, bent, thick, thin and so on, are also very common in the acting profession. One could almost say that eccentricity in the hand, combined with communicative skill, is a prerequisite for acting ability.

On many occasions, I have been consulted by young people who have asked, "Do I have acting ability?" Unless the hand displays a number of unusual features my reply is invariably, "Keep to amateur productions or part-time acting only." The life of an actor contains so many ups and downs, so much fierce competition and strain, so many unpredictable situations, that normal people just don't fit in.

The writer — most writers have a long little finger which is a sign of skill with words. Long, square-tipped little fingers go with those whose talent for words includes carefully picking exactly the right way to phrase a thought every time they speak or write. A pronounced fork at the end of the Head Line (diag. 5.33) is traditionally called "the Writer's Fork", as it often occurs with novelists and short-story writers.

MISCELLANEOUS MARKINGS

THE TEACHER'S SQUARE

This little pattern (diag. 5.34) indicates a talent for teaching, lecturing or instructing. Anyone with this mark is sure to teach others at some time in their life, whether it be in a regular school or by giving swimming instruction, pottery lessons etc. Sadly, experienced school teachers seldom have this mark! Time and again, a young person with this square takes up teaching only to discover that the profession requires more than just a talent for imparting knowledge. Some drop out after a few years, disillusioned perhaps by the educational "system", but forever after they will return intermittently to teaching others in one capacity or another. So often does this phenomenon occur, in fact, that I am tempted to re-name this marking "the Ex-teacher's Square".

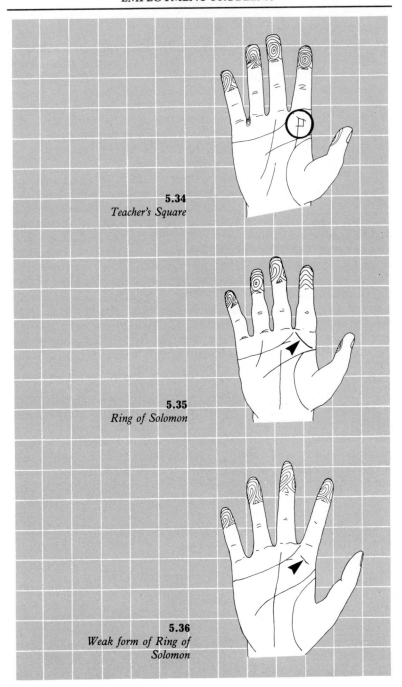

5.34
Teacher's Square

5.35
Ring of Solomon

5.36
Weak form of Ring of Solomon

THE RING OF SOLOMON

Traditional palmists associated this mark (diag. 5.35) with mastery of the occult sciences. In fact, the truth is much more mundane than that, though equally interesting. Solomon's Ring indicates a talent for understanding other people. It shows psychological insight into other people's minds, their hopes and fears and dreams. Obviously, many top occultists will have this mark, not because it indicates psychic ability but because a good palmist, astrologer or magician needs to be an expert at understanding the human condition.

It is quite possible to be a good judge of people without this mark. But anyone who does possess it will certainly have this talent. Some trace of Solomon's Ring is found in many hands, as it is not rare. Full, clear development of the ring is uncommon and is confined to those with a specific talent. In diagram 5.36 you can see a weak form of this line and diagrams 5.37 and 5.38 show two strong forms of the line. Lawyers often have this mark. Indeed, of the limited number of legal persons who have visited my office, none has been without it. The classic lawyer's hand also has a forked Head Line which enables him or her to see both sides of an issue (this is the Writer's Fork which we met earlier). A combination of this Head Line with the Ring of Solomon found on a competent hand would point strongly to law as a profession.

THE MISSING FATE LINE

When the Fate Line is completely missing from a hand, the person is bound to be unusual. The absence of this line indicates an inability to settle down into an orthodox or steady pattern of life. *On a good hand*, this can lead to a life of many different jobs, most of them handled successfully. Such a person seldom spends more than a few years at any given employment, often drifting in and out in a matter of months. *On a poor hand*, the lack of a Fate Line will almost certainly indicate a drop-out, possibly a criminal, probably a drifter with no roots and little chance of success. Only a few hands have no Fate Line whatsoever. The degree of ability and willpower shown by the rest of the hand will determine whether you are dealing with an aimless no-hoper or a potentially successful entrepreneur with a finger in many pies.

The earlier palmistry books maintained that the absence of a Fate Line indicated a dull, uneventful life. Many palmists even claimed that Eskimos had no Fate Line, for this reason! Quite apart from the fact that none of those palmists ever met an Eskimo, it is difficult to see how the extreme harshness of an Arctic life could possibly be described as "dull and uneventful". What is uneventful about battling for your life against blizzards,

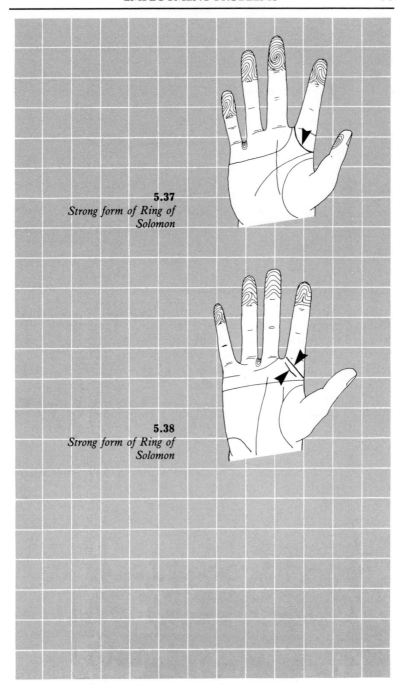

5.37
*Strong form of Ring of
Solomon*

5.38
*Strong form of Ring of
Solomon*

polar bears and starvation? In my experience, missing Fate Lines often accompany a life of endless adventure, totally lacking in stability and a steady lifestyle.

The parents of a child with no Fate Line must be urged to ensure that the youngster is trained for some specific work quite early in life, most certainly by the teenage years. Such a youngster will have no inclination to train in anything special so you must give him or her future security by insisting that some form of definite job training be undertaken. You may be sure that later the work will be abandoned for something else, but at least if you have given him a skill to fall back on, he will not be cast adrift completely in his young adult years.

The Fate Line often develops in the hand during the first decade of life. In young children, poor or broken Fate Lines usually grow more substantial as they reach the teen years. There is no need to worry if your seven year old does not have much of a Fate Line yet.

THE MEDICAL STIGMATA
There is a little pattern which is very often found on the hands of medical people. It is known as the Medical Stigmata and is a little patch of vertical lines beneath the little finger (diag. 5.39). People with this pattern are drawn to helping others and are therefore attracted to medicine and social work. The Medical Stigmata is extremely common on the hands of nurses, yet among some doctors the mark is not quite so common. This is doubtless because some people become doctors for money and prestige rather than because of any real interest in medicine or helping others! Doctors almost invariably have long hands with well-developed little fingers and strong Head Lines, but without the nerve lines that commonly accompany long hands. Such a hand bearing the Medical Stigmata would virtually have to be that of a doctor (diag. 5.40).

A hand with many fine lines and a Medical Stigmata may turn towards social work rather than medicine (diag. 5.41).

Naturopaths and other non-orthodox healers often possess a Medical Stigmata in conjunction with the Poison Line (described in Chapter VI) or with signs of ESP (described in Chapter IX, Lesson 10). Strongly sloping or curving Head Lines, indications of being self-employed, also characterise these people (diag. 5.42).

An odd marking, called the St Andrew's Cross (diag. 5.43), is traditionally found on the hands of anyone who has saved the life of another. If you do find such a mark on a hand with medical inclinations, chances are that the owner is a doctor or nurse.

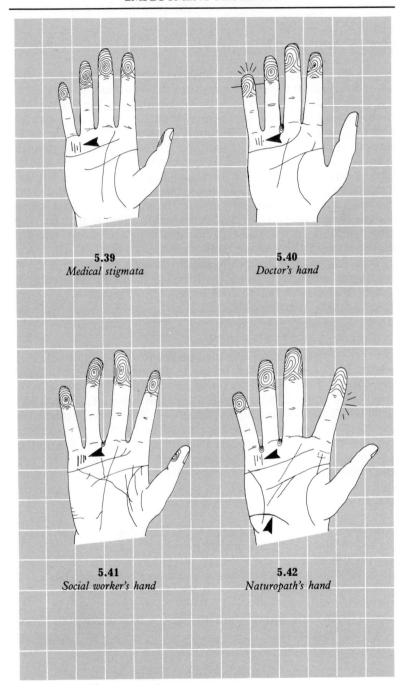

5.39
Medical stigmata

5.40
Doctor's hand

5.41
Social worker's hand

5.42
Naturopath's hand

AVERAGE WORKERS
AND POOR WORKERS

So far we have covered seven broad groups of employment. But what do you do if none of the features described applies to you? In the first place, you may still be successful in a particular field though you have none of the appropriate marks. Such cases are rare, but not unknown. Secondly, there is a great mass of respectable and worthwhile employment which does not require specific abilities and indeed, is not congenial to people who do have a strong leaning in a particular direction. The production industries, the retailing industries, clerical and secretarial work are the sorts of jobs suited to most "average hands", i.e. those containing no specific talents. Even within these industries, it is often possible to specialise in one aspect of the work which is more suited to the average hand than any other.

Very few people are really unsuitable for work, unless the whole hand reveals a badly disturbed personality. However, to finish this chapter, let us look at three formations which often lead to difficulty in employment.

WIDELY SPACED FINGERS

We have seen a number of times earlier in the book how fingers which lie close together reveal a conventional, law-abiding personality. People with such fingers live their lives according to the social conventions prevalent around them. Fingers which have wide gaps between them (diag. 5.44) belong to the rebels and free-thinkers who are often a source of headaches for those who employ them. Some degree of space (diag. 5.45) is a good thing. Too much space usually indicates a person who will never be a good employee unless the hands contain many positive features to outweigh the wide-spaced tendencies or unless the job is the sort to go with the free-thinking mind.

If you want an employee who is independent, original, innovative and stimulating to be around, pick a wide-spaced person. If you want someone who will do what you tell him, do *not* pick such a person! He may serve you well for two weeks, then walk out on you without so much as a backward glance. He will not play the game by the rules. Leave him alone, but give him an incentive to work, and he will outdo three-quarters of the rest of your staff. Expect him to behave like other people and you'll be disappointed.

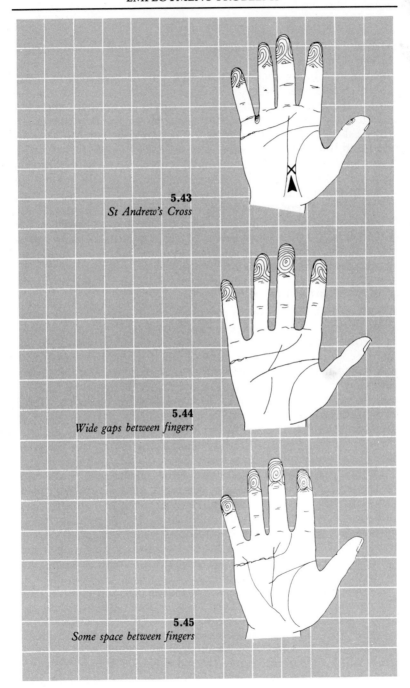

5.43
St Andrew's Cross

5.44
Wide gaps between fingers

5.45
Some space between fingers

SHORT-JOINTED LITTLE FINGER

Have you ever met someone who seemed incapable of organising things? This sort of character lives in a perpetual muddle, with nothing ever being accomplished in a simple way. The marking which reveals this trait is an abnormal shortness of the middle joint of the little finger (diag. 5.46). As long as the work of such a person does not include organisational tasks, there is no reason why he should not be a good worker. The moment things have to be organised, however, confusion sets in! Most people have all the finger joints more or less of an equal length. Disturbances to this pattern are not common, but when you find one it will probably be in the little finger rather than on any other digit.

Sometimes, there appear to be only two joints in the finger (diag. 5.47). This shows an unconventional, unorthodox streak in the personality. In other instances, there are actually four joints instead of the usual three (diag. 5.48), a pattern which has much the same significance as a long little finger.

THE FLEXIBLE THUMB

People with flexible thumbs are among the most charming in the world, yet rarely do they succeed in business. Cheerful, friendly, easy-going and unreliable, the bent-thumbed individual is not often a good worker. The keynote of this personality is flexibility. Ask her to help you and she's more than willing. Ask for a loan, and she can't give it to you fast enough. Ask her to take half-an-hour off work to get you to the grocer and she's behind the wheel with pleasure. She generally has half-a-dozen projects going at once, and here's the crunch. For while it is barely possible that she's a genius, juggling all these things together, it's far more likely that she's overdue with the lot of them!

The really flexible thumb is one which effortlessly bends back 90 degrees at the top. If the thumb is a big, strong one (diag. 5.49) its owner has a strong personality to go with his ultra-flexible nature and accordingly will emphasise the better aspects of adaptability. But a small or weak thumb (diag. 5.50) which bends backward accompanies a less determined personality, one where vacillation, uncertainty and an inability to stick to things are apparent.

Flexible-thumbed people are fun, interesting and entertaining. They always appear to be on the verge of some great success, yet they somehow never manage to achieve it. The few who do succeed are generally self-employed in a varied, changeable occupation (e.g. landscape gardener, novelist, animal trainer). Other mild-mannered flexible-thumbed people manage to settle into a job with an understanding employer who takes complete

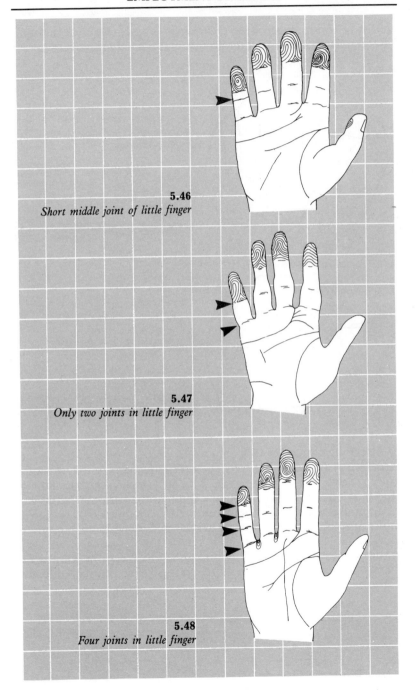

5.46
Short middle joint of little finger

5.47
Only two joints in little finger

5.48
Four joints in little finger

charge of them, controlling their actions (e.g. the civil service). The majority of them really do not make good employees.

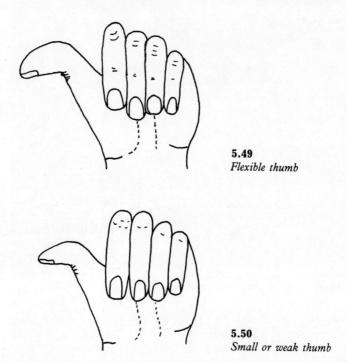

5.49
Flexible thumb

5.50
Small or weak thumb

At the beginning of this chapter, it was stated that desire and determination can enable any person to succeed at a job for which they are not completely suited. This is a most important rule in all vocational guidance. Properly applied, the information in this chapter can work wonders in guiding people of all ages into their most suitable occupations. It has been derived from a study of innumerable hands, not from a set of theories encased in some antique palmistry book. Why not set to work now looking at the hands around you and check for yourself just how reliable this information can be.

HOW TO DEAL WITH DIFFICULT PEOPLE

Clients often say to me, "You've told me all about my good points. So now how about my faults?" So many people seem to think that their good and bad qualities must be balanced equally, as if every positive feature must be accompanied by a negative one. In fact, most people are basically decent, with far more good attributes than nasty ones. Is it any wonder then that most hand readings paint a fairly attractive picture of the person whose hands are under examination?

Of all the people you know, probably 95 per cent of them are easy to get along with. You will have no difficulty in dealing with them, regardless of whether the association is a business or personal one. The remaining 5 per cent are a different story, however! We all know "difficult" people. In every group there is someone with a rough personality, the one everyone else tries to avoid. Can palmistry help you to understand these people? Of course it can. In this chapter, we are going to cover certain oddities sometimes found in the hand which go with disturbances to the personality. A few of these are listed in Chapter III. Now it is time to deal with more of them.

THE CLUBBED THUMB

The first of our oddities is a particular type of thumb; short, stubby and often swollen (diag. 6.1). It is known today as the Clubbed Thumb. In the old literature of palmistry, you will find it described with a thoroughly gruesome title: the Murderer's Thumb. This thumb is quite rare, yet not rare enough to mean

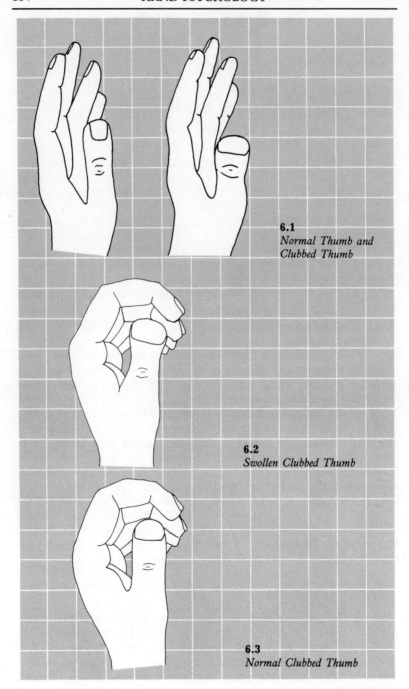

6.1
Normal Thumb and Clubbed Thumb

6.2
Swollen Clubbed Thumb

6.3
Normal Clubbed Thumb

you are never likely to encounter one. Approximately one person in a hundred possesses it. So if you keep your eyes open, sooner or later you will spot one. People with this rare thumb are subject to occasional loss of control, such as fits of violent anger or hysterical crying. Fortunately, this does not happen often, but when it does, the person may be quite dangerous.

The old name, the Murderer's Thumb, was given to this oddity last century because it was believed that a person with it was capable of injuring another person during the periods of loss of self-control. In fact, such a person is no more likely to be a murderer than anyone else. There is no actual record of a murder being committed by someone with the Clubbed Thumbs of which we speak.

People with these thumbs only lose control when they are under psychological pressure such as being teased, frustrated or badly annoyed. At all other times they appear quite normal, although an observant person may note that they get a bit "touchy" in their emotional reactions. Things may go well for months or years until one day some particular irritation causes the Clubbed-Thumbed person to explode. Then, for a short time, that person will be out of control until the fit of anger passes. It is most important to note that not all Clubbed-Thumbed people explode into actual violence. It may take the form of a nervous crying fit or some other non-violent form of hysteria.

The Clubbed Thumb is always short and stubby but some have a definite swollen appearance (diag. 6.2), while others do not (diag. 6.3). The swollen type is more prone to the violent sort of breakdown though this is not an absolute rule. There is some interesting evidence that the Clubbed Thumb may be related to the brain.

The brains of some epileptics show a deformity and there is known to be a section of the brain called "the thumb centre". These two facts, together with the explosive nature of the attacks experienced by Clubbed-Thumbed people, strongly suggest that this type of thumb is linked to an actual brain defect which produces the attacks.

If you know a person who possesses this thumb, you need to practise tact in her presence. Be polite and always take care to explain to the person what you are doing and why you are doing it. Explanations go a long way towards avoiding misunderstandings. If you yourself happen to have a Clubbed Thumb, you will by now have realised that your condition is not unique. You possess a congenital oddity and it is up to you to learn how to control it.

The first and most substantial rule is to avoid tension-producing situations. If something is annoying or upsetting you, find a way to solve it before you reach a crisis. Don't just wait, hoping it will go away.

Secondly, practise keeping calm when annoyed. Do this at all times in order not to let the small irritations of life upset you. Often an accumulation of small problems will mount up to a major crisis. If you can deal with each small problem calmly you can avoid an uncomfortable build-up of anxiety.

Two cases will serve to illustrate the Clubbed Thumb. The first is a young girl who was in a class with me at university many years ago. She was a brilliant student, quiet, pleasant-natured and methodical in her approach to study. I noticed on first meeting her that both her thumbs were clubbed. Being only an amateur palmist in those days, I was surprised to find such a person with thumbs of that type. At the end of the year, this girl topped the class in her final exams. When her parents told her the news one morning, she burst into tears, announced that she would have to do the course again to prove it was not simply good luck, locked herself in her room for two days and refused to come out. At the end of that time, she came back to normal and has subsequently gone on to do advanced studies. Her two-day breakdown was a classic Clubbed-Thumb phenomenon, except that such attacks can usually be measured in hours instead of days.

The second case concerns a member of a certain mystical organisation which teaches various meditative techniques. This man is very strongly built, with two thick and heavily clubbed thumbs. They are perhaps the most extreme case I have ever encountered. Over a period of some months, I got to know the owner of these thumbs, noting that he was very quietly spoken, careful in his speech and yet rather "touchy" when there was opposition to his own ideas. He would sit listening to what others said, all the time giving the impression that he was trying to prevent himself from angrily shouting at them. During heated discussions, I saw him rise from the table with eyes glaring, fists doubled, only to quietly repeat through clenched teeth, "I don't agree with you," before reseating himself. His self-restraint was visible.

One day, out of pure curiosity, I asked him whether he ever lost control of himself. His reply surprised me. "Not at all!" he began. "I used to lose control, long ago. But I have two sons, and one day I woke up in the street with an axe in my hands, to find that I had chased my elder boy three times round the house and out into the road threatening to kill him. When I say 'woke up', that's exactly what I mean. I literally didn't know what I was doing until I regained consciousness out in the street. I decided then and there that it would never happen again and to date it has not.''

This man is surely the most remarkable Clubbed-Thumbed person I have met. By iron self-control and years of mental discipline, he has conquered his own congenital defect. Some aren't so lucky, perhaps because they don't become so aware. Gordon Craig, the illustrious English stage designer and one-time lover of dancer Isadora Duncan, had a set of Clubbed Thumbs. Any book on his life will confirm how his peculiar temper and nasty rages kept his personal relationships in a turmoil.

Clubbed Thumbs tend to run in families, so if we have one member of a family with them the chances are that others will have Clubbed Thumbs as well. It is rarely passed from parent to child direct. The Clubbed-Thumbed person will usually mention that there is an uncle, an aunt or a grandparent with the same formation. There is some evidence that either males *or* females in a family are affected rather than both sexes.

THE SIMIAN LINE

6.4
Simian Line

Our next hand oddity is more common than the Clubbed Thumb, being found on as many as one hand in 12. It is the Simian Line, the sign of inner tension (diag. 6.4). On the great majority of hands there are three main lines, the Heart Line, the Head Line and the Life Line. On a small proportion of hands, the Head and Heart Lines are missing and instead there is a line running right across the palm, approximately where the Head Line would normally be. Earlier palmists used to argue over whether it was a Head Line or a Heart Line, failing to realise that this special line is a combination of the two.

There is a general rule that the more clearly and simply formed a Simian Line is, the more simple the qualities it represents; whereas the more complicated the Simian pattern, and its

attendant lines, the more complicated the person will be. Here is
a list of the qualities which are always associated with the Simian
Line.

1. The owner will never feel at peace: all through her life
    there will be a sense that things are not quite satisfactory,
    that in some way the answer to true peace of mind has not
    yet been discovered.
2. There will be energy. Anything a Simian-Lined person
    does is done with vigour. Physical strength or the inner
    strength of determination, or both, will be found.
3. The person will have trouble doing things in moderation.
    If she studies, she studies hard. If she works in a factory,
    she works twice as hard as her neighbour. If she fights, she
    fights like the devil.
4. Opinions are always definite. To the Simian-Lined
    person, every action is either "right" or "wrong". There
    is no such thing as "partly right" or "partly wrong".
    There is a saying that illustrates this: "The Simian-Lined
    man takes his kids to the beach and says, 'All right, you
    lot, now you're here and you're going to damned well
    enjoy yourselves!'"

Besides the four points above, there are two more which often
occur. First, there may be strong opinions on religion. And
second, there is often some creative ability such as painting,
pottery or even poetry. It must be obvious by now that the
Simian-Lined person is something of a social misfit. They are by
no means bad folk, but they are certainly not average citizens.
Before going into detail about how to deal with Simian-Lined
people, there is some background information which will prove
useful in understanding this aspect of palmistry.

The medical profession knows the Simian Line formation well
because it is always found in the hands of Mongol children, those
unfortunate youngsters who, because of a genetic defect, are
afflicted with an oddly shaped body and a limited intelligence.
All books on Mongolism describe the Simian Line but many
doctors seem to be unaware that the line is common with several
types of mental retardation besides Mongolism. Indeed, Simian
Lines are more common with normal folk of limited intelligence
than with normal folk of average intelligence. The word
"simian" refers to apes, the simians. Virtually all monkeys have
the line. It is well to remember, however, that the line does occur
on people of high intelligence as well.

The Simian Line is also more common among Asian people
than among the black- and the white-skinned races. In an Asian
community, a palmist could expect to encounter Simian Lines

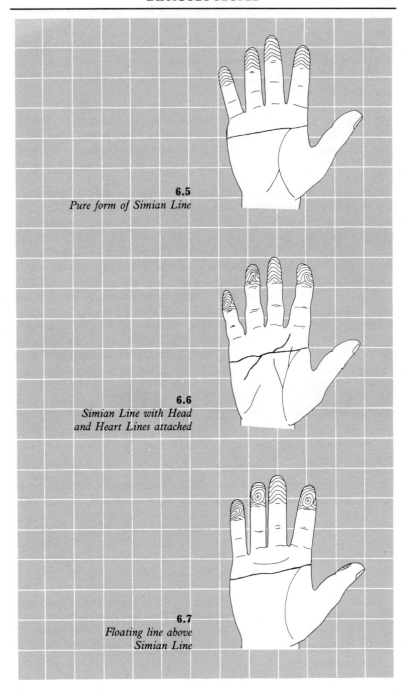

6.5
Pure form of Simian Line

6.6
Simian Line with Head and Heart Lines attached

6.7
Floating line above Simian Line

about twice as frequently as in an African or European area. I therefore suspect that the interpretation applied to this line may be less reliable with Asians than when it is applied to the others.

The Simian Line comes in various forms. Its pure form can be seen in diagram 6.5, while in diagram 6.6 you can see a Simian Line with a piece of Head Line and Heart Line attached.

In diagram 6.7 there is a common pattern of a Simian Line with a line floating above it which is actually a remnant of a Heart Line. Diagram 6.8 shows a half-formed Simian Line. The full Head Line and Heart Line are there, but a Simian Line is formed as well.

It is an interesting fact that the very name "Mongol" is related to the common finding of the Simian Line among Asiatics. An early researcher into Mongolism, Dr Crookshank, noticed that Mongol children look like Asiatics, having high cheek bones and slanting eyes, and he also noted that the Mongol or Simian Line was found both in the hands of some Chinese sailors and a Chinese statue of the Buddha. This led him to postulate that Mongol children were in some way related to the Asian racial type and hence the name Mongol from Mongolian.

Finally, doctors have found that Simian Lines are associated with certain types of congenital heart defects. In these cases, there are also accompanying skin-ridge patterns, notably arch fingerprints and a high axial tri-radius (diag. 6.9). Anyone with a Simian Line would be well advised to avoid putting any strain on the heart, i.e. don't smoke, don't become overweight, don't indulge in sudden exercise or physical efforts such as lifting a piano and do ensure that you get regular, moderate exercise such as walking, all through your life. There is no certainty that the heart is weak, but it is a definite possibility and therefore care should be taken.

Now let us consider what can be done with Simian-Lined people, assuming that the person is not subnormal in intellect. First, there is the matter of that lack of inner peace which plagues those who have this line. Whereas the average person may find satisfaction in a job or the home or a good marriage, the Simian-Lined person may obtain all these things without feeling that his life has been fulfilled. A Simian-Lined person may have fame, money and success and still ask, "What's the point of it all?"

There is no complete answer to this problem. You can, however, help a Simian-Lined person by discussing this chapter with him and if you can get him to read it so much the better. A Simian-Lined person can be encouraged to make the best of things rather than reaching for the unobtainable. Many of these people find it hard to form deep relationships with others.

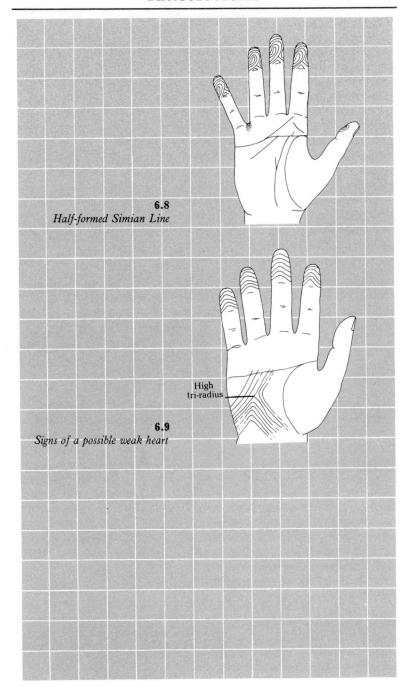

6.8
Half-formed Simian Line

6.9
Signs of a possible weak heart

High
tri-radius

Divorce or failure to marry at all is not uncommon with them. True, some Simian-Lined people do marry successfully, and in their own emphatic way may be devoted to their spouse. But such a person is also obstinate, and may stay in an unsuccessful marriage long after someone else would have given up.

Remember that Simian-Lined people are always tense inside. If you can help them to relax, good. If you can help them to understand themselves, to realise that all Simian-Lined people have these special qualities marking them out as different, you will have gone a long way towards answering the questions which are burning in the heart of every Simian-Lined person whether they voice those questions or not.

In Chapter VII you will find an account of the religious aspects of the Simian Line. Religion is one of the ways people try to find peace of mind, which is why it appeals to some Simian-Lined folk.

The second key to handling someone with a Simian Line is in the word "creativity". The driving energy which is dammed up inside these people sometimes finds its outlet through a creative field. Henry Miller is a good example of a man with the line who found this outlet through his writing. Nikita Kruschev found it in the cut and thrust of politics. He had a pronounced Simian Line in his right hand. Simian-Lined people have gone into sculpture, carving, metalwork, pottery, landscape gardening, tapestry-making, gunsmithing and many similar fields. The sense of *making* something fulfils a definite psychological need for these people. When such a person is busy creating something, he is generally at his most calm and happy. Annoyance and frustrations which have built up during the day can disintegrate in an hour of creative effort. A job which involves creative effort will make a Simian-Lined person happier than almost any other activity. It follows that anyone with this line who does not have a creative hobby should be encouraged to find one. Since these people are difficult to manipulate, the encouragement may need to be quite powerful. It is worth making the effort, nevertheless.

Someone who does have such a hobby should be encouraged to exploit it whenever possible. Remember that creativity can be therapeutic. Simian-Lined people are often misfits, but equally as often there will be fields in which they can excel. With one person it may be physical strength, with another it could be a creative skill. Exploiting these special abilities will always bring out the best qualities in the person concerned.

There are certain hands possessing the normal Heart, Head and Life lines where the Heart and Head lines are placed closer together (diag. 6.10) than is normal (diag. 6.11). There are obvious similarities between this formation and the Simian Line

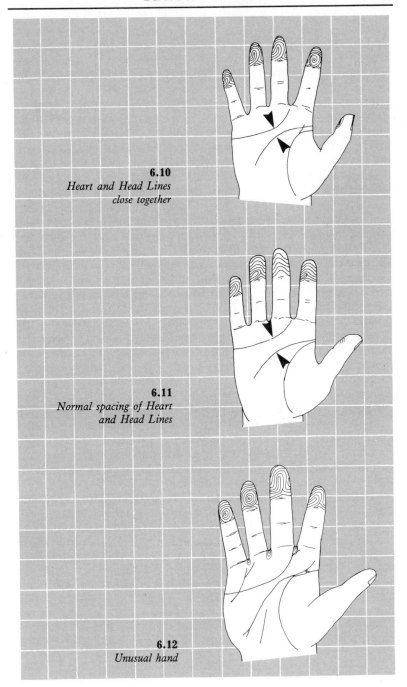

6.10
*Heart and Head Lines
close together*

6.11
*Normal spacing of Heart
and Head Lines*

6.12
Unusual hand

which has just been discussed. It does not give Simian-Line
tendencies, but instead is associated with narrow-mindedness.
People with this formation are almost incapable of seeing the
other fellow's point of view. They take everything personally,
seeing things from their own perspective only. The famous
palmist Noel Jaquin used to call the space between the Head and
Heart Lines the "vision metre", since people with a wide space
here have a "broad vision of life" and those with a narrow space
have a "narrow view of things". People with widely spaced Head
and Heart Lines are uniformly friendly, good-natured and tolerant
of others while narrow-spaced folk are often intolerant, narrow-
minded and sometimes difficult to get along with.

A person with narrowly spaced Head and Heart Lines makes a
poor judge whether the judgment be a beauty show, a dog show or
a murder trial. Her own personal opinions and feelings will
always dominate the judgment made. Such a person will hear you
criticise the make of car she drives and will accuse you of being
her enemy as a result. In the midst of a tornado, she will
telephone the electricity company to complain that the power
has gone off in her living room. Can anything be done with such a
person? To a client with this marking, I would explain all the
foregoing points and then urge the client to strive to see other
people's points of view. "Learn to put yourself in the other
person's shoes," I would say. "Ask yourself, when you find
yourself disagreeing with someone, why does he see it differently
from me?"

A palmist is privileged to offer advice where other people would
not dare. If you have to deal with someone who has this narrow
space between the lines, the only thing you can do is to tactfully
point out to him exactly why you disagree and try to persuade
him to look at your view of the situation. In diagram 6.12 you can
see a sketch of the hand of an unusual man. As you can see, he
has the narrow space in addition to a very sloping Head Line. The
hand itself is a strong simple one so this man cannot be a neurotic
type in spite of his imaginative Head Line. In fact, he is an
occultist, a student of mythology and magic. Many of his views
are unusual and he is frequently heard to say, "You are all wrong.
My view is the correct one." When he is asked how he knows this
to be, he invariably replies, "I just know. I feel it inside."

THE NEUROTIC HAND

6.13
Nervous person's hand

Tact and diplomacy are also needed in dealing with a person with a nervous or neurotic hand type (diag. 6.13). There is an account of this hand type in Chapter IV, along with several suggestions as to how such people can be helped, so we need not repeat this information here. People with such hands worry endlessly over all sorts of small matters. Their lives are always far too complicated for comfort. Nervous people are sensitive to their surroundings. This includes you, since you are an influence upon all those you meet. In the company of a nervous person, it is a wise plan to speak more slowly than usual. Careful speech always has a calming effect on a worrier. This is a very simple rule, yet not easy to carry out since often the worrier upsets those around him instead of absorbing their calm. It is possible to soothe a nervous person with your speech, however. Try it and see.

THE POISON LINE

6.14
Poison Line

Long, slim hands with a multitude of lines often possess the so-called "Poison Line", which indicates a craving for excitement and a susceptibility to drugs (diag. 6.14). This line has particular significance for two classes of difficult people: drug addicts and hyperactive children.

The simplest form of this line is a short, straight bar on the Mount of Luna (diag. 6.15). Although usually associated with nervous hands, this line can be found on any type of hand. Doctors call this part of the palm the Hypothenar Area and for this reason I usually refer to this form of the Poison Line as the Hypothenar Bar. There are three points to remember about the line: allergy, addiction, and the craving for excitement. Let us take them in order.

Whenever this line is found, the owner will react strongly to chemicals, drugs and medications. In nine cases out of 10, there will be one or more specific allergies such as an allergy to penicillin or to flower pollen. In 10 cases out of 10, the person will have a history of unusual reactions to medications.

Some people with this line seem to be virtually impervious to the effects of anaesthetics. This naturally creates problems when the need for a surgical or dental operation occurs. Others with the same line react violently to the same anaesthetic. One girl with a Hypothenar Bar is known to vomit incessantly for 24 hours whenever she recovers from an anaesthetic, much to the distress of the hospital staff.

People with the line have been known to "get a buzz" from drugs which have no such effect on other people. One person gets high on cold tablets. Another reacts strongly to ordinary tobacco. Coffee and tea addictions are common with those whose hands bear this mark. Children with the line are prime candidates for hyperactivity and reaction to sugar and food additives. A parent who finds this line in the hands of a child should take the utmost care of that child's diet, watching carefully for any changes in the youngster's behaviour which might relate to changes in the diet.

Another feature which has been observed in the hands of hyperactive children is a series of star-like patterns formed among a mass of intersecting lines (diag. 6.16). If you find such a pattern in your child's hands, there can be little doubt that diet is affecting the child's life. The allergic effects of the line can be summed up as "strong, unpredictable reactions to chemicals and drugs of all kinds".

It is a curious fact that those with the line often seem to have a subconscious awareness of their own peculiarity which leads them to abandon drugs and chemicals completely. The line is quite often found among ex-smokers, ex-coffee drinkers, ex-sugar addicts, etc. Vegetarians may have the line. Among naturopaths and other natural healers the incidence of Poison Lines is much higher than among the general public. Some palmists have

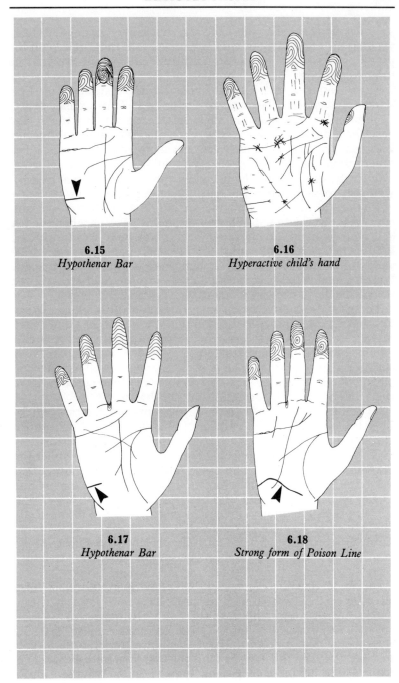

6.15
Hypothenar Bar

6.16
Hyperactive child's hand

6.17
Hypothenar Bar

6.18
Strong form of Poison Line

speculated that the presence of the line among healers, vegetarians and other spiritually minded folk indicates a certain psychic awareness or nature-affinity. This is at present an unproven theory.

So far, we have dealt with the physical implications of the line under the general heading of "allergy". The second point, "addiction", overlaps this. Besides the strong reactions just described, it seems that those with the line are more easily addicted to both physical and psychological pleasures than others. Imagine a dozen people who enjoy going to the movies. Who is the one eventually attending three or four times a week, who gets irritable when she hasn't been for a few days? The one with the Poison Line. Imagine an office with all the workers waiting for morning tea. Who starts getting nervous when the tea bell sounds a minute late? And who has been eating pickled sandwiches with chilli sauce for 14 years, increasing the sauce yearly until there is more of it than there is pickle? Right again. Poison-Lined people become addicted far more easily than those whose hands do not carry this mark.

There is also a strong tendency towards thrill-seeking. Drugs can and often do provide the stimulation which a Poison-Lined person craves, but at times other forms of thrill-seeking occur. Exhibitionists may have the line. People who "turn on" by getting on-stage in front of large audiences could well have Poison Lines. Skydivers, racing-car drivers, even drug couriers have been found with this formation in their hands.

Of course, not all these possibilities apply at the same time. The thrill-seeking public performer may quail at the thought of jumping from an aircraft. The six-sugars-in-the-coffee person may look askance at his pill-popping teenaged son who has inherited the family Poison Line. The only thing which is certain is that the pattern of allergy, addiction and thrill-seeking will apply one way or another to anyone who has this line.

There is an important difference between the two forms of the line: the short, straight Hypothenar Bar (diag. 6.17) and the long, curving pattern (diag. 6.18). Quite simply, the second form of the line is associated with stronger symptoms than the straighter form. It is a more acute form of the Poison Line.

For some inexplicable reason, those with the stronger form often become associated with the more dangerous forms of illegal drugs, e.g. heroin, amphetamines and the powerful hallucinogens. As previously stated, some palmists suspect that the Hypothenar Bar goes with a sort of nature-consciousness. It is possible that the full Poison Line goes with some subconscious attraction to the more dangerous forms of drugs. Whether this be true or not, there are many cases of people who have the rare, complete Poison Line who have either experimented with or become hooked on illegal drugs. I would go so far as to say that I have never seen a completely developed Poison Line in the hands of an adult who has not dealt with "hard" drugs at some time.

Accordingly, I would advise any parent with a youngster possessing this marking (be sure you understand exactly what it looks like) to do the utmost to discourage that child from having anything to do with drugs. And if you, the reader, happen to have the marking, my earnest advice to you based on 18 years of dealing with other people's lives is: leave drugs alone! We live in a drug-ridden society; coffee and tea are taken by millions of people without a second thought. When first introduced to Europe, these products were recognised for what they were. Today they are accepted unquestioningly. Tobacco and alcohol are drugs which have caused millions, not thousands, of deaths. Sugar, found in our cigarettes, canned food and even our daily bread, was first brought into Europe as a medication, to be prescribed only by doctors for the seriously ill. The humble aspirin is a potent drug as is the contraceptive pill.

In the midst of this plethora of chemicals the one thing most vitally necessary is discrimination. To lump all drugs into just two categories, legal and illegal, is useless. The question is not which drugs does the law forbid us to touch but rather which drugs should we avoid for our own good and safety. With the so-called "hard" drugs, there can be only one answer and that is to avoid them completely.

Clubbed Thumbs, the Simian Line and the Poison Line, signify three very different types of difficult people. Of course, there are endless small "difficulties" which crop up besides the main ones we have dealt with here, but these will be discussed in Chapter IX along with general descriptions of what the various parts of the hand signify. And, let's face it, everyone is "difficult" at some time!

One final point. You may occasionally meet someone who gets violently angry yet does not possess a Clubbed Thumb. Or you may find a narrow-minded person without a narrow space between the Head and Heart Lines. And you will certainly find that there are a very few people who do have a violent allergy without any sign of a Poison Line. *What you will not find*, however, is someone with one of these marks in his hands who does not have the accompanying qualities. It is always possible for human qualities to be marked in a different way or even not to be marked at all. So never jump to conclusions about what to expect in someone's hands before you have had a good look.

THE SEARCH FOR MEANING: RELIGION AND YOUR HANDS

The next time a religious crank stops you in the street or knocks on your door, take a good look at his hands. You may be able to discover why he behaves the way he does. Perhaps you have little interest in the church yourself, but religion does have a way of touching our lives whether we like it or not. The businessperson who only attends church at Christmas time discovers one day that her important client has certain religious beliefs which affect business conduct. Tom and Mary, quiet members of the local church for 20 years, are astounded when Tom Jr comes home announcing that he's joined the Supreme Enlightenment Movement and must now rise at midnight to chant his mantra. Independent Susan, recently moved to a new neighbourhood, finds that the door-knocking evangelists are the only people who have approached her in weeks, so she invites them inside.

Palmistry can show you why people turn to religion. It can help you understand why you hold the views or the doubts that you do. Palmistry will *not* give you the answers in every case, however. The hands always reveal a person's psychological drives, but there may well be times when some incident or experience shapes your religious attitudes in a way your hands will not show. Earlier writers on palmistry often made statements about religion based upon theory, not on actual examination of the hands at all. (In a similar way, they described the hands of different races and hands supposedly suited to different types of employment without ever bothering to find representatives of the races or professions they were describing.) Every statement in this book is based on practical experience. All the comments about religion as shown through palmistry have been checked and rechecked by the examination of actual hands and the questioning of the people concerned.

Listed below are the three palmistic indications which predispose a person towards religion. If you have any of these in your hands, the chances are that you have definite religious opinions.

THE LONG INDEX FINGER

7.1
Long index finger

The person with this formation (diag. 7.1) possesses a strong ego, and a strong sense of his own identity. This can result in pride, self-confidence, a desire to do well in all fields and sometimes gives leadership ability as well. It also inclines the person to think about his own identity: "Am I a good person? What is life all about? How can I make the best of things?" Many people go through a period of self-questioning like this during adolescence. Religious conversions occur most frequently between the ages of 14 and 20. For the person with a long index finger, the adolescent period will almost certainly be the time when religious questions are examined and religious attitudes are established.

A high proportion of long-index-fingered folk have definite religious opinions which developed in the teenage years. But even those who have no religion at all will admit that in those years they did think about the subject. For these people, a meaning and purpose to life is essential. In the teenage years, the majority of them consider religion because of its claims to provide the meaning of life. Oddly enough, it is the strong ego of the man or woman with the long index finger which often makes him or her decide against belonging to a particular church. Such a person does not want to be bossed around and definitely wants to make up his or her own mind, on all matters. Strong though the desire may be to find a purpose for living, the desire to think and act as an individual may well be stronger. Long-index-fingered people do not take kindly to being told what to believe or how to act. Accordingly, some youngsters whose search for direction takes them into a church may find that their strong ego takes them out again!

One young woman with a healthy index finger length who was raised as a Catholic tells her story like this: "When I was a kid I loved all the ritual, the colours, the prayers and all that. Then, while I was at school I thought I would grow up to be a nun. I used to say my prayers every night and read my Bible. When I was 12, I had an astral projection and the nuns told me that I mustn't talk about it. Also, I found that my brother and I could sometimes read each other's minds, but one of the nuns told me it was a trick of the devil. After that, I started thinking for myself. And now I don't go to church at all."

This young woman had a very long index finger and was a high school teacher, recently completing a university degree. Both her story of having swung from wanting to be a nun to then leaving the church altogether and also her position as a teacher are typical of people with a long first finger.

For those who have considered the church, but found it is not the answer, there are two alternative paths. One is to examine other religions outside those of one's upbringing. Among the young people who turn to the religions of the East, often those with doctrines of reincarnation and the need to search within through meditation, there are many who possess the long first finger. The second path is to formulate your own ideas about life and, perhaps, about God. As stated at the beginning, virtually all long-index-fingered people have some religious leaning but this may consist of a personal belief in a divine pattern to the universe and in life after death rather than adherance to a particular religious denomination.

There is a tradition recorded in most 19th century palmistry books that a long first finger is the mark of a priest. There is some truth in this. Not all men with this formation become priests, but many priests do have the distinctive finger. Among high church dignitaries, such as bishops and archbishops, the long first finger is very common indeed, if we are to judge from the score or more whose hands have been published in books or photographed in the newspapers. Of course, we can see why such people are drawn to the church and it is a similar principle which ensures that so many church officials have this marking. The strong ego is often drawn to leadership and what role is more leading than that of a priest or bishop?

Intelligence, willpower and ability are all needed to get ahead in any field. But when these are *not* accompanied by a long index finger, the person will have little desire to be an administrator or supervisor. Conversely, a long index finger does not show the capacity to reach a high position *unless* other strong factors are present. But the owner will certainly have a desire to achieve in life and if she has any ability she will definitely get to the top of her field.

THE CURVING, SLOPING HEAD LINE

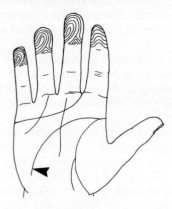

7.2
Deeply curving,
sloping Head Line

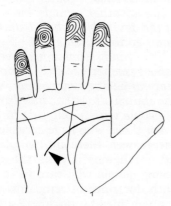

7.3
Common curving,
sloping Head Line

When the Head Line runs downward towards the bottom corner of the hand, not in a straight, sloping path but with a rich curve (diag. 7.2), a particular type of imagination is indicated. A man or woman with this line has little interest in practical, mundane affairs, but is instead drawn to the world of imagination. Ideas which sound fantastic or unbelievable to an average person are often completely accepted by someone whose hand has a Head Line running in this fashion.

Fortunately, this type of line is quite rare, although lines similar to this but not so strongly developed are fairly common (diag. 7.3). This line will still show imaginative tendencies but none as extreme as those of a person with the first type of curve. Before showing how this relates to religion, we must look at the whole range of behaviour which goes with this formation. And what a range it is!

In the first place, he or she will be interested in imaginative or creative matters: poetry, mysticism, magic, mythology are the sorts of subjects which appeal. A child with such a Head Line may delight in stories of elves and goblins, ghosts and fairies. An adult who likes to read novels and who has a Head Line of this type may be into Superman movies, science fiction and other imaginative types of literature.

Secondly, the owner will almost certainly believe in the spiritual side of nature. This belief may include the acceptance of fate and destiny and a belief in prediction, fortune-telling and good and bad luck.

Thirdly, the owner is likely to believe in theories and ideas which more rational people would not accept. People with such lines have been known to believe in contact with UFOs, the International Jewish Conspiracy, the imminent end of the world, the return of Jesus, the dangers of vaccination, the evils of eating canned food and a host of other similar ideas. This sort of Head Line reveals a mind which is prone to accepting all sorts of strange beliefs.

Fourthly, such a person is likely to go round in a dream world. There may be moodiness and there will certainly be daydreaming. Before you conclude that all these folk are quite crazy, you must carefully note the following points.

1. The more strongly the Head Line droops, the stronger the pattern may be, and a moderate slope will require a more moderate interpretation.

2. Even with a perfect example of the line, not every point listed above will apply. With every person you meet, most of the above will apply, but in each particular case some parts will apply more than others. The overall picture will always be consistent with these points, but details will vary from case to case.

3. Some of the more extreme ideas and beliefs of these people may sometimes turn out to be correct. History gives many examples of "strange" beliefs turning out to be true where orthodox opinions were false. Such occasions occur in every period of history and will undoubtedly continue to do so in the future. Here are just two examples from very recent times. Firstly, the strange people who claimed that a drug called Thalidomide caused birth deformities while the drug companies themselves denied this and even "proved" that it didn't. And, secondly, the strange people of the 1960s who claimed that the CIA was persecuting them. The 1970s Freedom of Information Act in America proved they were right.

A person with such a line may be a happy, well-adjusted human being just as often as someone who has none of these tendencies. Now, how does all this relate to religion? A high proportion of these people with sloping Head Lines are attracted to unusual religious groups. In this, the last quarter of the 20th century, one can list such groups as the Eckankar movement, the Moonies, the followers of the assorted Indian Gurus, the Hari Krishna devotees etc. Fifty years ago, the list would have been different and, of course, it will change again as each new generation comes along.

Not many people have extreme drooping Head Lines but if you visit any of the groups mentioned above you will be sure to find that such Head Lines are common. Younger people with this marking often comprise the bulk of the membership and are generally very dedicated to their faith. Interestingly, older people who have this Head Line and who join such groups are seldom as dedicated as the young enthusiasts for the good reason that they have been in such organisations before and, for them, the current religious belief may be tinged with the residue of belief from other, earlier convictions.

Unfortunately, among the so-called "fringe" religions, there are some whose influence is downright harmful. In their time, the Quakers and the Salvation Army were branded as eccentric and heretical, but no-one ever seriously suggested there was anything harmful about them. On the other hand, some of the modern sects are notorious for brainwashing, financial exploitation of members, destructive and anti-social behaviour and similar practices which are blatantly negative. It is a tragedy that such sects prey upon people who have nothing evil in their nature at all, but who are misled by the teachings of the cult. Young folk with drooping Head Lines are always in danger of being taken in by such cults.

We cannot leave this subject without mentioning that established churches and even governments have sometimes been known to attack small denominations for devious reasons. For example, one very tiny Indian group has been used by a particular government as an excuse for building up the national secret police force, supposedly to combat the "danger" posed by a handful of devotees to the cult. And of course many established religions have a history of bloodshed and exploitation far more horrific than any of the "fringe" religions. All these facts need to be borne in mind when you have to deal with someone who has joined one of the odd religious groups.

There are several important pieces of advice to remember when dealing with young people who have become involved with a religious cult. If you have a son who possesses the drooping Head

Line, you should do all in your power to inform him about the subject. Start by letting the youngster read this chapter. If you can, find television programs or magazine articles about different groups and get the youngster to look at them. What you must do is to let your child see several different points of view and to become informed about some of the different religious groups. If you do this, there is much less chance that your child will be taken in by the first fringe religion that comes his way. Do not neglect to consider the good points as well as the bad points with each religion.

If you yourself believe strongly in a particular faith, you would still do well to let your adolescent learn about other religions. Any young person with such a Head Line is likely to be attracted to the unusual areas of life. You cannot protect him by giving only your point of view, for sooner or later he will encounter others.

If you have to deal with someone who has joined a sect you do not approve of, you must at all times be sympathetic to that person. Do not allow yourself to fall into the trap of thinking, "This is a bad sect, so I should be angry with a person who belongs to it." In the first place, remember that the person is a victim of the sect, and deserves help and sympathy, not antagonism. Secondly, remember that antagonism achieves nothing. You will only drive a devotee further into the cult if you antagonise her. It will not help to get her out. And it is not easy to remember these points when you are being pestered by some wild-eyed evangelist from the Flat-Earth Religious Revivalists, but you should strive to do so. Do not ridicule or scorn such a person. Be sympathetic. But tell him that he is mistaken. Don't say, "I am right," but rather say, "You are wrong. Your religion is misleading you. You think you are doing right, but actually this religion is leading you to do wrong."

An authoritative statement like this, presented in a sympathetic manner, has an excellent chance of penetrating a brainwashed young mind. Religion gives a person a form of support or security. You must offer friendship and support, even kindness to the devotees of a cult if you are to have any hope of getting someone out. A final point of advice: learn as much as you can about the teachings of the sect, about its history and about the arguments used to support its beliefs. In a discussion with any devotee, she will be prepared with all the answers while you are not, so make it your business to gather as much knowledge as you can. Ask your minister or do research in the local library.

Cult leaders who brainwash devotees are always afraid of an opponent who is armed with real knowledge. The devotees of odd religions seldom know anything about the history or origins of their own sect other than the very biased account given them by their leaders. Also, they generally have little knowledge of other cults similar to their own. People who are eagerly awaiting the return of Jesus or the end of the world are almost invariably quite unaware of the countless times in our past when people have been led to believe in these same delusions. They know nothing of the past, and so have no way of seeing the delusion. Enlighten them! Find out about the subject yourself. There are many books available on the history of the various unorthodox beliefs.

THE SIMIAN LINE

7.4
Simian Line

You will find a full account of the Simian Line in Chapter VI. It is the curious bar line that runs across the hand, replacing the usual Heart Line and Head Line. The Simian Line (diag. 7.4) is a sign of inner tension, which may be creative or destructive, or both. This tension usually has a profound effect on religious attitudes.

The first person to note the connection between Simian Lines and religion was Fred Gettings, who records in *The Book of the Hand* that he found an abnormally high number of Simian Lines in the hands of attendants at a religious meeting. I have found exactly the same thing in a branch of the Theosophical Society. In fact, there are religious overtones to all Simian Lines (excepting those on mentally retarded people), but these overtones can range from great religious devotion to avowed atheism!

Atheism as a belief is not common except in some communist countries. Many people have no real belief in God, but can scarcely be called atheists since they never think about religion at all. The true atheist is a person who has considered religion and rejected it. Atheism is not uncommon among Simian-Lined people. The inner tension experienced by a person who has this line nearly always drives him to consider religion as a source of calmness, contentment and satisfaction. If the person cannot accept religion, he emphatically rejects it. There are no half-measures where Simian-Lined people are concerned. Many, though by no means all of these people, are rather crude and defiant in their approach to life and for such individuals atheism may have a strong appeal.

Among the cruder specimens of Simian-Lined folk (and remember that not all people with a Simian Line fall into this group) there are sometimes found religious beliefs of a superstitious and fundamentalist nature. A Simian-Lined person who considers religion and decides to accept it is likely to have the same emphatic attitude as the atheist. I have known people of this type who ruled their life by the Bible and generally by the Old Testament with its harsh, "Thou shalt and thou shalt not" rules. It is a remarkable fact that atheists with Simian Lines have also been known to convert to fundamentalist Christianity. Here is a case to illustrate this point.

Simon North was a sergeant in the army who married at 35 and produced four children. He possessed powerful hands with complex lines and a perfectly formed Simian Line in both hands. A tense man, he confined himself to a few limited interests: cars, mechanics and drinking beer. Occasionally, religious evangelists from the Jehovah's Witnesses or the Mormons called at the family home, and when this happened Simon would drive them from the home with a stream of curses. He announced that he had no sympathy with such people.

Eventually, Simon's children left home and, not long after, he and his wife separated. A few years before these events, Simon accepted a magazine from a door-knocking evangelist before throwing the man out. But now, in the privacy of his garage, he read the magazine through. From that point on, he began to study the Bible and, though he never joined the church, he became convinced that the Bible was the word of God. When his son announced his homosexuality, Simon astounded the family by declaring that according to the Bible this was an abomination and he ordered the young man out of his life.

Today, Simon has the strength and vitality common with many Simian-Lined people and is as active in his later years as he was in his youth. After the divorce came through, he began to rethink his beliefs. One day he began to take an interest in psychical matters and spiritualism. He is still convinced of the truth of the Bible teachings, but he has widened his beliefs beyond the narrow bounds which once restricted them.

Occasionally, a Simian Line occurs in the hands of a person of

high intelligence and even refinement. This is a rare phenomenon, but when it does occur there is a chance that the person
will climb high in a religious field. Beryl Hutchinson, one of
Britain's finest palmists, noted from a television program that
Pope John XXIII had a Simian Line. Sephariel, the famous
astrologer and occultist of the 19th century noted that Madame
Blavatsky, founder of the Theosophical Society, possessed the
line. And one of the most saintly and spiritual men I have ever
known, the founder of a great charity and holder of three
university degrees, has Simian Lines in both his hands.

OTHER PATTERNS

The long index finger, the drooping Head Line and the Simian
Line are the only three configurations which have a definite
relationship with religious matters. Of the three, only the Head
Line pattern lends itself to "problem solving" as this book sets
out to teach, but it is well worth studying the other two to
understand why people behave the way they do.

There are three skin-ridge patterns worth mentioning,
although they are not of great importance. When all the
fingerprints are whorls (diag. 7.5), the person is invariably self-
contained, individualistic and thoughtful. Strongly developed
ideas and opinions are always present with people with these
fingerprints, especially those who have a complete set of whorls.
Even unintelligent people who have whorls are thinkers, as far as
their limited abilities will allow. These people hold opinions on
most subjects, although they often have a secretive streak which
ensures that however much they might talk about one subject,
they might also be deliberately quiet about others. I have seen
people with complete sets of whorls who were deeply involved in
a particular religion or philosophy and whose hands gave no other
clue as to why this should be.

Between the base of the second and third finger, there is
sometimes a skin-ridge pattern known as a Loop of Seriousness
(diag. 7.6). It is found on most people who have a fundamentally
serious, reliable attitude to life. Occasionally, in religious circles,
you will encounter a serious, earnest person who studies her
religion and leads her life strictly according to what she considers
to be right and proper. The earnest young person who explains, "I
joined the church because I saw so much evil-doing around me
and I knew there must be a better way of life," usually has a big
Loop of Seriousness in her palm. There is a theory that when the
loop runs to one side under the ring finger (diag. 7.7), the person

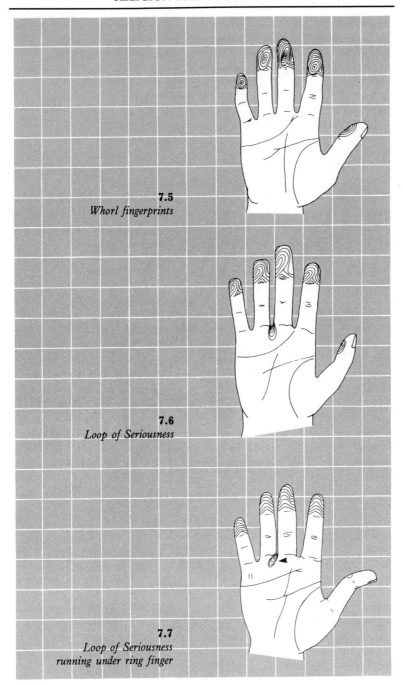

7.5
Whorl fingerprints

7.6
Loop of Seriousness

7.7
*Loop of Seriousness
running under ring finger*

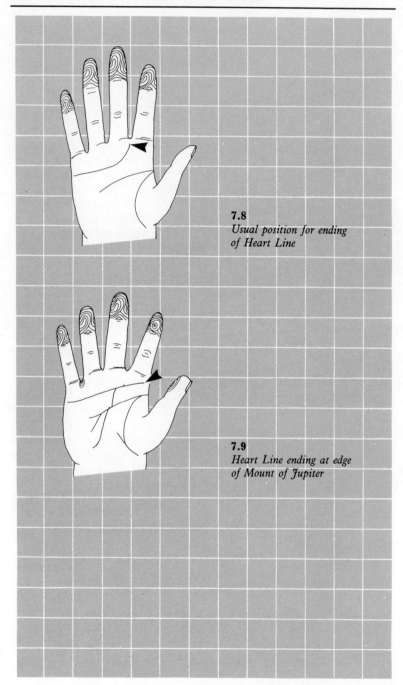

7.8
Usual position for ending of Heart Line

7.9
Heart Line ending at edge of Mount of Jupiter

will have preaching or missionary tendencies. One researcher claims that missionaries for the churches often have this skin pattern.

There is also a Heart Line pattern which sometimes links up with religion and missionary tendencies. Properly speaking, it shows humanitarian inclinations. The usual position for the end of the Heart Line is between the first two fingers (diag. 7.8). It may lie a little to either side of this position and may be either at the very edge of the skin between the fingers or about a centimetre below on the palm. In a very few hands, the Heart Line sweeps right out onto the Mount of Jupiter under the first finger (diag. 7.9) and this pattern shows a humanitarian tendency in the owner. Such people have a desire to do good to all those around them and to devote themselves to caring for others. It is a rare pattern, but when found the interpretation is quite reliable. I have seen this line in the hands of a woman working among the paupers of India and in the hands of an astrologer who tirelessly sorts out the tangled lives of his clients as well as practising healing for all those who are sick or in pain.

This is not a religious pattern, but since caring for the needy has traditionally been part of the work of certain churches, people with this Heart Line sometimes find their way into the churches. When such a person joins a religious organisation, it is invariably the *practical* side of the church work that occupies him.

This completes the account of religion in your hands. Of course, you will be sure to find some religious people who show none of these markings. Some of these cases can be accounted for by the person's upbringing, since many adherents to the churches are there simply because they were brought up to belong to a particular faith. Others may have come to religion through some particular incident, rather than through a psychological need. Nevertheless, the foregoing points will explain a good deal. There are also certain configurations which definitely do *not* go with religious faith. People with widely spaced fingers, for example, are never found among the believers in any group which has fixed ideas and teachings.

I would like to close this chapter with some comments on the connection between palmistry itself and religion. The orthodox churches have never opposed palmistry, in spite of Cheiro's claim to the contrary. But many of the fundamentalist churches have concluded that all psychic phenomena, spiritualism, etc. are the work of the devil. The reader is at liberty to decide for himself or herself whether the devil exists or not, but this is the teaching of some church groups. Since palmistry is not a psychic subject, but a purely scientific study of the human hand, it cannot fall under this classification. Any church member who thinks that it does is simply displaying ignorance of what palmistry actually is.

Some palmists believe that the marks and signs of the hand reveal the lessons and experiences of earlier incarnations, with their resulting implications for this lifetime. Others see in the hands the work of God, who has given us our lives and our particular abilities. Whatever the attitude of the palmist may be, if palmistry is used to help us and is used as a tool for problem solving, it can only result in good which, after all, is the purpose of all religions.

C H A P T E R   V I I I

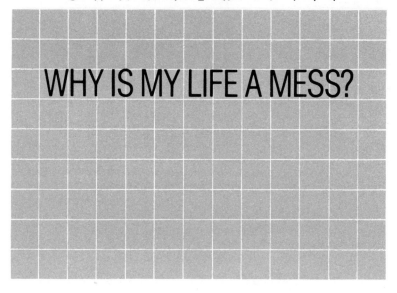

WHY IS MY LIFE A MESS?

"I've read your book, Mr Fitzherbert. I don't seem to have any mental or emotional hang-ups, yet my life is still in a terrible tangle. Can anything be done for me?" The answer to this question is probably *Yes*, since your hands undoubtedly reveal the reason for things going wrong. Sometimes the most gifted people manage to make a mess of their lives despite their above-average abilities.

OVER-ACHIEVEMENT

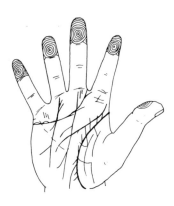

8.1
*Splayed fingers and
deep strong lines
indicate a high achiever*

Mandy is a dynamic, impressive young woman with boundless enthusiasm for everything that comes her way. She happens to be small, though perfectly proportioned and she whizzes about like a pocket edition of Wonder Woman. Mandy was the driving force

135

behind three successful business ventures before she reached the age of 25. When I first heard of her, she had just been appointed assistant editor of an influential women's magazine.

Mandy's love life is a disaster. She has lost count of the boyfriends she's had, most of whom parted from her with angry words or actual physical violence. Her relationship with her own sister has been distinguished by a black eye and numerous bruisings. Studying prints of this young woman's hands, I found no signs of emotional disturbance whatsoever. There was, however, one powerful indication as to why this dynamic person has such a disturbing life.

John is 30 and a computer engineer. He drives a super-speed, four-wheel drive car, is president of an athletics club, an expert mountain climber and he builds reproduction antique furniture in his spare time. He has had three wives so far and countless girlfriends. He also has an ulcer. John's clothes are the best, his pure-bred Samoyed is a champion. John belongs to several important societies and has won awards in six different sports. In spite of all his achievements, John is permanently in debt, suffers from erratic health and seldom manages to remain on friendly terms with anyone for more than six months at a time. His hands show the same pattern as Mandy's hands.

What is the common feature? Both John and Mandy are super extroverts with excess energy. When they put their hands down on a flat surface, all the fingers splay out like the arms of a star fish (diag. 8.1). They both have a large number of very deep, strong lines all over the palms, including wide-sweeping Life Lines. In short, they are both overly energetic.

The full-throttle person is a high achiever who commonly attempts to succeed in too many fields at once. The result, as with both John and Mandy, is that achievement never brings permanent results. Relationships with other people become strained. The super extrovert is always making new friends and all too frequently losing old ones. Other people simply cannot keep up and when friends become irritated with the overeager person, sparks begin to fly.

No-one has yet succeeded in giving advice to someone like this and yet there are ways in which the problem can be overcome should the extrovert want to change. The secret lies in careful planning and in the pursuit of moderation. Instead of blithely undertaking 20 things in the course of a day, the extrovert must learn to say no to at least half of them. People like Mandy and John delight in pushing themselves as far as their strength allows. This habit must be broken. They also delight in competition. What they need to learn is to confine this competitive spirit to a few areas, not to take on every human being and every challenge they meet.

The super extrovert is always in a rush, yet 80 per cent of that rush is totally unnecessary. Careful planning of their lives on a daily basis would eliminate much of this senseless darting and dashing and put order into their lives. Personal relationships are always a delicate area with these folk. They need consciously to practise the art of listening to others, paying attention to what others say. The Johns and Mandys of this world are far too busy talking about their own plans or giving advice to others to notice how impatient people may be getting with them.

There is a psychological disturbance known as manic depressive psychosis in which the sufferer's moods swing from periods of depression and lethargy to periods of excitement and high energy. In the manic, or active half of the cycle, the person behaves rather like the super extrovert. Conventional treatment for this problem involves the use of drugs, but there is a self-help technique which can be useful as well. It can also be recommended for the super extrovert.

Anyone can slow down his own manic or overexcited mood by careful control of speech and movement. Force yourself to speak slowly and softly, not in a loud voice. Pause for a moment before starting to speak. When you reach for something, or when you get up from your chair, move slowly. Ten minutes of controlling speech and movement like this will take the edge off anyone's excitement. A day of it will bring your mood close to normal again.

If you find yourself talking with someone who is in an overnervous or overexcited state of mind, you can often calm her somewhat by behaving in a calm manner yourself. If you can persuade the excited person to slow down too, so much the better. Calm, slow behaviour can even have an effect on a whole group of overstimulated people. In a room full of people shouting at each other, one firm, calm voice which first catches everyone's attention and then drops to a quiet, soothing level of speech can effectively quieten the whole room.

LACK OF ENERGY

At the opposite extreme to the super extroverts are those whose energy levels are too low. This problem can equally upset the lives of otherwise gifted people. Quite often the sufferer is only dimly aware that his energy level is below normal and so fails to realise that this is the cause of many problems.

8.2
*Life Line running close
to the thumb indicates
a low energy level*

One young woman, Leah, recognises her own physical lethargy but cannot see how it has affected her life. She possesses not only superb good looks but also a high intelligence. From childhood, a blood condition has slowed her physical movements. Being both attractive and clever, she has never lacked men to cater for her needs. She has, however, proved incapable of training herself for any job or profession. Poor stamina has prevented her from succeeding on her own. Besides her succession of rich boyfriends, she has involved herself in an endless series of get-rich-quick schemes. For Leah, lacking the ability to succeed in spite of her intelligence, the chance of making money without effort is irresistibly attractive. Consequently she has been cheated out of funds or lost money through unwise speculation countless times. Leah has yet to find a satisfactory boyfriend although her opportunities are endless. Men, however, respond to her physical attractiveness only, since the lethargy prevents her from being a stimulating companion. Being clever herself, she is quickly bored by men who are interested in her only for her looks. And so the circle turns.

Leah is fully aware of her physical disability, her lack of vitality, but at 35 years of age she has still not accepted that the emotional and financial difficulties are its direct outcome. She thinks that it's just a matter of finding "Mr Right" or the fastest way to a million and all will be well.

A variety of medical conditions can result in deficient energy but most will be marked in the hand in the same way. The Life Line, which should curve well out into the palm, runs instead almost in a straight line downwards and close to the thumb (diag. 8.2). In such cases, the line is often thin, sometimes broken up or islanded. The Life Line will simply look "weak" or washed-out. Anyone whose life is one long series of difficulties should check their own Life Line and compare it with diagram 8.2. A common effect of low energy is to make the sufferer feel pessimistic or depressed. Here is another typical case taken from my files.

Trudy was a 26-year-old single mother, endeavouring to raise her child alone. Although by nature a happy, cheerful person, she began to find single-parenthood a burden. Besides the factors of loneliness and limited income, her life seemed to be an endless procession of struggles and disappointments. She ate poorly and lost considerable weight, wanting to nap constantly and she even considered a temporary foster home for the child to give herself a break. When I examined her hands it was obvious what was wrong. Her Life Line was thin and frayed, a sure sign of energy depletion. Linking this to her loss of weight, it was not hard to see that she was suffering from malnutrition. It turned out that she had been cutting back on her own food in order to give her baby sufficient nourishment.

In Trudy's case, there is a happy ending. A few of her friends undertook to provide extra meals for her while another went over her budget and demonstrated how buying groceries in bulk could stretch her limited finances. The problems of poverty, and energy loss occasioned by poor diet now have been removed and her life is easier to handle.

OBESITY

8.3
Fat bottom phalanges are a major sign of obesity

Another problem related to diet is overweight. Fat people suffer the anxiety of being unattractive in the eyes of almost everyone else. This naturally leads to difficulty in personal relationships as well as damage in career and scholastic areas. The medical dangers of being overweight need hardly be spelled out in detail:

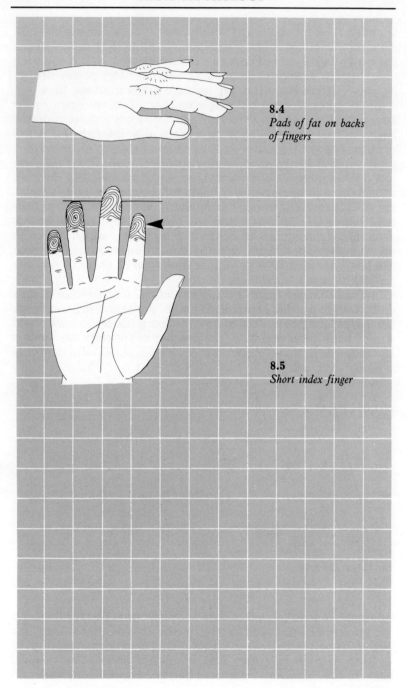

8.4
*Pads of fat on backs
of fingers*

8.5
Short index finger

suffice it to say that the life expectancy of fat folk is considerably lower than that of their thinner companions. The overweight person is likewise restricted in her physical activity.

At least four causes are commonly linked with being overweight: overeating, fluid retention, hormone imbalance and a metabolic imbalance created by overfeeding in childhood. By a study of hands, one can clearly distinguish the overeaters from those whose problem was created in the early years. Fluid retention is not identifiable through the hands and hormone imbalances may only be hinted at without being clearly evident.

The first thing to check for in the hands of a fat person is the bottom phalanges of the fingers. If they appear thick and puffy, you are dealing with someone who is both sensual and self-indulgent (diag. 8.3). For such people, food is simply one form of self-gratification. It is difficult to feel sympathy for someone who ruins his body purely through gluttony and such people seldom listen to advice on how to deal with the problem.

If the back of the hand reveals pads of fat, like little packets attached to the back of each finger base (diag. 8.4), you may conclude that the weight problem has been present since childhood. Parents who overfeed a baby or toddler can alter the metabolism of the child's body so that, as the child grows, virtually everything it eats can turn to fat. Adults who have this marking can make strenuous efforts to lose weight without success.

The only way of correcting the problem is to undergo a properly supervised fast. (However, fasting for longer than a few days without correct medical supervision and proper preparation is very unwise.) Prolonged fasting can totally change many body functions and can eliminate a fat problem set up in babyhood. However, such fasting is a serious business and anyone considering it as a measure for weight-control should consult an expert.

Fasting is not a recommended method nor an adequate one for dealing with overweight based on simple overindulgence. Proper control of the diet, as taught by such groups as Weight Watchers, is the correct way to deal with this fat. Regular short fasts such as one day per week, however, may help as an addition to a properly adjusted diet.

Fluid retention is a rare condition which cannot be readily diagnosed from the hands. Since it is impossible to suffer from this complaint without being aware of the fact, there is little need for the palmist to deal with it. Medical attention is essential for treatment.

Hormone imbalance may occasionally give a tendency towards obesity. Although there is no certain way of diagnosing from the hand, any deformity of the little finger or any oddity in the fingernails (especially unusually large, shiny nails) would warrant advising the person to seek a doctor's opinion on the matter.

The majority of fat people have swollen lower joints of the fingers, indicating sheer joy of eating and overindulging. There are cases of people who overeat for psychological reasons and for these a thorough investigation of the hand may reveal the cause. Romantic problems, work hassles and lack of self-confidence are the three most common causes.

Lack of self-confidence is revealed by a short index finger (diag. 8.5) which, in the worst cases can amount to an actual inferiority complex. We have touched on this feature in Chapters IV and V, where we described what happens when a short-index-fingered person attempts to overcome the problems of smoking and unemployment. Now it is time to deal with the problems which beset anyone who is unsure of herself, no matter what job or habits she possesses.

LOW SELF-ESTEEM

Talented and intelligent people can be afflicted by a sense of inferiority. Indeed, short index fingers are more common with such people than with those whose abilities are only average. The psychological weakness arises in childhood, sometimes as a result of the sensitivity which can be found in talented children, and sometimes from an unfavourable upbringing.

The only time a short index finger does not indicate a sense of inferiority is when it is carried jutting out from the hand (diag. 8.6). There are also other hand patterns which worsen the problem — tied Head and Life Lines (diag. 8.7), tied Fate and Life Lines (diag. 8.8A), a low-set little finger (diag. 8.8B) and a tri-radius in the skin ridges under the first finger which is misplaced close to the second finger (diag. 8.9).

People with short index fingers have difficulty with life. In company, they worry that others don't like them or are not satisfied with their behaviour. At work, they worry that their efforts are not adequate. They may be inclined to redo things many times over in the search for perfection and acceptance.

Short-index-fingered people anticipate criticism. In fact, they expect it. If you tell such a person, "Well done today, Harry," he thinks you are implying that he bombed out yesterday. The palmist must be particularly careful with these folk as almost any statement he makes can be misconstrued. In short, there is low

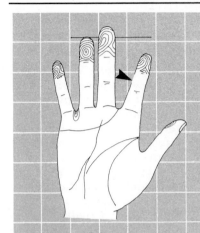

8.6
Short index finger jutting out

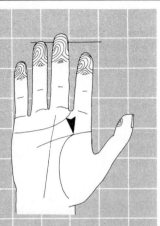

8.7
Tied Head and Life Lines

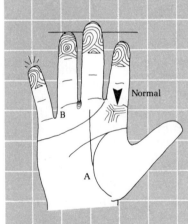

8.8
*Tied Fate and Life Lines (A),
and low-set little finger (B)*

8.9
Misplaced tri-radius

self-esteem in these people. For the owner of a short first finger, life is an uphill battle.

The majority of those whose problem occurs early in life find some way of overcoming it, as explained in Chapter V. Those few who do not, need careful counselling if they are to have any hope of success in the future. In particular, teenagers can benefit greatly from sympathetic advice from the palmist. Begin by pointing out that the short index finger is usually found on people with above-average talent or sensitivity. Then go on to stress the way an inferiority complex colours the way the owner sees things, often much worse than the situation actually warrants. Drive home to the sufferer that his own mind is playing a trick on him. Advise him to say to himself, whenever necessary: "This is just my own mind making me feel inferior when actually I am not really inferior at all." Your objective must be to make the person understand how unrealistic his self-doubt is. If he can be made to see that the self-doubt is an illusion, not reality, he has great hope of fighting to overcome it. Encourage him by pointing out that most sufferers manage to beat the problem. For some, it actually becomes the stimulus to greater effort. Here is a case history to illustrate not only the insecurity associated with the short index finger, but also how this feature can contribute to the problem of overeating.

Gloria was a pretty teenager but her alcoholic father's continual criticism resulted in her developing a painful inferiority complex. She married at 17 to escape her father and rapidly produced six children. Her husband, also a drinker, criticised her as well and in an attempt to prove her worth she had given birth to this succession of babies. In motherhood, she sought to assert herself, to prove there was good reason for her existence. Under the influence of her bad-tempered husband, Gloria became a compulsive eater. Her weight increased to the point where her appearance became quite grotesque. She also took to consulting fortune-tellers in the hope of hearing good things about the future of her life. When she came to me, I spotted her very short first finger right away. Since her fingers gave no sign of gluttony, these short indexes were the clue to her excess weight.

She told me, "Whenever I am worried or upset, I go straight to the refrigerator and eat myself senseless. The more I am put down, the more I look for solace in food." Gloria is an intelligent woman with good insight into her own predicament. In subsequent discussions with her, she told me that one of her hobbies was painting and I suggested that this would be a worthwhile activity to pursue to improve her self-esteem. Over the next few months, she devoted more time to her hobby. At my suggestion, she took some completed works to a small gallery and was so thrilled when they accepted them for sale on commission that she could barely swallow her dinner that night.

By the end of the year, Gloria had sold several paintings, and she had joined Weight Watchers. Her husband, pleased with the improvement, seemed less critical than he had been and actually began to discuss what went on at his wife's meetings. Gloria felt that life was considerably brighter and looked forward to even greater improvement through her own efforts.

One of the difficulties of counselling someone with a short index finger is that the person may require encouragement for years in order to achieve a permanent effect. The self-doubting mechanism ensures that the person will question every improvement and every positive suggestion. A palmist is rarely in a position to counsel for more than a short period, but in your day-to-day life, occasions may arise when you have to deal with a self-doubting individual. Patience and a clear understanding of the problem are the keys to success.

Perhaps the most disturbing manifestation of self-doubt is masochism. Anyone who has befriended a masochistic individual will know how such a person can create endless situations of trouble, turmoil and distress. Often, masochists possess short index fingers, though there are a good number with whom you must search for more subtle clues.

Carol is now in her 20s. A journalist, she has also spent periods as an actress and as a teacher. She holds two university degrees and she has a very short index finger. Her first affair, at 18, was with a kind-hearted boy only a year younger. Throughout the initial year of the affair, they had an excellent relationship. In the second year, she did everything in her power to break up the friendship, finally succeeding by arranging for her lover to find her with another man.

Her subsequent relationships included several married men, a sadist, two drug addicts and a professional criminal. In every case, the relationships brought nothing but despair, anxiety and physical strain. She abandoned her work as a teacher when it proved successful, lived for a while as an actress in dire poverty and subsequently left a good position as journalist to work for an editor who was a chronic alcoholic. By the time she was 28, she could look back on a score of disastrous incidents which had hurt her deeply. Nevertheless, when she encountered a palmist who took one look at her hands and diagnosed masochism, she flatly denied any such trait existed!

Can anything be done with such a person? Besides applying the same techniques as you would use with the short-index-fingered individual, the only hope is to spend long periods discussing and analysing the common patterns behind the disastrous events. Masochistic people resist looking at the way they create their own problems. If you can draw up a list and carefully point out exactly what the masochist is doing, it may be possible to stop repetition of the same "mistakes". If you couple this technique with the support and counselling recommended for a short-index-fingered person, the problem may be overcome.

Dealing with a masochist is perhaps the most frustrating and disappointing exercise anyone can undertake. Such people really do not want to be helped. Nevertheless, overcoming masochism not only helps the sufferer, but also countless others who are affected by this individual's behaviour. Although most masochists have defective first fingers, masochistic behaviour can occur in hands which do not have this feature. Any of the emotional oddities revealed by the Heart Line or the little finger may result in masochistic tendencies and only by learning about events in the life of the person can masochism be diagnosed. It is a fairly rare condition in its fully developed form but traces of it can be found in the lives of many people.

In Chapter IV there is a description of the neurotic or highly strung person's hand. A restless, unsettled mind always results in an unsettled life. Sometimes, quite ordinary people come under stress and when this happens the stress creates erratic behaviour which in turn leads to further stress. This sort of vicious circle results in breakdowns. From the hand, it is possible to watch the development of stress-created markings which are a warning sign that danger lies ahead.

STRESS

8.10
An island in the middle of the Head Line indicates sensitivity to stress

The first place to look to determine whether someone is susceptible to stress is the Head Line. If there is a clear island in the middle of the Head Line (diag. 8.10) it is a warning that the person is sensitive to stress. There are many people who can deal with difficult and stressful conditions without succumbing to them but individuals with islands in the Head Line are not so lucky. Under moderate or quiet circumstances, these folk can operate perfectly well but under high stress conditions they fall to pieces. The classic "nervous breakdown" is sometimes the outcome.

It is possible to determine the approximate date of such an event according to the position of the island. This does not mean that the person is "fated" to have a breakdown at a certain date but it does show that the natural sensitivity is more marked at this time than at other times. The individual should be particularly careful of stress at the time of susceptibility. An important point to note is that anyone with an islanded Head Line is always more susceptible to stress than normal and should consciously avoid any extended pressure or strain.

Amateur palmists are rather inclined to see signs of death and disaster all over the average hand. Do not assume that every little series of scratchings forms an island. Unless the island is very clearly marked and very noticeable, it does not warrant concern. Diagram 8.11 shows an example of a clearly formed island. Any island found at the commencement of the Head Line, at the point where it joins the Life Line (diag. 8.12) does not have any stress-related significance at all.

The second formation of the Head Line which needs to be mentioned is made up of a series of interlocking lines, forming a chain (diag. 8.13). Earlier palmistry books refer to this as a chained Head Line and, quite incorrectly, claim that it indicates poor mental powers. In fact, it is found only on persons of above-average intelligence and it indicates an alert but highly agitated mind. I have found this pattern repeatedly with female university students, particularly those with a small build. The chained pattern is thus partly related to physical energy and stamina and partly to the finely tuned nervous system.

In such people, there is little danger of actual nervous breakdown, but there is definitely a strong likelihood of minor nervous symptoms whenever stress arises. These range from nervous tremor and poor sleeping patterns, to needless worry, anxiety and a nervy tone in the voice and manner. When stress is removed, these symptoms tend to disappear.

There is one cardinal rule for any student with a chained Head Line or, indeed, anyone with this pattern marked in the hand. Pay proper attention to sleep and diet. Remember that the pattern indicates delicacy both in the physical and the psychological

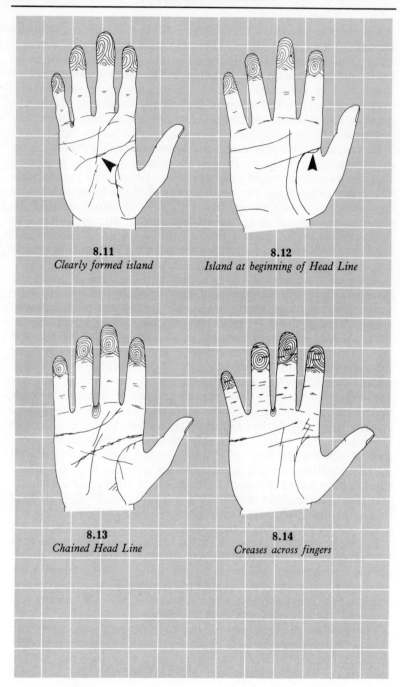

8.11
Clearly formed island

8.12
Island at beginning of Head Line

8.13
Chained Head Line

8.14
Creases across fingers

spheres. By far the best way to minimise stress for these people is for them to keep a careful watch on their physical well-being. Missing meals and eating junk food must not be allowed. Healthy eating of fresh fruit and vegetables, unprocessed and wholegrain products and the avoidance of any refined foods would be a sensible idea.

Some degree of physical exertion such as regular walking or bicycle-riding should accompany study or mental exertion. Although college students must expect to devote many hours each evening to their books, sleep should not be cut back as a result. Adequate rest is essential. All these points are simple commonsense and yet people with chained Head Lines repeatedly ignore them. By following a healthy lifestyle, their susceptibility to nervous strain as indicated by the Head Line can be minimised.

Under stressful conditions, even the most stable person can start to suffer and the indication of this anxiety shows up in the hand. A careful study of your own hands (adequate prints can be taken with a well-inked stamp pad) could produce interesting results, especially through periods of exceptional difficulty.

A classic indication of strain is the growth of horizontal creases across the tips of the fingers or anywhere else on the inner side of each finger (diag. 8.14). These are called bar lines and can come and go in the hand quite regularly. They are created by frustration. Anyone whose plans are being continually thwarted is liable to grow them. In particular, working in a dead-end job is likely to bring these bar lines out.

There is no simple cure for this problem. Anyone who notices bar lines appearing on the fingers should take stock of his or her life with a view to determining what frustration needs to be conquered. The point here is that many people can put up with adversity without realising the damaging effect it may be having upon health and personality. Discovering bar lines should be a warning that it is time to stop "putting up with things" and deal head-on with the annoyance.

All the lines, particularly the Head Line, can change under stress. Sometimes tiny hair lines start to grow through and across the Head Line. Sometimes the Head Line grows thicker, taking on a woolly appearance instead of its usual clear path across the hands. Any of these changes are a warning that stress is at work. Several British palmists have reported beneficial results in such cases through the use of herbal or homeopathic remedies. There is no evidence from the palmists' experiences that the conventional tranquillising drugs of modern medicine have any long-term effect. Their use is most suited to attaining temporary relief from stress while other measures are being applied for long-term effect.

In this chapter, we have dealt with the sort of problems that can mess up the lives of otherwise competent people. Of course, many difficulties may arise in the areas of romance or employment and in such cases the chapters on these particular subjects need to be considered as well.

Your hand is the ultimate guide to your life. As you have seen, by understanding the information it gives to you, it is possible to learn to solve your own problems. There is no reason why your life should not be a totally happy one, filled with satisfaction. Self-knowledge is the key to this end and by the study of your own hands that knowledge is available for you to use.

TEACH YOURSELF PALMISTRY (A COMPLETE COURSE IN TEN LESSONS)

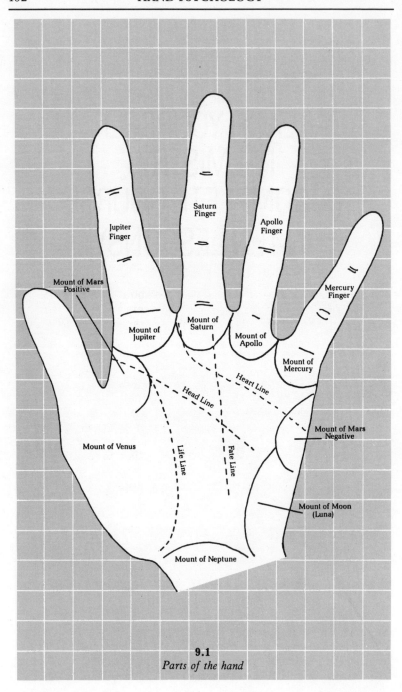

9.1
Parts of the hand

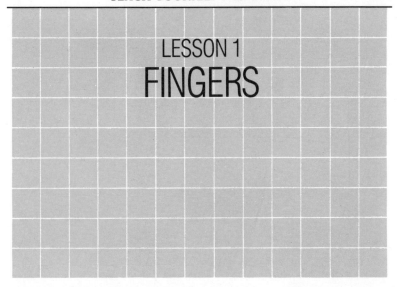

LESSON 1
FINGERS

To become a palmist, you need to learn about three main parts of the hand. These are: the shape of the fingers and hands; the skin-ridge patterns, especially the fingerprints; and the three main lines.

Our first lesson deals with the fingers, and you must start by memorising their names and meanings, as well as becoming familiar with the other areas of the hand (diag. 9.1).

The *first (or index) finger* is traditionally called Jupiter. It shows the degree of self-confidence, so from its size and shape can be judged things like leadership ability or shyness, bossiness or timidity.

The *second finger*, called Saturn, reveals the serious side of a personality. How it is developed will reveal business talent, reliability, steadiness or, if underdeveloped, a careless and frivolous nature.

The *third (or ring) finger*, called Apollo (the Sun), is a symbol of creativity and artistic qualities. A strong development goes with a talent for designing, drawing, etc.

The *fourth (or little) finger*, called Mercury, concerns both sex and communication. All sorts of sexual and romantic qualities are shown here, as well as the ability to speak, write or express oneself.

The *thumb* shows will, and overall strength of character. This digit is so important that it has been given a lesson of its own.

There is a basic principle that if any finger is long, it shows strong development of the accompanying qualities. If short, it shows the lack of those qualities.

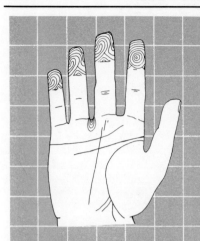

9.2

Hand of a bank manager. Note the long first finger

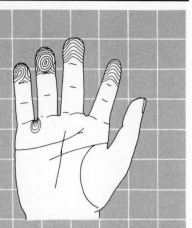

9.3

Hand of a self-employed house painter. Note the short first finger which is thrust outwards

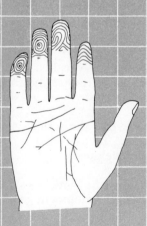

9.4

Hand of a shy shop assistant. Note the short first finger

9.5

Hand of a clerk whose hobby is collecting antiques. Note the curved first finger

Here are the meanings in detail:

THE INDEX FINGER
(SYMBOL OF SELF)
Diagrams 9.2–9.5
A *long* first finger reaches more than two-thirds of the way up the top joint of the middle finger. A *short* one reaches less than halfway up. A long index finger shows plenty of self-confidence and self-awareness, so the owner is sure of his or her own abilities, interested in self-development and advancement, keen to have things his or her own way, able to take charge of things, and possibly bossy or conceited.

If the finger is short, the reverse will hold true. A person with a short index finger is usually shy, afraid he or she is going to fail, and inclined to doubt and criticise himself or herself.

Quite often, a shy person with a short first finger tries very hard to overcome this personality problem. Such a person usually overreacts and becomes very aggressive and independent. In these cases, the finger is held jutting outwards.

There is one other form for the index finger: the *curved* shape, rather like a banana. This is related to the short form, indicating poor self-confidence. People with curved index fingers have a great need for security and therefore often have many hobbies and collect many possessions. They like to take precautions as well.

THE MIDDLE FINGER
(SYMBOL OF SERIOUSNESS)
Diagrams 9.6–9.8
A *long* middle finger is one which reaches high above the fingers on either side. It reveals a person who treats life seriously, who believes strongly in "getting ahead" and "being successful".

People with *short*, stubby middle fingers are careless and do not like to hold a responsible job. In hands like this, the middle finger is no longer than the first and third digits. Business people who deal with money and property usually have long, strong middle fingers. Hippies and drop-outs often have short ones. Most people have middle fingers which are neither very long nor very short.

THE RING FINGER
(SYMBOL OF CREATIVITY)
Diagram 9.9
There is only one rule with this finger: if it is *long*, then the

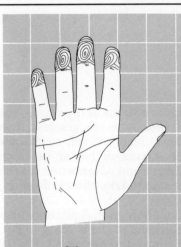

9.6
*Hand of an average
family man. The middle
finger is of normal length*

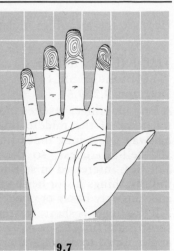

9.7
*Hand of the wife of the
average family man. She
has her own cosmetics
agency and looks after her
husband's pay packet.
Note the long middle
finger*

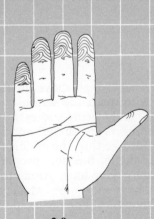

9.8
*Hand of an alcoholic man
who has been unemployed
for 20 years. Note the
short middle finger*

9.9
*Hand of a successful
woman potter and
sculptor. Note the long
ring finger*

person will have a creative nature. Usually this means an interest in art. For some unknown reason, this sometimes accompanies a gambling instinct, but not frequently enough to make this a rule.

Short ring fingers are so very rare that you will not need to bother about them.

THE RING FINGER AND
MIDDLE FINGER TOGETHER
Diagram 9.10
On some hands, these two fingers *bend towards each other*. This shows that at some time in the past, the person has sacrificed pleasure for duty, or stifled his or her own creativity in order to do something rather dull. Usually, this will have been something like looking after a sick or elderly parent, or giving up an exciting or creative life in order to take a steady job.

THE LITTLE FINGER
(SYMBOL OF COMMUNICATION AND SEX)
Diagrams 9.11–9.14
This is the only finger which symbolises more than one aspect of a personality. There are a good many shapes and forms which this digit can have.

A *long* little finger reveals a good ability to write or speak, and a strong sex drive. It is very common on people of above-average intelligence.

A *short* little finger reveals immaturity in emotional or sexual behaviour. This has been discussed in detail in Chapter III.

If the little finger is *low-set*, some childhood difficulty connected with a parent has affected the person's emotional outlook. Full details are in Chapter III.

If the finger *sticks out* from the hand, the person is experiencing a temporary emotional or sexual difficulty.

Some uncommon forms of the little finger (Diagrams 9.15–9.19)
If the finger *curves* or bends towards the ring finger, it indicates a shrewd mind. In a poor hand, this shrewdness can even extend to self-seeking dishonesty.

If the finger has only *two joint lines* instead of the usual three, the person is unconventional or deviant in behaviour.

If the finger has *four joint lines*, this has the same significance as a long digit.

If the *top joint is thick or swollen*, or even simply unusually long, the person is a great talker, probably an "ear basher".

If the *middle joint is very short*, the owner lacks organising ability.

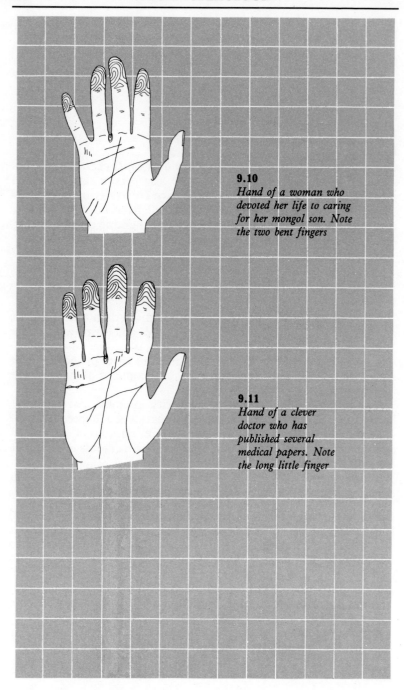

9.10
Hand of a woman who devoted her life to caring for her mongol son. Note the two bent fingers

9.11
Hand of a clever doctor who has published several medical papers. Note the long little finger

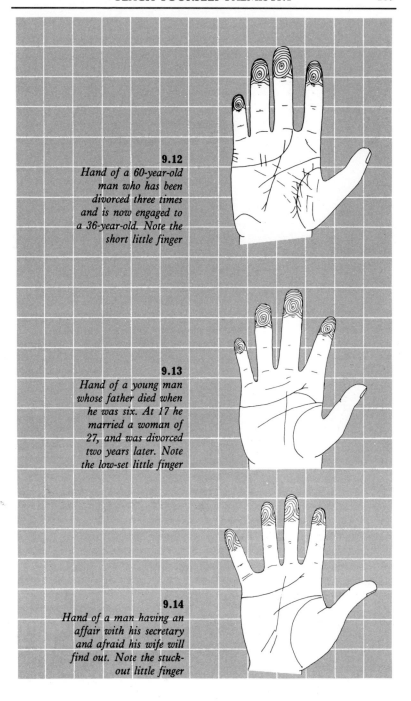

9.12
Hand of a 60-year-old man who has been divorced three times and is now engaged to a 36-year-old. Note the short little finger

9.13
Hand of a young man whose father died when he was six. At 17 he married a woman of 27, and was divorced two years later. Note the low-set little finger

9.14
Hand of a man having an affair with his secretary and afraid his wife will find out. Note the stuck-out little finger

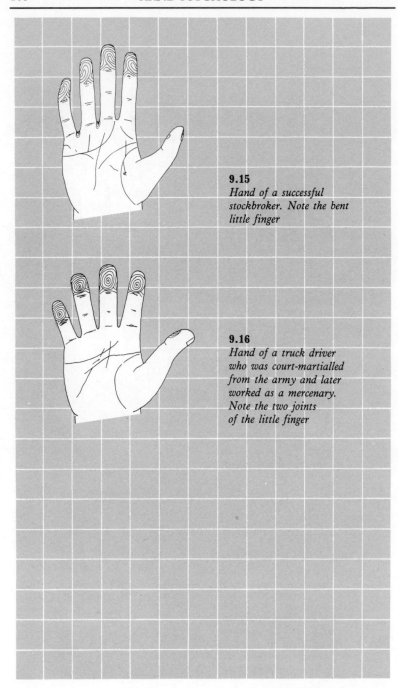

9.15
*Hand of a successful
stockbroker. Note the bent
little finger*

9.16
*Hand of a truck driver
who was court-martialled
from the army and later
worked as a mercenary.
Note the two joints
of the little finger*

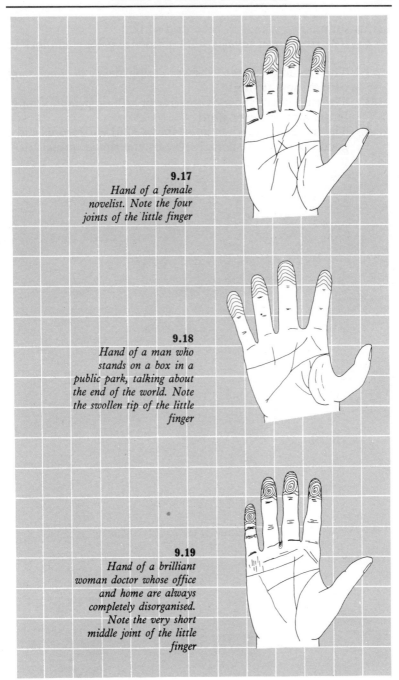

9.17
Hand of a female novelist. Note the four joints of the little finger

9.18
Hand of a man who stands on a box in a public park, talking about the end of the world. Note the swollen tip of the little finger

9.19
Hand of a brilliant woman doctor whose office and home are always completely disorganised. Note the very short middle joint of the little finger

Let us summarise what has been said so far:

1. The first finger reveals self-confidence if long and lack of it if short.
2. The middle finger shows seriousness if long and carelessness if short.
3. The ring finger shows a creative or artistic person if long, but is almost never short.
4. The little finger, when long, shows skill with words and a good sex drive. If short, it reveals emotional immaturity.

LESSON 2
GENERAL INFORMATION ABOUT FINGERS

LENGTH

Unusually long fingers are found on people who fuss over small details. They are finicky and particular about all they do.

Short fingers are found on quick-thinking, impulsive people.

SHAPE
Diagrams 9.20–9.21

Fingers with *knobbly* joints, called "knotty fingers", show a mind which loves to argue and reason things out. (This does not apply if arthritis has distorted the fingers.) Scientists, debaters, chess players and so on tend to have knotty fingers.

Smooth fingers belong to people who use intuition rather than pure reason. Artists, poets and humanitarians are the sorts of people who have smooth fingers. Smooth fingers are much more common than knotty ones. The shape of the fingers has nothing to do with intelligence, but a lot to do with the type of thinking a person uses.

Each finger is divided into three sections, called phalanges. According to how long or thick each phalanx may be, the personality will be different.

Long top joints on all fingers show a thoughtful person.

Long middle joints on all fingers show skill with business and practical things.

Puffy, thick bottom joints show greediness, self-indulgence and love of food and comfort.

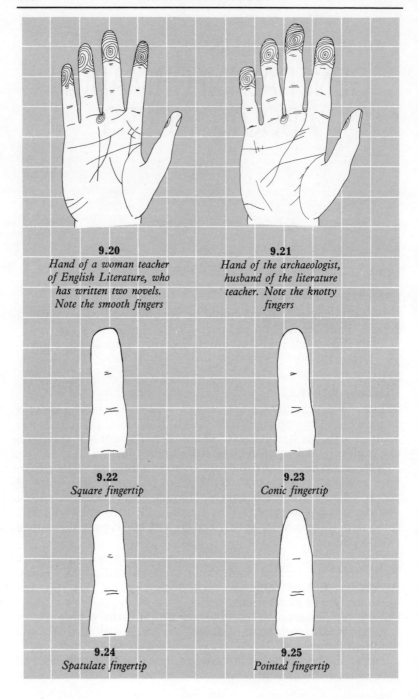

9.20
*Hand of a woman teacher
of English Literature, who
has written two novels.
Note the smooth fingers*

9.21
*Hand of the archaeologist,
husband of the literature
teacher. Note the knotty
fingers*

9.22
Square fingertip

9.23
Conic fingertip

9.24
Spatulate fingertip

9.25
Pointed fingertip

Pinched-in, thin bottom joints indicate a person who is fussy about what he or she eats. Such people avoid sensual self-indulgence.

TIPS
Diagrams 9.22–9.25
The tips of the fingers come in four main shapes.

Square fingertips (diag. 9.22) show a lover of careful, neat work. Such people like to follow a set method in any task they perform.

Conic fingertips (i.e. round) (diag. 9.23) are very common. They show an easy-going, ordinary way of doing things.

Spatulate fingertips (i.e. thick at the top) (diag 9.24) show a love of activity and outdoor life. Such people are also inventive.

Pointed fingertips (diag. 9.25) are rare. They show a spiritual or inspirational type of mind.

SPACING
Diagrams 9.26–9.32
Most people hold their fingers *slightly apart*, showing a moderate degree of independent thinking.

Very wide gaps between the fingers show a non-conformist, someone who is not afraid to "break the rules".

Fingers which *hug together tightly* show a completely conformist mind. For example, a burglar with close-spaced fingers (diag. 9.26) would break into houses by the same method every time, and would remain living in the same district for years (in between prison sentences).

A burglar with widely spaced fingers (diag. 9.27) would be more likely to dabble in sideline activities like bank robbery and extortion and his convictions would probably be scattered through six different states. This man would be capable of giving it all up, however, since his mind is not as fixed as his close-fingered counterpart.

Very extroverted people, and young children, put their hands on a table with all their fingers *splayed outwards* (diag. 9.29).

A gap between the first and second fingers shows the ability to make decisions for yourself and for people around you. Many managers show this pattern.

A gap between the second and third fingers usually occurs only when all fingers are widely spaced. It shows independent thinking about basic values in life.

A gap between the third and fourth fingers shows independent or unconventional thinking about sex and relationships. Often, but not always, this leads to trouble in the romantic side of life.

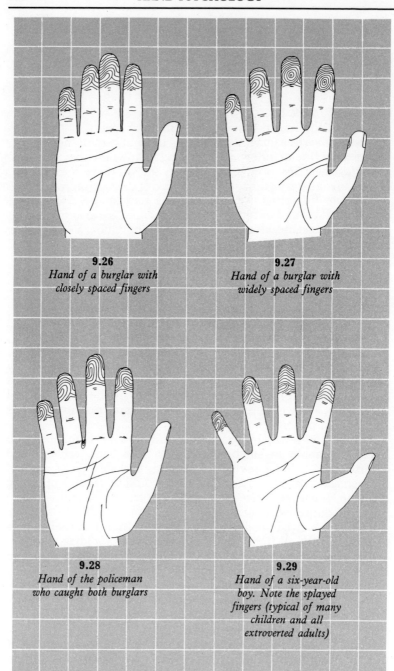

9.26
*Hand of a burglar with
closely spaced fingers*

9.27
*Hand of a burglar with
widely spaced fingers*

9.28
*Hand of the policeman
who caught both burglars*

9.29
*Hand of a six-year-old
boy. Note the splayed
fingers (typical of many
children and all
extroverted adults)*

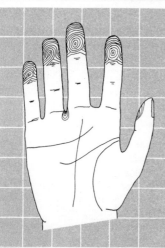

9.30
*Hand of the head buyer of
a big department store.
Note the wide space
between first and second
fingers (decision-making
ability)*

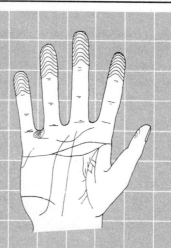

9.31
*Hand of a successful but
unconventional female
artist. Note the widely
spaced fingers (independent
thinking)*

9.32
*Hand of a corrupt
politician who has an
"arrangement" with a
massage parlour. Note the
wide space between third
and fourth fingers
(unconventional
relationships)*

9.33
*Hand of a female archery
champion. Note the
pinched-in base phalanges
(self-discipline) and
spatulate fingertips
(outdoor activity)*

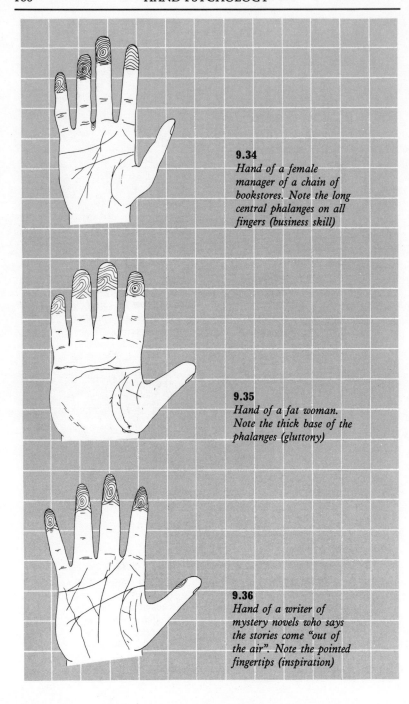

9.34
Hand of a female manager of a chain of bookstores. Note the long central phalanges on all fingers (business skill)

9.35
Hand of a fat woman. Note the thick base of the phalanges (gluttony)

9.36
Hand of a writer of mystery novels who says the stories come "out of the air". Note the pointed fingertips (inspiration)

Here is a list of questions relating to the lines of the hand, together with the answers in the right-hand column. Cover the answers and test yourself on the information in this lesson.

Questions

1. Name one common sign of a society drop-out.

2. Which finger is often long on the hand of an artist?

3. What is the typical writer's feature?

4. Which feature shows complete disorganisation?

5. How is the desire to be a leader indicated?

6. Someone who always goes his or her own way has what feature?

7. What sort of fingers are found on people who do not like to debate and argue?

8. What feature indicates a love of outdoor life?

9. What is the sign of gluttony?

10. What shows a bossy person?

11. Name a common feature of stamp and coin collectors.

12. Very tidy people have what sort of fingers?

13. Which people are quick to think and act?

14. A shy person is likely to have what feature?

15. If a child has a difficult time with a parent, what will you be likely to find in his or her hand?

16. How do children's hands differ from those of adults?

Answers

1. *A short middle finger.*

2. *The ring finger.*

3. *A long little finger.*

4. *A short central phalange on the little finger.*

5. *By a long first finger.*

6. *Widely spaced fingers.*

7. *Smooth fingers.*

8. *Spatulate fingertips.*

9. *Fat bottom phalanges on the fingers.*

10. *A long first finger.*

11. *Curved first fingers.*

12. *Square-tipped fingers.*

13. *Short-fingered people.*

14. *A short first finger.*

15. *A low-set little finger.*

16. *When placed down, the fingers splay out.*

17. What sort of tips usually go with smooth fingers?

18. How would you recognise a fussy, particular person?

19. Which sign is associated with intellectuals and thinkers?

20. Which formation indicates excessive talkativeness?

21. How would you recognise an unadventurous person?

22. Which people love to solve puzzles and problems?

23. Name a sign of extrovertism.

24. Picky eaters have which feature?

25. Name two typical business signs.

17. *Rounded ("conic") tips.*

18. *By the long fingers.*

19. *Long top phalanges on the fingers.*

20. *A long or thick (swollen) top phalange on the little finger.*

21. *By the closely spaced fingers.*

22. *People with knotty fingers.*

23. *Fingers splayed out.*

24. *Thin bottom phalanges.*

25. *a. A long middle finger.*
b. Long middle phalanges.

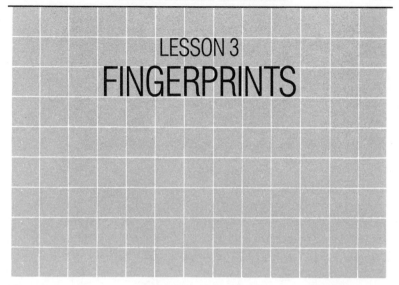

LESSON 3
FINGERPRINTS

Fingerprints are tremendously important, because they represent the most basic and unchangeable elements of our personalities. We can learn to modify these basic traits, but we can never completely get rid of them.

Technically, the study of these fine ridges in the skin is called "dermatoglyphics". Ridge lines in the skin run all over the palm and soles. In Lesson 10, we will study the patterns in the palm, but for the moment we are concerned only with the patterns on the tips of the fingers.

There are just three main types of prints:
1. The *whorl* (diag. 9.37), which is the sign of the individualist and the thinker.
2. The *arch* (diag. 9.38), which is the sign of the practical doer.
3. The *loop* (diag. 9.39), which is the sign of the balanced, middle-of-the-road person who fits in with others.

WHORL
Diagrams 9.40, 9.41
A person whose fingerprints are mainly of the whorl type will be individualistic, not just "one of the crowd"; thoughtful, and his or her ideas and opinions will be clearly formed; secretive, able to keep things to himself or herself; and often talented in some way.

Whorls come in two types, *spiral* and *concentric* (diags 9.40, 9.41). They are much the same in meaning, but the qualities of the concentric type are a little stronger.

Positive qualities of people with whorl fingerprints include

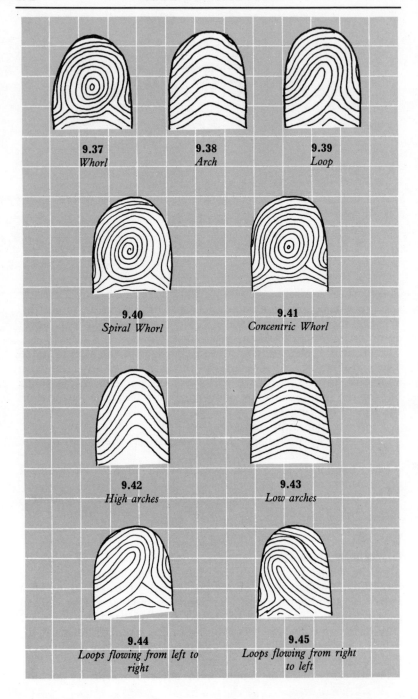

9.37
Whorl

9.38
Arch

9.39
Loop

9.40
Spiral Whorl

9.41
Concentric Whorl

9.42
High arches

9.43
Low arches

9.44
Loops flowing from left to right

9.45
Loops flowing from right to left

their intensity and general ability. Negative qualities include isolation, being too much wrapped up in themselves.

ARCH
Diagrams 9.42, 9.43
A person whose fingerprints are mainly of the arch type will be suspicious, never believing anything until it is proved; good with his or her hands, good at making or mending things; reliable, hard-working, able to get things done; practical, aiming at efficiency; and reserved, preferring to control his or her own emotions.

Positive qualities of the people with arch fingerprints include steadiness, realism and usefulness. Negative qualities include reluctance to accept change and a lack of responsiveness.

Some arches rise up *high* (diag. 9.42) while others are *low* (diag. 9.43). People with higher arches are usually more skilful and idealistic.

LOOP
Diagrams 9.44–9.48
A person whose fingerprints are mainly of the loop type will be adaptable and fit in with other people; easy-going; good at dealing with people and making the best of whatever is available; and likeable. (Whereas arch people and whorl people are sometimes popular and sometimes not, everyone gets on well with a loop dominant person.)

Positive qualities of the person with loop fingerprints include flexibility and all-round capability. Negative traits include lack of individualism.

Loops can flow from *left to right* (diag. 9.44) or *right to left* (diag. 9.45). There is no significant difference between the two types.

SOME EXTRA NOTES ON THE THREE TYPES OF PRINTS
Diagrams 9.49–9.54
Although fingerprints are classified according to type, there are always differences between one print and the next. These notes will help you interpret the subtle differences.

There is a general rule that strong, clear fingerprint patterns intensify the meaning of each type and bring out the higher qualities.

Only experience and intuition will help you in interpreting subtle differences like this but they are well worth looking for.

1, is a good way.

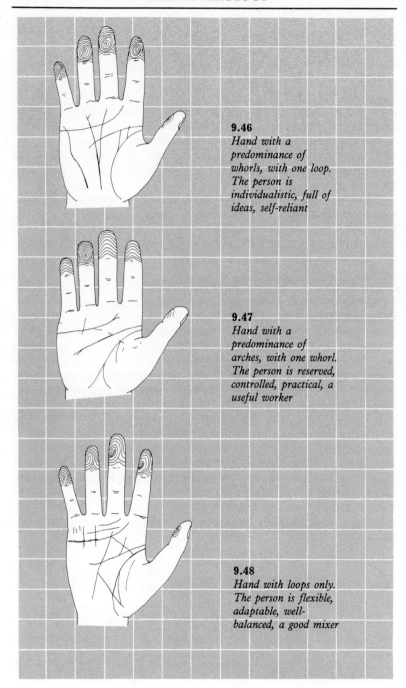

9.46
Hand with a predominance of whorls, with one loop. The person is individualistic, full of ideas, self-reliant

9.47
Hand with a predominance of arches, with one whorl. The person is reserved, controlled, practical, a useful worker

9.48
Hand with loops only. The person is flexible, adaptable, well-balanced, a good mixer

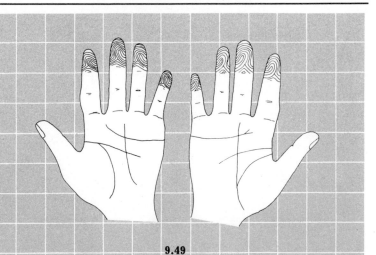

9.49

All ulnar loops. The base of each loop slopes from the little finger side of the hand

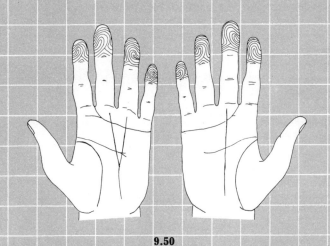

9.50

First and second fingers have radial loops, the others are ulnar loops. The base of each radial loop slopes from the thumb side of the hand

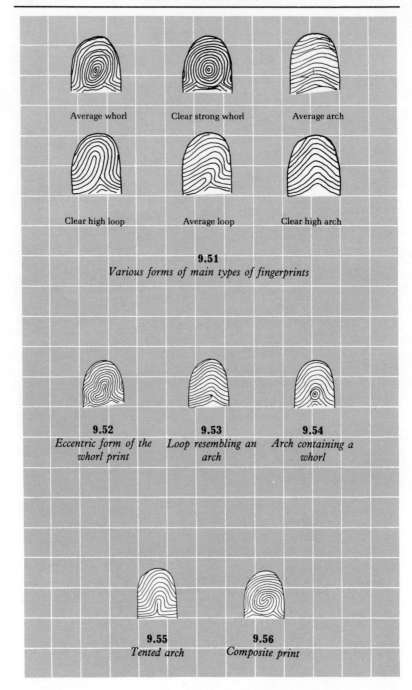

Average whorl   Clear strong whorl   Average arch

Clear high loop   Average loop   Clear high arch

9.51
Various forms of main types of fingerprints

9.52
Eccentric form of the whorl print

9.53
Loop resembling an arch

9.54
Arch containing a whorl

9.55
Tented arch

9.56
Composite print

There are also cases of eccentric or strangely formed prints which invariably accompany strange or unusual personalities.

Loop prints are classed as *"ulnar"* or *"radial"* depending on whether the base of each loop starts on the little finger side of the hand (the ulnar side) or on the thumb side (the radial side). As you can see, this means that an ulnar loop slants either left or right depending on which hand it is on.

Radial loops have all the qualities of an ordinary loop, except that the owners are a little more individualistic or rebellious.

OTHER TYPES OF PRINTS
Diagrams 9.55–9.56

The arch, loop and whorl account for 80 per cent of all fingerprints. However, there are two rarer prints which you need to recognise.

One is a *tented arch* (diag. 9.55), so-called from the little vertical line in the middle, like a tent pole. It is a sign of enthusiasm. People with tented arches become deeply involved in everything they do. Qualities of the ordinary arch are also present. Note carefully that a tented arch is not just an arch with high curving ridges. It must have the little "tent pole" in the middle to be a true tented arch.

The other rare print is a *composite print* (diag. 9.56). It is related to the whorl and is composed of two loops curling around each other. The owners of these prints see two sides to each and every question and often experience difficulty in making up their minds. They also have the ordinary whorl qualities.

LESSON 4
FINGERPRINTS ON INDIVIDUAL FINGERS

If all the fingers have the same type of print, there is no difficulty in interpreting the character. Indeed, if the prints on the first and second finger are the same, this will show the person's main characteristics. Quite often, however, one finger has a different sort of print from the others. This is easy to interpret if you remember the basic meaning of each finger. (See Lesson 1.)

Loops are the most common type of print and they reveal average, middle-of-the-road qualities whenever they occur.

INDEX FINGER

The index finger expresses the self. Prints on this finger relate to personal interests and goals.

A *whorl* on the first (Jupiter) finger shows individualism, the ability to form one's own ideas.

An *arch* on the Jupiter finger reveals practical ability in dealing with personal hobbies and interests, but not in other areas of life.

A *tented arch* on this finger shows special enthusiasm for personal projects and personal beliefs.

A *composite* on this finger shows changeability in personal beliefs and attitudes and goals.

SECOND FINGER

The second finger expresses the serious or stable side of a personality, especially ability in work or business.

A *whorl* on the second (Saturn) finger shows individualism in a person's working life. This often leads the owner to select unusual work.

An *arch* on the Saturn finger shows practical skills in work or employment. Occasionally, an intelligent person prefers to work at a simple, physical job and such people usually have this finger-print pattern.

A *tented arch* on this finger shows enthusiasm for work or business.

A *composite* on this finger shows changeable and uncertain attitudes to work or business, often culminating in an endless search for "the right job".

THIRD FINGER

The third finger is indicative of the artistic side of the personality.

A *whorl* on the third (Apollo) finger indicates artistic ability.

An *arch* on the Apollo finger suggests a craft hobby such as carving, enamelling, sculpture or embroidery.

A *tented arch* on this finger shows a special enthusiasm for some form of art. This is very rare.

A *composite* on this finger shows that the owner's artistic taste is variable. Therefore the taste may be constantly changing in clothing or decor.

LITTLE FINGER

The little finger (Mercury) nearly always bears a loop, unless all the prints are of another type. It is so rare to find an isolated print on this finger that no certain interpretations can be laid down. Remember that the little finger relates to the unconscious side of the personality.

However, here is a special rule to remember: when the last two fingers, Apollo and Mercury, are marked with whorls, and if the other prints of the remaining fingers are of another type, the person's subconscious mind is unusually active. This leads to vivid or precognitive dreaming, and also hunches or mental impressions of all types.

THUMB

The thumb often bears an isolated print which will reveal how the owner sets about doing things, his or her method of action.

A *whorl* on the thumb shows an individualistic way of getting things done.

An *arch* indicates practicality and directness in setting about tasks.

Tented arches hardly ever occur on a thumb, but *composites* are quite common. This is the most usual place for a composite print to appear. Such a print shows a habit of doing one thing and then immediately wishing you had done something else! It can lead to indecision in carrying out ideas.

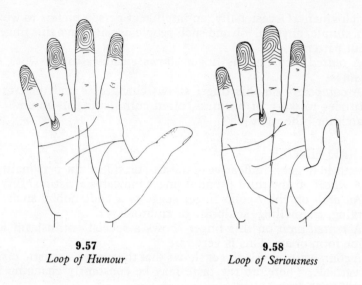

9.57
Loop of Humour

9.58
Loop of Seriousness

LOOPS OF HUMOUR AND SERIOUSNESS
Diagrams 9.57–9.58
Besides the fingerprints, there are two patterns in the skin of the palm which are so important that they should be looked at as well. (Other palmar patterns are dealt with in Lesson 10.) Please remember that fingerprints are of very great importance and must never be left out in your analysis of a hand.

A clear loop in the space between the Mercury and Apollo fingers (diag. 9.57) shows a sense of humour, a happy or optimistic approach to life. Those with this loop are better at enjoying themselves than at "getting ahead" in the world.

A clear loop in the space between the Saturn and Apollo fingers (diag. 9.58) is a sign of seriousness. It is very common among successful business people.

These loops are studied in greater detail in Chapter V.

VARIETIES OF PATTERNS
Diagrams 9.59–9.71
Here are some hands to illustrate the variety of fingerprint patterns. Full sets of composites and full sets of tented arches are very rare. However, two or three of these prints on one hand are enough to give a strong sense of the appropriate qualities.

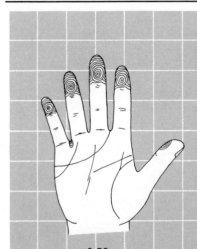

9.59
*All whorls. The person
is thoughtful, self-
contained, an
individualist*

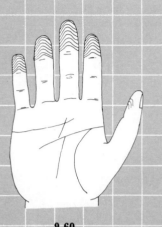

9.60
*All arches. The person
is practical,
emotionally reserved*

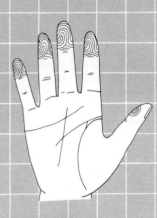

9.61
*All loops. The person
is easy-going, adaptable*

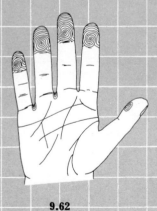

9.62
*Hand of a talented
actor who is very
changeable and
unpredictable.
Note the predominance
of composites, one
whorl, a loop on the
thumb*

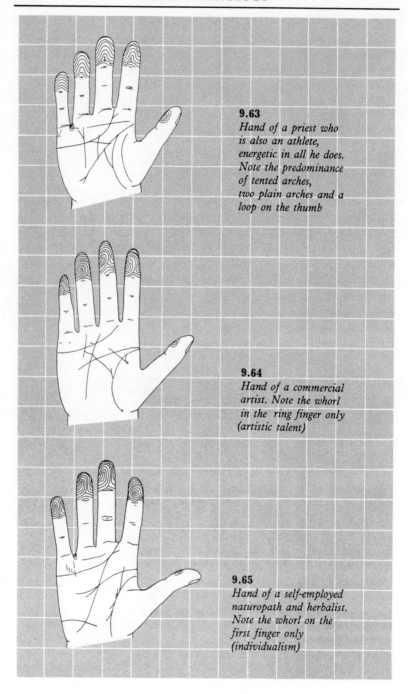

9.63
*Hand of a priest who
is also an athlete,
energetic in all he does.
Note the predominance
of tented arches,
two plain arches and a
loop on the thumb*

9.64
*Hand of a commercial
artist. Note the whorl
in the ring finger only
(artistic talent)*

9.65
*Hand of a self-employed
naturopath and herbalist.
Note the whorl on the
first finger only
(individualism)*

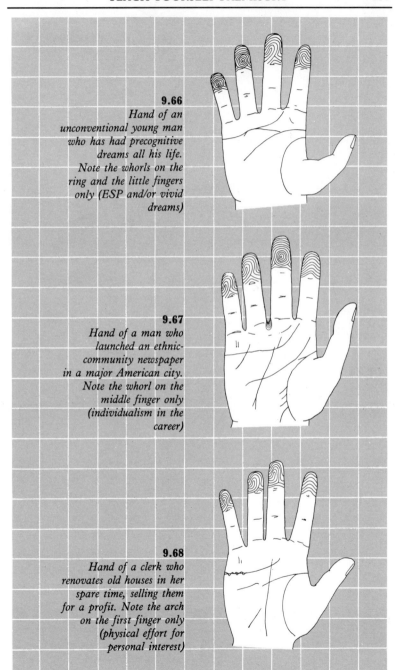

9.66
Hand of an unconventional young man who has had precognitive dreams all his life. Note the whorls on the ring and the little fingers only (ESP and/or vivid dreams)

9.67
Hand of a man who launched an ethnic-community newspaper in a major American city. Note the whorl on the middle finger only (individualism in the career)

9.68
Hand of a clerk who renovates old houses in her spare time, selling them for a profit. Note the arch on the first finger only (physical effort for personal interest)

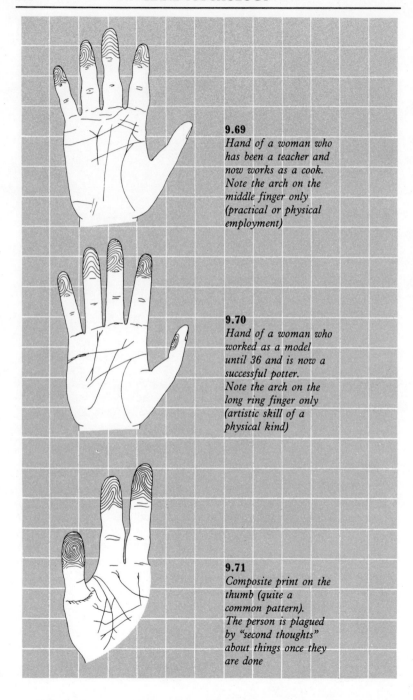

9.69
*Hand of a woman who
has been a teacher and
now works as a cook.
Note the arch on the
middle finger only
(practical or physical
employment)*

9.70
*Hand of a woman who
worked as a model
until 36 and is now a
successful potter.
Note the arch on the
long ring finger only
(artistic skill of a
physical kind)*

9.71
*Composite print on the
thumb (quite a
common pattern).
The person is plagued
by "second thoughts"
about things once they
are done*

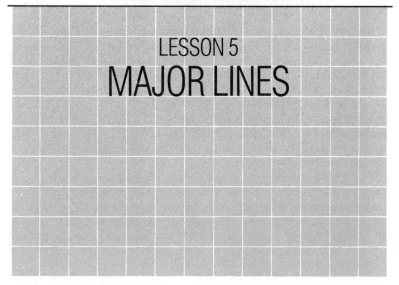

LESSON 5
MAJOR LINES

There are three major lines in the hand (diag. 9.72) and about a dozen less important ones.

The *Heart Line* reveals a person's emotional and sexual nature.

The *Head Line* reveals mental abilities.

The *Life Line* reveals physical strength, energy and stamina.

Students of the occult believe that the human being is an immortal soul who periodically reincarnates into a new body and a new personality. The "new person" of each incarnation has its own physical, mental and emotional nature. The *real person* lies behind and above the body, its thoughts and its feelings. These three main lines in the palm are symbols of the three basic parts of a person's nature *for this lifetime*.

THE HEART LINE
Diagrams 9.73–9.79

The Heart Line, the emotional symbol, may take one of two main forms — curved or straight.

The typical *curved* Heart Line sweeps up between the first and the second fingers. Such a person is warm, emotional and affectionate; shows his or her feelings through gestures and actions; and plays an active or dominant role in love affairs.

The typical *straight* Heart Line runs horizontal below the fingers. Such a person is cool, thoughtful and seldom very passionate; shows his or her feelings through thoughts and words more than through actions; and plays a quiet or receptive role in love affairs.

Although people with straight Heart Lines may appear to be

less emotional or less sexy than those with curved ones, this is not really the case. They just have different ways of showing it! Here are some examples of the different emotional reactions of the two types.

Anger with a loved one The person with the *curved* Heart Line shouts, stamps, threatens and gesticulates.

The person with the *straight* Heart Line cries, sulks, makes cutting remarks or suffers in silence.

Falling in love The person with the *curved* Heart Line is flushed, excited and eager for marriage.

The one with the *straight* Heart Line acts in a caring, considerate, interested manner and tries to be as attractive as possible.

Sorrow over a parting The *curved* Heart-Lined person howls, acts suicidal . . . but gets over the sadness and finds someone else.

The *straight* Heart-Lined person mopes, worries, can't get it out of his or her mind and never completely gets over the heartbreak.

Requirements for a lover The person with the *curved* Heart Line looks for a lover who is attractive, emotional and demonstrative.

The one with the *straight* Heart Line hopes for a lover who is interesting, sincere and compatible.

There is really no need to memorise all these points, as long as you clearly understand the basic principle behind them.

Both the curved Heart Line and the straight Heart Line can take a number of forms. When the *curved line ends under the first finger* (diag. 9.73), it shows a person who will pick his or her lovers very carefully. This person wants only the best.

When the *curved line ends under the second finger* (diag. 9.74), the sexual nature is strong and very direct. There is not much "choosiness" about the choice of lover with this type of formation!

A *straight Heart Line which is so short that it reaches only as far as the middle finger* (diag. 9.75) reveals a lack of real emotional involvement. Even if the sex drive is strong, there is little capability for real loving and caring.

A *very long straight Heart Line* (diag. 9.76) indicates the ability to love in an idealistic, self-sacrificing way. Those who dedicate their lives to helping and caring for others often have this Heart-Line formation.

If there are *two branches on the Heart Line* (diag. 9.77), each branch adds something to the emotional nature. Such people have complex emotional patterns.

If there are *three or more branches* (diag. 9.78), the owner is highly emotional in matters of love.

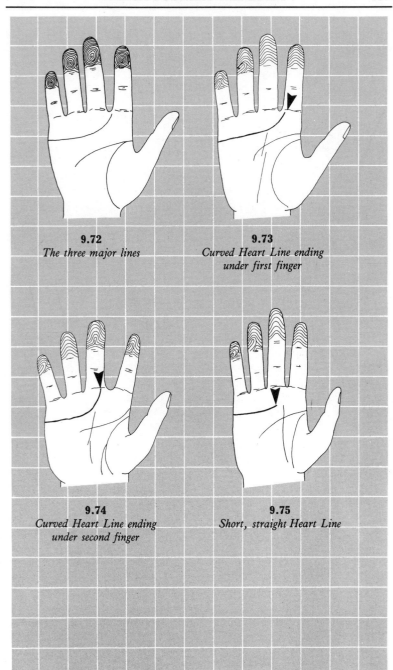

9.72
The three major lines

9.73
*Curved Heart Line ending
under first finger*

9.74
*Curved Heart Line ending
under second finger*

9.75
Short, straight Heart Line

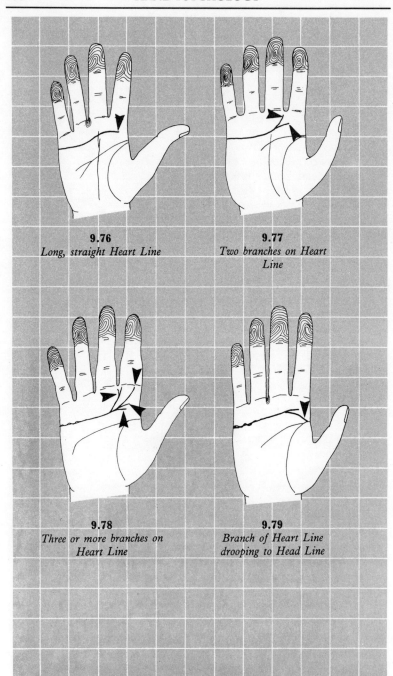

9.76
Long, straight Heart Line

9.77
Two branches on Heart Line

9.78
Three or more branches on Heart Line

9.79
Branch of Heart Line drooping to Head Line

A *branch drooping to the Head Line* (diag. 9.79) is a sign of emotional sensitivity. Such people are easily hurt or disappointed if anything goes wrong in a love affair.

THE HEAD LINE
Diagrams 9.80–9.97
The Head Line reveals how a person thinks, although it does *not* show how intelligent he or she is. It shows the type and class of intelligence but not how much ability a person actually has.

The average Head Line ends somewhere under the ring finger.

A *short* Head Line shows a person whose thinking is simple, practical and straight-to-the-point. Such people do not mess around and do not waste words in idle chatter.

A *long* Head Line shows that the thinking is careful, detailed and comprehensive. Such people go into things very thoroughly.

Remember that this is not a matter of intelligence. The length of the line shows only how complex or detailed a person's thinking is, *not* how clever he or she may be.

The path that the line follows may be horizontal or it may slope. The line itself may also run straight or in a curve.

A *straight* Head Line may run across the hand or slope downwards. In diagram 9.80, A, B and C are all straight Head Lines. The straight line always indicates clear, concentrated thinking, no matter where the line runs to.

A *curved* Head Line shows a person whose mind likes to experiment and play with new ideas. This is true no matter where the line actually runs to. In diagram 9.81, A, B and C are examples of curved Head Lines.

Horizontal Head Lines belong to people who always look at the useful or practical side of a matter.

Sloping Head Lines are found on those who look at the imaginative or creative side of things.

Chains (diag. 9.82) in the Head Line show a sensitive, highly strung mind.

One or two *islands* (diag. 9.83) in the Head Line show that the person may crack up under pressure such as intensive study or mental strain.

Wavy (diag. 9.84) Head Lines show an original, unusual mind. People with these lines originate new ideas and fresh points of view.

A *fork* (diag. 9.85) in the Head Line shows the ability to see more than one point of view. Novelists often have this pattern, which is known as the Writer's Fork.

Most Head Lines are lightly joined to the Life Line at their

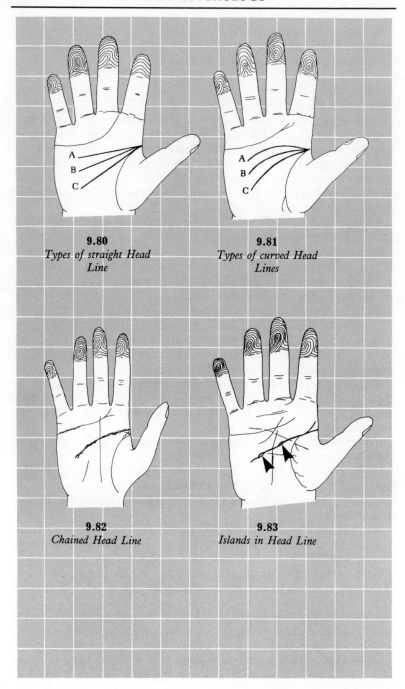

9.80
Types of straight Head Line

9.81
Types of curved Head Lines

9.82
Chained Head Line

9.83
Islands in Head Line

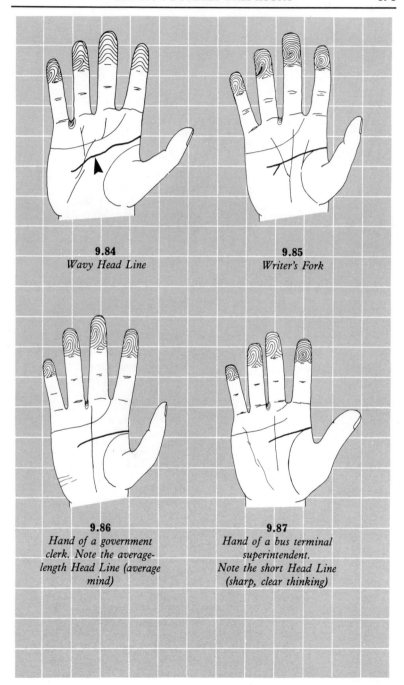

9.84
Wavy Head Line

9.85
Writer's Fork

9.86
*Hand of a government
clerk. Note the average-
length Head Line (average
mind)*

9.87
*Hand of a bus terminal
superintendent.
Note the short Head Line
(sharp, clear thinking)*

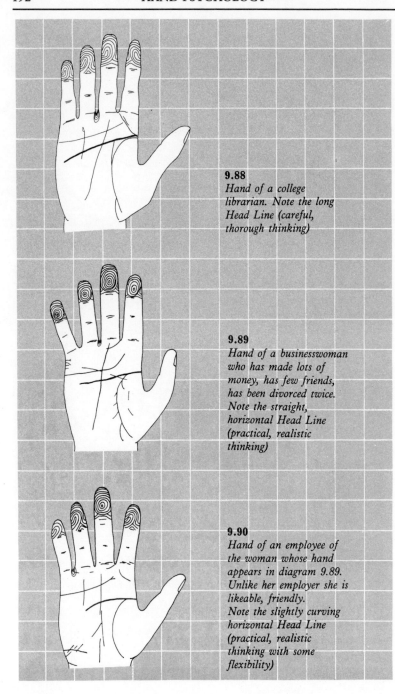

9.88
*Hand of a college
librarian. Note the long
Head Line (careful,
thorough thinking)*

9.89
*Hand of a businesswoman
who has made lots of
money, has few friends,
has been divorced twice.
Note the straight,
horizontal Head Line
(practical, realistic
thinking)*

9.90
*Hand of an employee of
the woman whose hand
appears in diagram 9.89.
Unlike her employer she is
likeable, friendly.
Note the slightly curving
horizontal Head Line
(practical, realistic
thinking with some
flexibility)*

9.91
Hand of a mathematics professor with special interest in space—time theories.
Note the long, straight, steeply sloping Head Line (thorough, complex, clear, concentrated thinking, with concern for the imaginative or creative side of life)

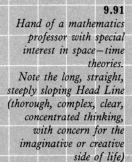

9.92
Hand of a film scriptwriter specialising in horror movies who has had a nervous breakdown.
Note the long, steeply curving Head Line (flexible, complex, highly imaginative thinking) and the island in the Head Line (susceptibility to pressure, strain)

9.93
Hand of a writer of imaginative tales, quite stable and sensible but a bit eccentric.
Note the average-length, straight horizontal Head Line with downward-sloping fork (practical mind with some imagination as well) and the Writer's Fork

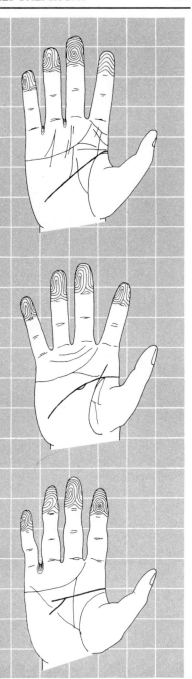

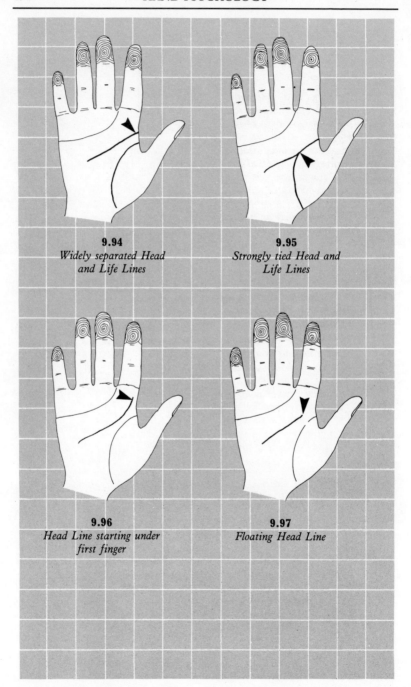

9.94
*Widely separated Head
and Life Lines*

9.95
*Strongly tied Head and
Life Lines*

9.96
*Head Line starting under
first finger*

9.97
Floating Head Line

commencement. A few are separated from the Life Line and others are tied to it for a centimetre or more.

Widely separated lines (diag. 9.94) belong to impulsive, uninhibited people who make their minds up quickly. They are found on folk who learn to think for themselves when young, usually in childhood.

Strongly tied lines (diag. 9.95) belong to people who are cautious and slow to commit themselves. They usually indicate that the person was completely under the influence of the parents during childhood; this influence can often continue past 20 years of age.

A rare form of line *starts under the first finger* (diag. 9.96), on the Mount of Jupiter, not on the edge of the hand. This shows a highly independent, well-developed mind. It is an excellent marking, and is always the sign of a high achiever.

A few, very relaxed, carefree people have Head Lines that are *separated even from the edge of the palm* (diag. 9.97), and which float in the centre of the hand.

THE LIFE LINE

Diagrams 9.98–9.106 *(9.101 to 9.106 are examples of lines in combination)*
The Life Line is an index to how much energy, strength and vitality a person possesses.

Running fairly close to the thumb (diag. 9.98A), it shows poor strength and energy.

Running in a wide curve (diag. 9.98B) through the palm, it shows excellent vitality and strength.

Chains (diag. 9.99A), or a thin, feathery effect, indicate overall delicacy of health.

Little lines rising (diag. 9.99B) indicate an active personality, one who does things.

Outward swinging lines (diag. 9.99C) indicate restlessness, love of travel.

Any strong line parallel to the Life Line (diags. 9.100A,B) indicates energy and the probability of longevity.

Most of the small marks on or beside the Life Line relate to events at particular times of the life. The length of the Life Line does not show the length of the life, and short lines are sometimes found on very simple palms for no other reason than that all the lines on such a palm are short, thick and simple. A short Life Line does not mean an early death.

Earlier palmistry books refer to pattern 9.100A as the "Line of Mars". In fact, pattern 9.100B, formed by a curve and displacement of the Fate Line, has exactly the same meaning, which is an abundance of vitality.

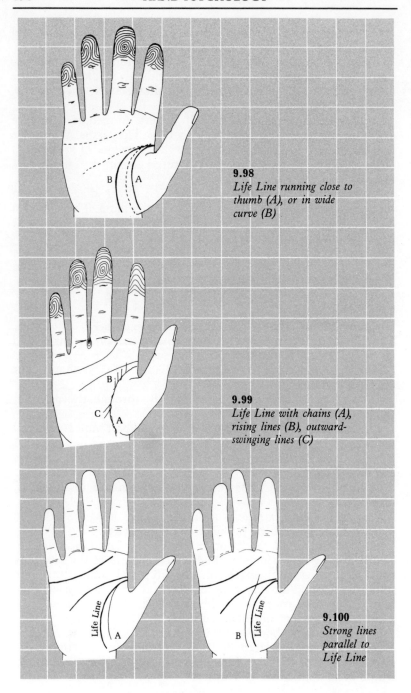

9.98
Life Line running close to thumb (A), or in wide curve (B)

9.99
Life Line with chains (A), rising lines (B), outward-swinging lines (C)

9.100
Strong lines parallel to Life Line

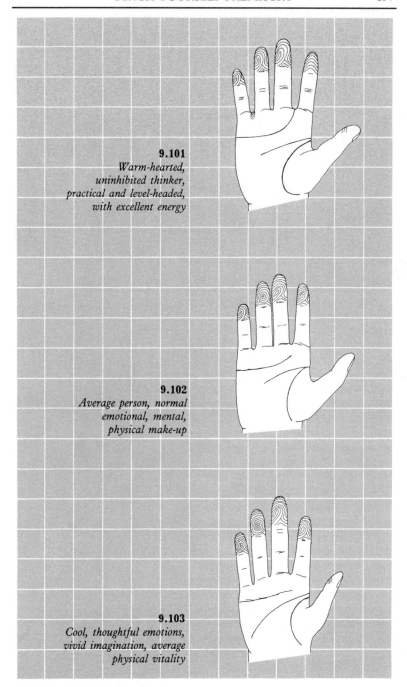

9.101
*Warm-hearted,
uninhibited thinker,
practical and level-headed,
with excellent energy*

9.102
*Average person, normal
emotional, mental,
physical make-up*

9.103
*Cool, thoughtful emotions,
vivid imagination, average
physical vitality*

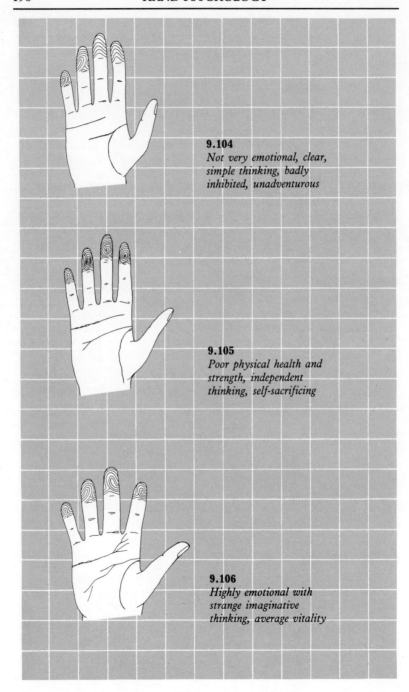

9.104
*Not very emotional, clear,
simple thinking, badly
inhibited, unadventurous*

9.105
*Poor physical health and
strength, independent
thinking, self-sacrificing*

9.106
*Highly emotional with
strange imaginative
thinking, average vitality*

THE SIMIAN LINE
Diagrams 9.107–9.110
There is a freak formation found in some hands, in which the
Head and Heart Lines blend into a single line across the palm. It is
called the Simian Line (diag. 9.107). This line indicates a tense
personality, which is never completely relaxed; difficulty in
relating to other people; and concentration, determination and
energy.

The line is common among mentally retarded people, although
many people of normal or above-average intelligence have it as
well. (In the hand of a mentally retarded person, it should always
be interpreted merely as a sign of that condition.) Interpretation
of Simian Line hands is quite complex, and for a full description
you need to read Chapters VI and VII.

Questions	*Answers*
1. What does a short, straight Heart Line indicate?	**1.** *Lack of emotional warmth.*
2. What is shown by a horizontal Head Line?	**2.** *A practical, realistic attitude to things.*
3. How would you interpret a thin, weak Life Line?	**3.** *Poor health and lack of vitality.*
4. When Head and Life Line are tied, what does this show?	**4.** *Caution, unadventurous in thinking, and an inhibited childhood.*
5. What is the meaning of a long, straight Heart Line?	**5.** *Idealism, perhaps a missionary spirit.*
6. What does a Head Line running down towards the bottom of the hand indicate?	**6.** *Imagination.*
7. How would you interpret a short Head Line?	**7.** *It shows clear, simple thinking processes.*
8. Explain a fork on the end of the Heart Line.	**8.** *This shows two sides to the emotions.*
9. What is shown by a strongly curved Heart Line?	**9.** *Warmth, emotionalism, demonstrativeness.*
10. What does a long Head Line mean?	**10.** *Careful, thorough thinking processes.*
11. Explain a Life Line that runs in a wide curve.	**11.** *This shows strength and energy.*

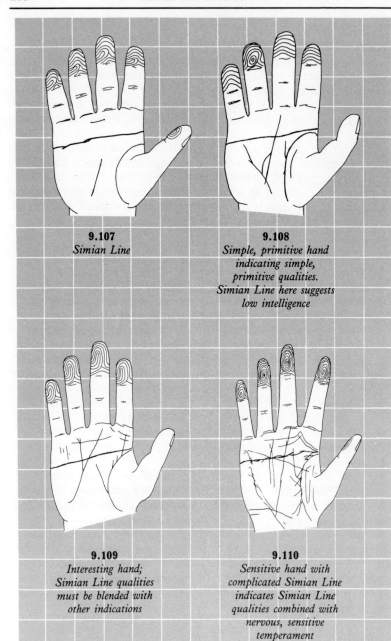

9.107
Simian Line

9.108
*Simple, primitive hand
indicating simple,
primitive qualities.
Simian Line here suggests
low intelligence*

9.109
*Interesting hand;
Simian Line qualities
must be blended with
other indications*

9.110
*Sensitive hand with
complicated Simian Line
indicates Simian Line
qualities combined with
nervous, sensitive
temperament*

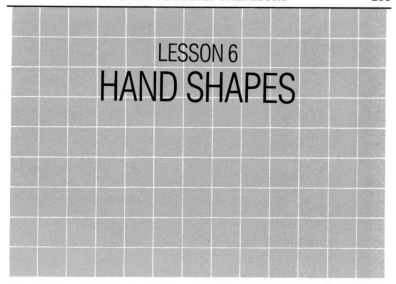

LESSON 6
HAND SHAPES

By now, you will have noticed that certain basic ideas are repeated in the fingers, lines and the fingerprints. For example, is it not obvious that smooth fingers, rounded fingertips, and loop fingerprints are all much the same? And is not the difference between widely spaced fingers and close-together ones similar to the separated or tied junction of the Head and Life Lines? In practice, it is very common to find hands where all the pieces fit together like a jigsaw puzzle.

One way this happens concerns the actual shape of the hand. If you run a pencil around your hand on a sheet of paper, you will obtain the outline of its shape. The shape of your hand bears a relationship to the type of lines and type of fingerprints your hand carries.

The system of hand shapes which I use was first put forward by Fred Gettings, and is a marvel of commonsense and reliability. Other systems have been put forward, notably by Dr Charlotte Wolff and the Frenchman, Casimir D'Arpentigny (who created the first method of classifying hands, still used by some traditional palmists today).

The Gettings system is based upon the fact that the palm may either be long and narrow, that is, rectangular in shape, or short and wide (square). The fingers may be either long or short, thus producing four hand types.

The *Earth* Hand (diag. 9.111) has a square palm and short fingers. It denotes a steady, simple person.

The *Water* Hand (diag. 9.112) has a long palm and long fingers. People with such a hand are sensitive and thoughtful.

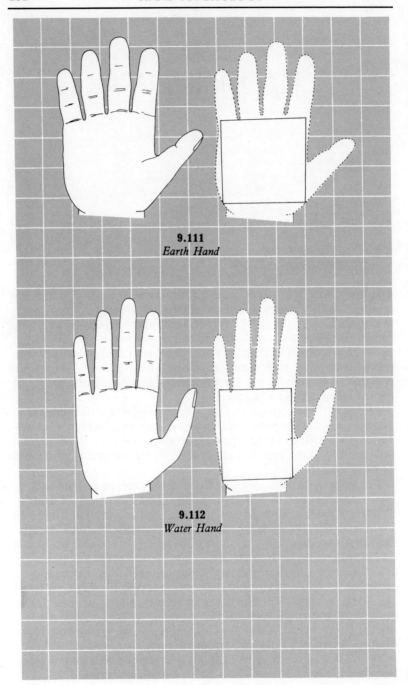

9.111
Earth Hand

9.112
Water Hand

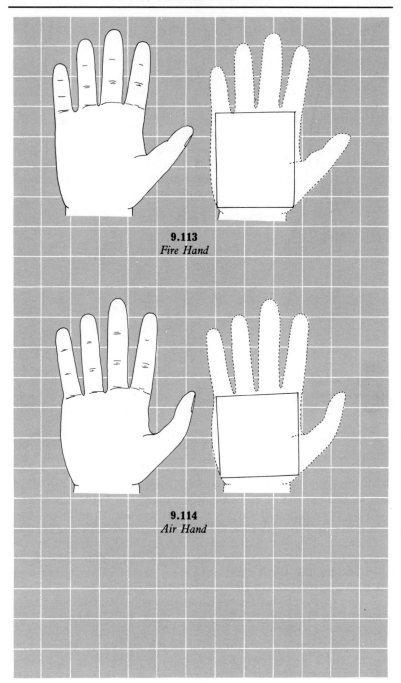

9.113
Fire Hand

9.114
Air Hand

The *Fire* Hand (diag. 9.113) has a long palm and short fingers, and is found on busy, energetic people.

The *Air* Hand (diag. 9.114) has a square palm and long fingers, and is found on lively, talkative, inquisitive people.

The four names, earth, water, fire and air, are taken from ancient occult writings, such as the traditions of alchemy. These traditional names are useful, just as the traditional names for the parts of the hand are useful too. Some palmists like to abandon these names in order to sound modern, while others have developed alternative names of their own. For the sake of uniformity, it is well worth maintaining these traditional names, as most palmists have done for generations.

THE EARTH HAND

9.115
Typical lines and fingerprints of an Earth Hand

On an Earth Hand, the palm is square and the fingers are short (diag. 9.115). The line pattern is usually very bare and simple and it is common to find arches or low loops on the fingertips. People with this type of hand are slow, careful and practical. They dislike change and often concentrate on one activity. The Earth-Handed person is "in tune" with nature, and so is most often found in the country. He or she is emotionally stable and simple.

Occasionally, you will find an Earth Hand with one or two strange markings in the skin ridges or the lines. This can indicate that besides the earth qualities, there are other complications, such as a special talent or unusual intelligence.

A trap to watch out for on Earth Hands is that most appear to have a long little finger! This must never be interpreted in the usual way because in fact the finger only *appears* to be long in comparison with all the others, which are short and stubby. Never read a big Mercury Finger on an Earth Hand as you would do on an average hand.

THE WATER HAND

9.116
*Typical lines and
fingerprints of
a Water Hand*

The palm of a Water-Handed person is rectangular, the fingers are long (diag. 9.116). There are usually a great many fine lines, including lots of long, vertical lines on this type of hand. The prints are commonly loops. This hand is extremely common among women.

Water-Handed people are gentle, refined, peaceable, graceful, sensitive and tasteful. For these people emotions are more important than pure reason. They are influenced by people and circumstances.

When this hand is found on a male, it indicates intelligence, as well as the above-mentioned qualities. Extremely feminine women, particularly fashion models and some actresses, often have exaggerated forms of the Water Hand. On such females, the whole hand looks as if it has been stretched out.

THE FIRE HAND

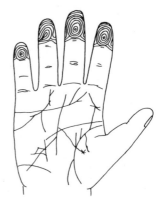

9.117
*Typical lines and fingerprints
of a Fire Hand*

The palm of a Fire-Handed person is rectangular, the fingers are short (diag. 9.117). There is always a large number of strong, clear lines on this type of hand, and whorl fingerprints are the most commonly found.

The Fire-Handed person is active, busy, runs around doing things and is always on the go. He or she is excitable and emotional. The Fire-Handed person influences other people and controls situations. ·

Fire-Handed people are nearly always extroverts and fun to be around.

THE AIR HAND

9.118
Typical lines and fingerprints
of an Air Hand

On the Air Hand, the palm is square, the fingers are long (that is, at least as long as the palm and often longer) (diag. 9.118). The prints are loops, usually high ones, and the lines are thin but clear, strong and well-formed.

The Air-Handed person is mentally alert, curious, and likes to learn. He or she is very good at talking or writing, is emotionally well-balanced and rarely gets upset. He or she likes finding out how things fit together.

Air-Handed people often enter the communications professions. They appear to other people to be cheerful and happy because of their emotional stability but they themselves think that this stability is not very real.

GENERAL COMMENTS ON THE FOUR TYPES

Of course there are times when one hand type has fingerprints or lines which belong to another type. These hands are found on people with mixed characters, often rather unusual ones. There are also a few hands which fit into no class at all, because the palm is halfway between the square and rectangular shapes, while the fingers are much the same length. Such indeterminate hand shapes show a diversified personality, one which is impossible to classify.

Palmistry students always find the Air Hand the hardest to identify at first glance. If you are looking at a hand and cannot decide its type, the fingerprints and line pattern may help determine whether it is an Air type or not.

Here is a test to cover the information in this section. Cover the right-hand side of the page while you work out the answers.

Which hand types exhibit the following characteristics?

1.	Likes to learn and investigate.	1. *Air.*
2.	Dislikes change.	2. *Earth.*
3.	Likes the countryside.	3. *Earth.*
4.	Gentle and peace-loving.	4. *Water.*
5.	Warm and emotional.	5. *Fire.*
6.	Influenced by their surroundings.	6. *Water.*
7.	Good at communicating.	7. *Air.*
8.	Taste and refinement.	8. *Water.*
9.	Slow and careful.	9. *Earth.*
10.	Energetic and busy.	10. *Fire.*
11.	Influences other people.	11. *Fire.*
12.	Hard-working and practical.	12. *Earth.*
13.	Lively but emotionally stable.	13. *Air.*
14.	Excitable.	14. *Fire.*

What sort of lines and fingerprints are most commonly found on each of the hand types?

1. Earth.	1.	*A few simple lines, arch or low loop prints.*
2. Water.	2.	*Many fine, tangled lines and loop prints.*
3. Fire.	3.	*Many strong, clear lines and whorl prints.*
4. Air.	4.	*Several clear, thin, well-marked lines and high loops.*

HAND TYPES COMBINED WITH OTHER FEATURES
Diagrams 9.119–9.131

So far, we have covered fingerprints, fingers and the main lines. We have also shown you how these fit together into the four hand types. Now let us have a look at some hands and see how these elements of palmistry can be combined to give a picture of the people whose hands these are found on. Each analysis is followed by the kind of reading a palmist would give.

In diagram 9.119 we have a typical Water Hand with the fingers smooth and quite close together. Neither the Heart nor the Head Lines are very impressive. The fingerprints are all loops except for the ring finger.

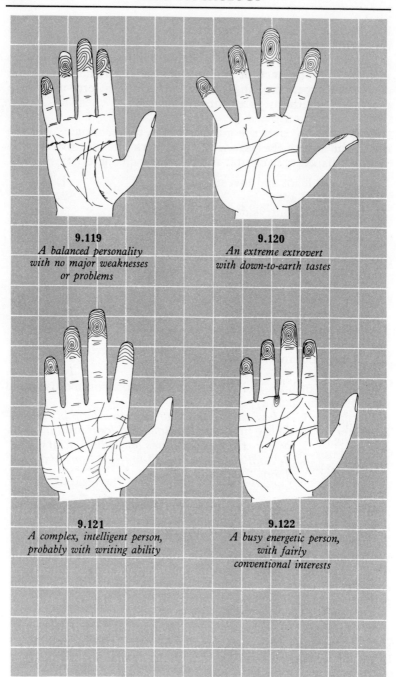

9.119
*A balanced personality
with no major weaknesses
or problems*

9.120
*An extreme extrovert
with down-to-earth tastes*

9.121
*A complex, intelligent person,
probably with writing ability*

9.122
*A busy energetic person,
with fairly
conventional interests*

Reading "You are a gentle, feminine person and are good at fitting in with the people around you. You have a balanced personality with no major weaknesses or problems. You are rather set in your ways, not particularly adventurous. In fact, you are thoroughly normal. You appear to have some artistic ability and this is probably your most important talent, which you should certainly use and develop."

Diagram 9.120 shows an Air Hand with all the fingers splayed out. Unlike most Air Hands, all the fingerprints are whorls and the lines are quite bare, strong and simple.

Reading "You are an extreme extrovert. You love putting on a show and attracting attention. You have lots of ideas and love sharing them with people around you. However, in spite of all this talking and carrying on, you are actually quite simple and down-to-earth in your tastes and inclinations."

The hand in diagram 9.121 is also an Air type, but unlike the last one, it has a great many sensitive lines. The first finger is short, the little finger is long and strong. The middle finger appears long too, while the prints are whorls and one arch. Study the Heart and Head Lines carefully.

Reading "You are a complex, sensitive, intelligent person with a talent for communication, probably writing. You are rather shy, even introverted. You are interested in ideas, probably in learning and studying. Although you doubt yourself a good deal, you have real ability in fields like writing and possibly art. You have plenty of imagination as well."

Diagram 9.122 is a pure example of the Fire Hand. The fingers are all of normal length, and set close together.

Reading "You are a busy, active, energetic person but you are not at all unconventional, so all your energy and enthusiasm are confined to everyday affairs like your home and your job. You are an intense person and work hard and well at the limited field of things which interest you."

Diagram 9.123 is another example of a Water Hand. Compare it with the first example, and see how much longer and clearer all the lines are. The prints are all loops. The first and fourth fingers are very long.

Reading "You are a thoroughly feminine person, gentle, sensitive and refined, with a good deal of talent which you know how to use. You are extremely self-confident and used to getting your own way in whatever you do. You have intelligence and the ability to put across your ideas in writing or through speech."

Diagram 9.124 shows a rather average hand except for the fingertips. It may be a Water type, but really it does not fit well into any of the four categories. The fingers are all close, the

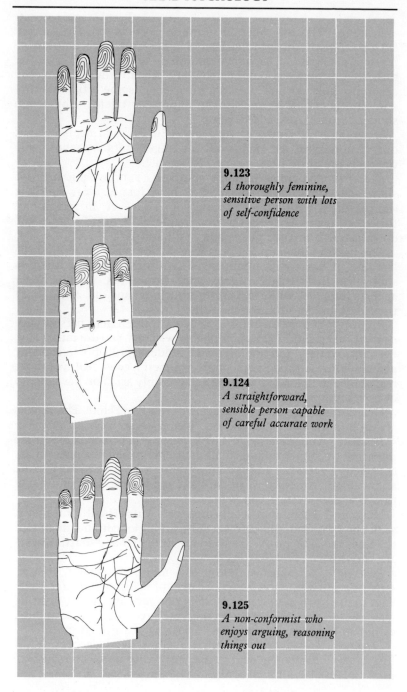

9.123
A thoroughly feminine, sensitive person with lots of self-confidence

9.124
A straightforward, sensible person capable of careful accurate work

9.125
A non-conformist who enjoys arguing, reasoning things out

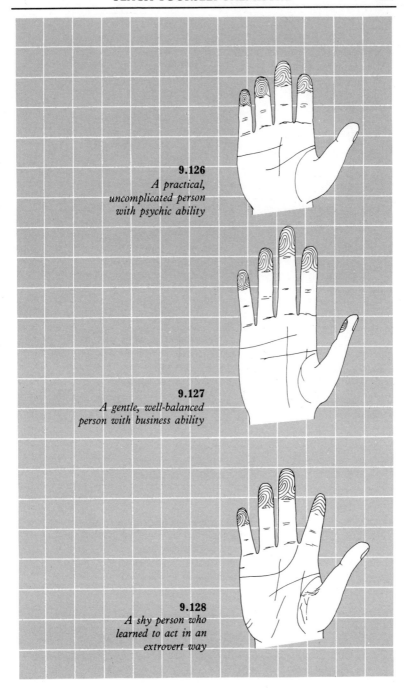

9.126
*A practical,
uncomplicated person
with psychic ability*

9.127
*A gentle, well-balanced
person with business ability*

9.128
*A shy person who
learned to act in an
extrovert way*

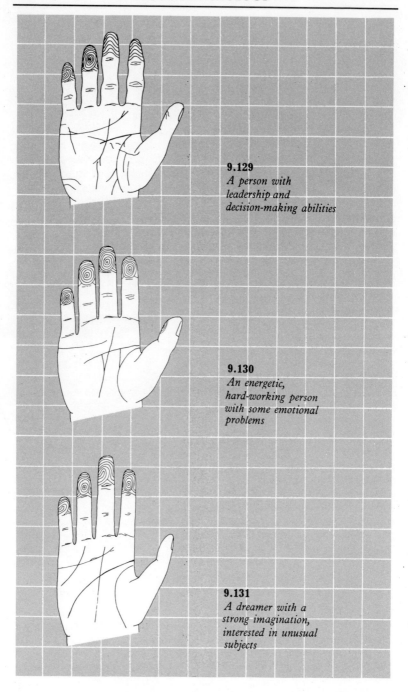

9.129
*A person with
leadership and
decision-making abilities*

9.130
*An energetic,
hard-working person
with some emotional
problems*

9.131
*A dreamer with a
strong imagination,
interested in unusual
subjects*

prints are loops with one mixed print on the first finger. The lines are simple. The fingertips are all very square.

Reading "You are a straightforward, middle-of-the-road person. You are set in your habits, sensible rather than imaginative. Everything you do is done carefully, and accurately. You like to get things just right and you would be successful in a career where careful, accurate work is needed."

Diagram 9.125 is another Water Hand. It has many unusual lines and very knotty fingers. The index finger is long, and there are three different types of prints. The fingers are wide apart.

Reading "You are a distinctly unusual person. You are a non-conformist, used to going your own way, and as you are self-confident you generally get what you want. You are quite nervy and sensitive in spite of your strong character. You love arguing, reasoning things out, and you have a variety of interests and abilities."

Diagram 9.126 is a pure Earth Hand: square palm, short fingers, very simple lines. The only unusual feature is the two whorls on the ring and little fingers.

Reading "You are a simple, uncomplicated person. You are very practical and hard-working, good at getting things done. You would fit well into country life, rather than life in the city. You have a sixth sense, psychic ability."

These eight examples will show you the way a palmist works. In practice, the short reading given with each could be extended to twice the length. Notice how the bare bones of the facts about each hand can be "fleshed out" when you come to making the actual reading.

Diagrams 9.127–9.131 are five more examples — to test you on how well you have been learning! Note down the points you notice about each hand. Then make up a descriptive paragraph to go with each. (The answers follow.) Though naturally your paragraphs will differ from mine, you should be able to see the important features in each example.

Answers

Diag 9.127. Water Hand. Loop fingerprints. Lines fairly simple. Heart Line straight, Head Line very straight and horizontal. Very long middle finger.

Reading "You are a feminine, gentle, well-balanced person. You are very level-headed, serious and reliable and would do well in a business or commercial career."

Diag. 9.128. Fire Hand. Loop prints with one arch on the first finger. Lines fairly simple. Heart Line well-curved, Head Line average. Index finger short, and jutting out.

Reading "You are a busy, active, energetic person. In your youth, you were shy and to overcome this you learned to act in a brave, outgoing, independent way. Today, you appear to others to be very confident and extroverted, but inside you are still afflicted by uncertainties and self-doubts. You are warmhearted and affectionate. Sales work or perhaps your own business would suit you.''

Diag. 9.129. Fire Hand. Two arches, one whorl and a loop. Average lines, but the Head Line is very short and straight. Index finger long and held separate (spaced) from the others.

Reading ''You are a busy, active, energetic person and very independent. You have leadership ability and a gift for making decisions. You are practical, skilled with your hands and your thinking is clear, simple and realistic. You also have a scientific mind and love reasoning things out. You are suited to being in charge of some scientific, mechanical or practical business and could well run a business of that kind of your own.''

Diag. 9.130. Fire Hand. All whorl fingerprints. Lines fairly simple. Straight Head Line. Very short, straight Heart Line. Little finger low-set.

Reading ''You are a busy, hard-working, energetic person. You are hard-headed and practical and something of an individualist. Your emotional life is not very well adjusted. Your childhood relationship with your parents was disturbed and today your emotions are rather stunted. You seldom really care for anyone.''

Diag. 9.131. Water Hand. Lines fairly simple. Heart Line straight and Head Line extremely long. Two whorls and two loops.

Reading ''You are thoughtful, sensitive, gentle and a feminine person. You are a dreamer, someone with a very strong imagination. You are interested in unusual, imaginative subjects such as the occult and at times you can be unrealistic in your thinking.''

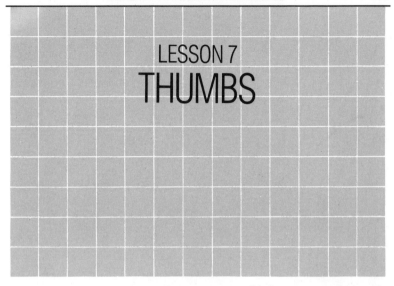

LESSON 7
THUMBS

The thumb is so much a thing unto itself that it can almost be studied without reference to the rest of the hand. Thumbs are vitally important, and must be looked at to judge the overall strength of the personality.

Thumbs can only be studied in actual living hands. Prints and diagrams of hands cannot accurately reproduce the thumb. For this reason, thumbs are not mentioned a great deal in this "Teach Yourself Palmistry" section, but this should not deter you from reading this part carefully and applying the knowledge whenever you actually come to read a hand.

The thumb shows how much drive and forcefulness a person has and how he or she applies that drive and forcefulness. So you see, the thumb is virtually showing what sort of person you are and in this sense is as important as the whole of the rest of the hand. There is an important rule here which a beginner finds hard to apply: "The more ordinary the thumb, the more ordinary the person." You will start to understand this rule when you have looked at a good many thumbs and have had a chance to decide what "ordinary" thumbs look like.

There are two sections to the thumb: the *top* section is connected to willpower while the *bottom* section shows one's reasoning power. We can measure the thumb by length, breadth and thickness.

The *length* (diag. 9.132) shows how hard you will try to get what you want.

The *breadth* (diag. 9.133) shows how much you will push and shove to get what you want.

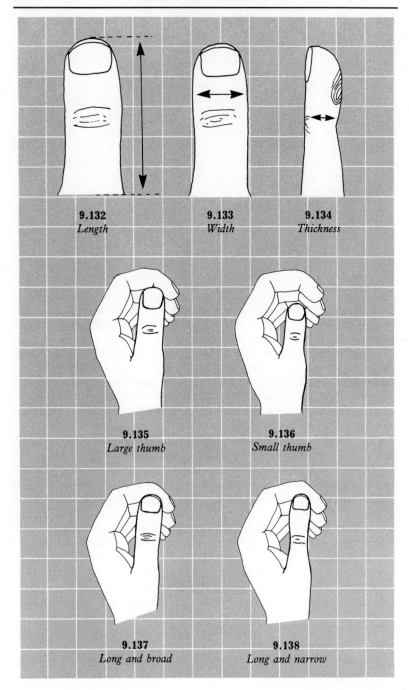

9.132
Length

9.133
Width

9.134
Thickness

9.135
Large thumb

9.136
Small thumb

9.137
Long and broad

9.138
Long and narrow

The *thickness* (diag. 9.134) shows whether you do things in a blunt way or in a subtle way.

However, in reality these things can all overlap or mix up together, which is why you must try, with practice, to assess the whole thumb at once. But that will come later.

Large thumbs, (fairly long, fairly thick and broad) (diag. 9.135), go with very strong personalities. These are the sort of people who usually get their own way in any situation.

Small thumbs (diag. 9.136) go with more gentle people, the sort who say "yes, sir" and "no, sir", to others. Small-thumbed people are usually ruled by their emotions.

Long, broad thumbs (diag. 9.137) show people who will try hard to reach their goals and who will push hard and work hard to get them. They are not afraid of competition and will probably reach the top in the end.

Long but fairly narrow thumbs (diag. 9.138) show people who will try to reach their goals but do not have much driving force. They are certainly not aggressive and do not like competition. They will probably work well but quietly and persistently and may become skilled or qualified in some profession. But they will not push their way to the top. If they ever get to the top, it will be because someone decided they were right for the position and put them there. This sort of thumb is quite commonly found on intellectuals.

Small but broad thumbs (diag. 9.139) show not much sticking power or much determination but loads of push and drive. Such people will make a lot of fuss and may be rather fierce, but in the end they won't get very far. They'll push to get their own way but they are not achievers. Remember that they are largely ruled by their emotions, and emotions are very changeable things.

Small, narrow thumbs (diag. 9.140) reveal altogether weak personalities. However, it is not impossible for such people to possess some particular talent or ability, in spite of the overall personality weakness.

Thumbs that have an especially *wide top*, wider than the rest of the thumb (diag. 9.141), show aggression and pig-headedness; a real fighter.

Conversely, if the *top is fairly narrow* and the bottom is wider (diag. 9.142), there is a lack of real willpower.

Sometimes, the *bottom section is pinched in*, or "waisted" (diag. 9.143). This shows refinement in the reasoning ability, so that such people can be (if they choose), tactful, persuasive and clever. Most people have the sides of the lower section parallel, making it neither thick nor thin.

If the *bottom section is swollen out* (diag. 9.144), there will be

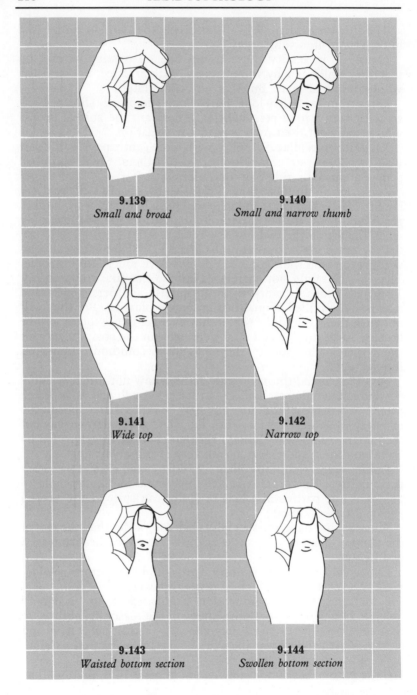

9.139
Small and broad

9.140
Small and narrow thumb

9.141
Wide top

9.142
Narrow top

9.143
Waisted bottom section

9.144
Swollen bottom section

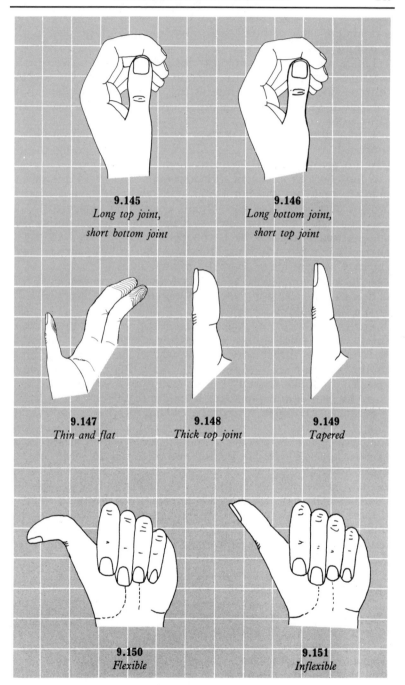

9.145
Long top joint,
short bottom joint

9.146
Long bottom joint,
short top joint

9.147
Thin and flat

9.148
Thick top joint

9.149
Tapered

9.150
Flexible

9.151
Inflexible

a complete lack of tact, persuasiveness and cleverness in the reasoning ability.

This is not quite the same thing as intelligence. Of two equally intelligent people presenting a lecture, the one with the waisted thumb will give more interesting ideas and employ more entertaining phrases than the other, even though both present the same lecture.

A *long top joint with a short bottom joint* (diag. 9.145) is supposed to show someone who gets on with doing things, without giving much thought to them.

A *long bottom joint and short top joint* (diag. 9.146) is said to indicate a person who thinks and talks and plans about what to do, but who often does not actually get around to doing it.

Looking at a thumb sideways, if the whole thumb looks thin and flattened (diag. 9.147), the person is not very strong or energetic in a physical sense, but his or her mind is active. He or she may be nervous or a worrier as a result.

A *thick top joint* (diag. 9.148) shows a blunt, no-nonsense way of doing things. This is the person who tells you exactly what he or she wants and is going to do.

The *tapered* or "spoke-shave" *tip* (diag. 9.149) shows a more subtle way of doing things. This person asks you what you think, and finds the nicest way of telling you bad news. A thick-thumbed person who wants to kill you will get a gun and shoot you. Your "spoke-shaved" thumb enemy will wait till you have curry for dinner and slip some arsenic into the curry powder.

Perhaps the most interesting aspect of the thumb is its *flexibility* of the top joint. In some thumbs, the joint can bend right back (diag. 9.150), while in others the joint is as stiff as an iron bar (diag. 9.151). The flexible thumb (often misinterpreted as being "double jointed") is the sign of a changeable, adaptable nature, while the stiff thumb has opposite traits. Negative qualities of the flexible thumb include an inability to stick at things, extravagance, unreliability and the habit of doing too many things at once. Positive qualities include an easy-going nature, generosity and a good sense of fun. Stiff-thumbed folk are persistent, dependable and sometimes a bit dull!

A thumb which is always *held close to the side of the hand* shows a careful and probably a stingy person.

However, thumbs which usually *stick out from the hand* (diag. 9.152), or can easily stretch out in this manner, show a relaxed, relatively carefree personality.

There is a rare type of thumb called the *"Clubbed Thumb"* where the top joint is abnormally short, the nail very broad, and the whole thumb thick and sometimes even swollen

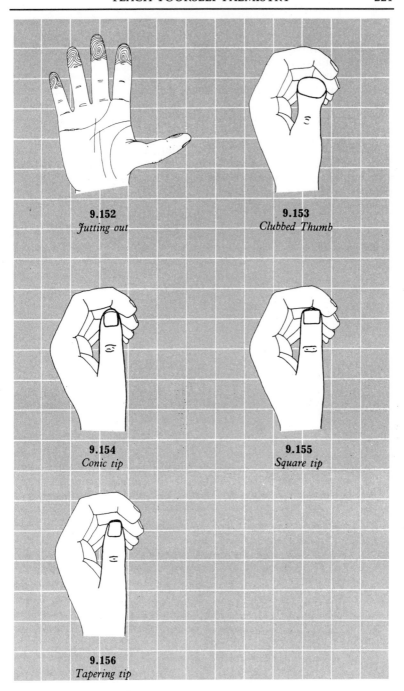

9.152
Jutting out

9.153
Clubbed Thumb

9.154
Conic tip

9.155
Square tip

9.156
Tapering tip

(diag. 9.153). Owners of this type of thumb are subject to occasional bursts of emotionalism, e.g. tears or anger. Full details are to be found in Chapter VI.

The tip of the thumb, seen from the nail side, is usually more or less rounded. It is a classic *conic tip* (diag 9.154). Round tips have no particular meaning.

Square-tipped thumbs (diag. 9.155) go with a love of fairness and justice.

When the *sides of the top joint taper in* (diag. 9.156), whether to a rounded or to a square tip, the owner has more natural gracefulness of movement and action than a person whose top thumb joint has parallel sides.

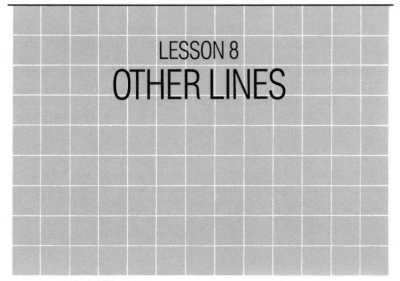

LESSON 8
OTHER LINES

Some general observations on lines are warranted before we begin studying the remaining lines in detail.

A multitude of fine lines is always a sign of a highly strung personality. Many Water Hands possess a mesh of intersecting lines, created by the nervous, sensitive mind of the person on whose hand they appear. If you study several Water Hands, you will see what a pattern of lines like this looks like.

Occasionally, you will find a hand on which every space is covered with multiple tangled lines. This is a dangerous formation, showing that the whole nervous system is badly overstrained.

Men tend to have far fewer lines than women. It is unwise to conclude that this shows men are insensitive.

There is a popular misconception that the lines are simply folds in the skin. This is quite untrue, as should be obvious to anyone by the number of lines which do not follow the folds of the hand and the fact that manual workers usually have few lines while non-manual workers have many. The fact that this cannot be explained even by the counter-theory that working with the hands makes the lines go away, is demonstrated when mentally active nervous people indulge in manual labour. Their many-lined hands remain exactly the same no matter how many years they remain at work.

Proof that the lines are created by the nervous system and not by muscular use of the hands is easily found.

1. Old people have clear lines in their palms, but if senility sets in the lines fade and blur almost to the point of disappearing. As the mind decays, so do the lines.

2. The Fate Line, or line of social adjustment, is commonly missing or fragmented in the hands of young children, but appears or consolidates between the ages of seven and 10, when the youngster begins to act like a person, instead of a creature of instinct.
3. Prints taken before, during and after a person goes through a "nervous breakdown" register a great increase in the number of lines when the breakdown actually occurs. There is a direct relationship between a person's nervous state and the number of lines in the hand.
4. Certain rare cases of concussion of the brain have been observed to cause immediate and total obliteration of the lines. Most cases of concussion do not have this effect. At least one case of severed nerves in the arm has also been observed to obliterate the lines. Both of these phenomena disprove the "fold" theory.
5. The end of the Heart Line, which relates to emotional and sexual attitudes, commonly develops and changes around puberty.
6. Electric-shock treatment, once used extensively in mental hospitals, has been observed to have a profound effect on the lines in the hands, causing breaking and starring. The electricity operates through the nervous system.
7. The relationship between certain lines on the palm and aspects of personality has been established by psychological testing as well as by simple observation. This proven relationship could not exist if the lines were merely skin folds.
8. The suggestion that Head and Heart Lines are caused by the folding of the fingers is disproved by the fact that the Simian Line, and not the dual Head and Heart Lines, coincides with the bending of the fingers. If folding was responsible, a Simian Line would be present in every hand. This so-called natural fold is in fact found only on certain exceptional people, those who are psychologically different from the norm.

THE FATE LINE
Diagrams 9.157–9.171
The Fate Line is a vertical line running from the bottom of the hand towards the middle finger (diag. 9.157). It may be short or long, straight or crooked.

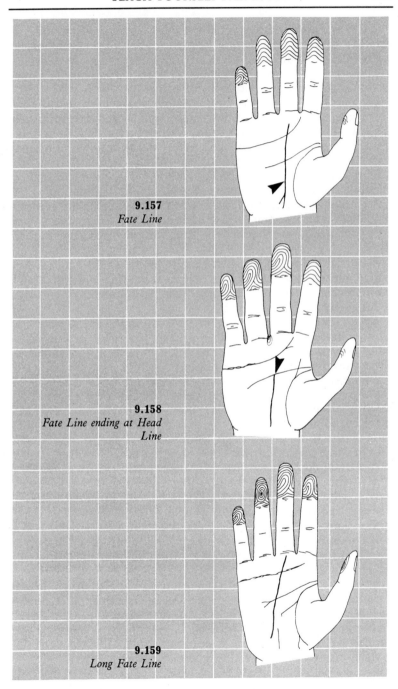

9.157
Fate Line

9.158
Fate Line ending at Head Line

9.159
Long Fate Line

The Fate Line reveals your attitudes towards work and the
stability of your life. *Strong* Fate Lines belong to people who
settle into a set pattern of life, such as a career. *Weak* lines belong
to less settled, unstable people. Events, particularly career
changes, can be registered upon this line.

Fate Lines *rising from the very bottom of the palm*, thus
making a long line, are found with people who settle into their
life path at an early age; for example, the person who completes
schooling, gets through college and moves into a profession based
directly upon that training.

Conversely, Fate Lines *arising well above the wrist* belong to
people whose early adult years are varied and flexible.

A Fate Line which *stops at the Head Line* (diag. 9.158) is found
on people who lose their sense of direction by the middle 30s or
40s. Such people are inclined to "drift" in the second half of their
lives.

Most Fate Lines end approximately at the Heart Line. A line
which clearly *runs almost to the middle finger* (diag. 9.159)
indicates the ability to keep active into old age and is often a sign
of longevity.

A Fate Line which *begins in the bottom quarter of the hand, but
is tied to the Life Line* (diag. 9.160), records a restricted or
dominated childhood. People who are pushed into a career by
their parents often have this mark.

A Fate Line *commencing from the Mount of Luna* (diag. 9.161),
the outer bottom corner of the palm, indicates a preference for
relating to people, or to the public in general. Such people
gravitate to jobs where there is a lot of contact with the public.

Two or more Fate Lines are found only on people who pursue
two or more careers at the same time.

A Fate Line which *runs into the Heart Line*, in such a way as to
extend the Fate Line to the first finger (diag. 9.162), indicates a
person who becomes totally and obsessively involved with his
career. Specialists are the only people to show this rare line.

The complete *absence* of a Fate Line indicates a person who
lacks stability and is unlikely ever to settle into a set pattern of
life. This commonly results in many different jobs and homes and
indeed, an adventurous, unorthodox life.

This lack of social stability, revealed by the missing line, is
common among alcoholics, drug addicts, delinquents, criminals
and all sorts of social misfits. It is therefore a danger signal.
Occasionally, the line is missing in an otherwise talented and
capable hand. Such people become successful, self-made business
people, often in several fields at the same time.

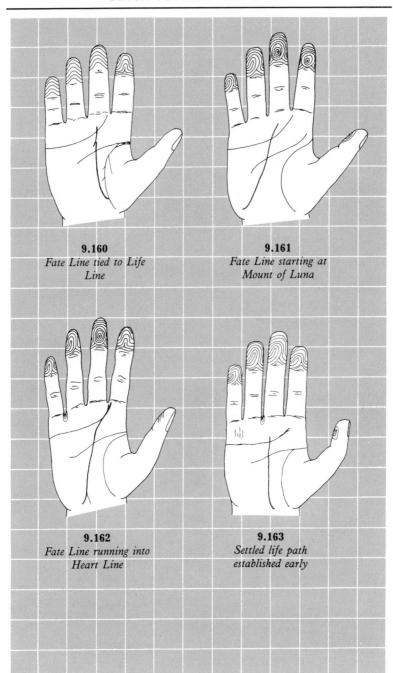

9.160
Fate Line tied to Life Line

9.161
Fate Line starting at Mount of Luna

9.162
Fate Line running into Heart Line

9.163
Settled life path established early

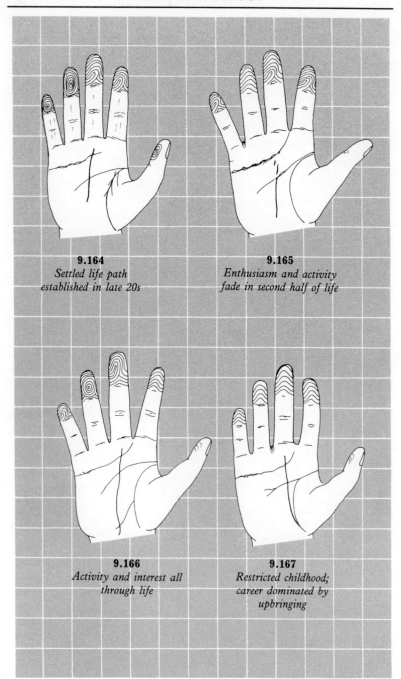

9.164
*Settled life path
established in late 20s*

9.165
*Enthusiasm and activity
fade in second half of life*

9.166
*Activity and interest all
through life*

9.167
*Restricted childhood;
career dominated by
upbringing*

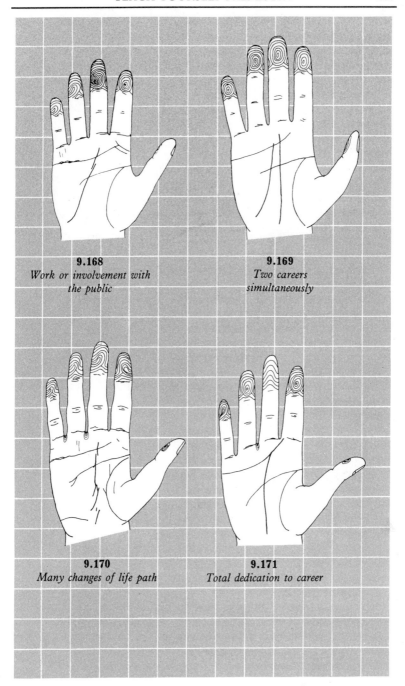

9.168
*Work or involvement with
the public*

9.169
*Two careers
simultaneously*

9.170
Many changes of life path

9.171
Total dedication to career

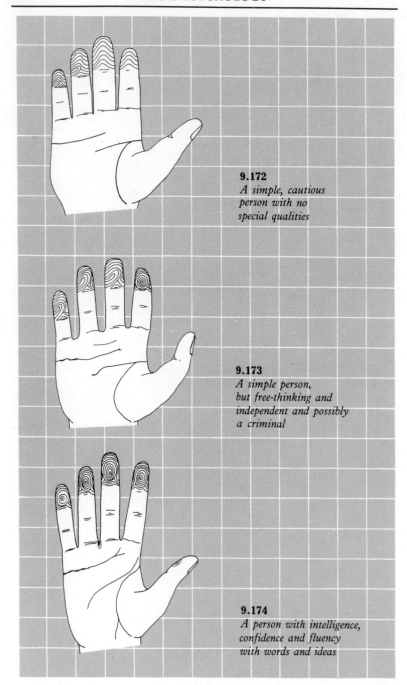

9.172
A simple, cautious person with no special qualities

9.173
A simple person, but free-thinking and independent and possibly a criminal

9.174
A person with intelligence, confidence and fluency with words and ideas

GENERAL COMMENTS ON THE FATE LINE
Diagrams 9.172–9.180
Old-fashioned palmists once believed that a long, straight Fate Line was a sign of great success. Certainly, many famous and successful people have this mark, but equally many dull, uninteresting people do as well. The line merely indicates a life dedicated to one path. Ability and talent are necessary to make that path one of public success. Classes of people who sometimes show strong Fate Lines are tramps and beggars. Such people who have pursued this lifestyle from childhood to death often have very long, bare Fate Lines.

Female hands are much more prone than male hands to show long Fate Lines, especially the classic female Water Hand.

Examine diagrams 9.172, 9.173 and 9.174, which show the hands of three very different people all without Fate Lines. What are the relevant features of each hand?

Diagram 9.172 shows a simple hand. All fingers are normal and very close together. Fingerprints consist of two arches and two loops. The hand has simple lines but no Fate Line. The hand shape is uncertain, possibly Fire or Earth.

Conclusion A simple, cautious person with no special qualities. The missing Fate Line indicates no sense of stability, but the close fingers counteract this. A dull, simple life.

Diagram 9.173 shows a simple hand, an Earth or Fire Hand. Fingers are spread apart. It has a short Saturn finger, poor index finger, and a stubby little finger with only two joints. Prints are loops, with one whorl on the Jupiter finger. The hand has simple lines, but no Fate Line.

Conclusion A simple person, but free-thinking and independent. Deviant tendencies (defective little finger) and poor stability (short Saturn). This person is *not* an upright citizen! He or she is a misfit, possibly a criminal.

Diagram 9.174 shows a long hand (Water type) but with whorl prints. It has long first and fourth fingers. The hand has simple lines of good quality and the Heart Line is forked. The Head Line extends almost from Jupiter. There is no Fate Line.

Conclusion This person has intelligence, confidence, fluency with words and ideas. Having no Fate Line, he or she will have an interesting, varied and unsettled life, but should be very successful in whatever he or she does.

Diagrams 9.175-9.180 show six more hands with various Fate Lines. On the following pages, you will find an analysis of each hand, integrating all the features.

Diagram 9.175 shows the very rare pointed fingers, a sign of inspiration and intuition. The fingerprints are all whorls, except one. There is a sensitivity line from the Heart Line down to the Life Line and two "idealistic" branches of the Heart Line onto Jupiter. The Head Line has two branches, curving down, and quite long. The Fate Line is tied to the Life Line. The hand is a Water Hand. Finger lengths are normal, though Saturn is a little long.

Conclusion An unusual, highly sensitive but stable person. Thoughtful, imaginative, feminine. The childhood years were restrictive.

Diagram 9.176 shows a very normal-looking Water Hand with no distinguishing characteristics. However, the lines are quite strong and well formed. There are no obvious weaknesses.

Conclusion The long, clear Fate Line suggests a life set on one path all the way through.

Diagram 9.177 shows a simple Fire Hand, with an Arch on the first finger, two whorls and a loop on Mercury. The Fate Line coming from Luna suggests contact with the public. There is a gap between the little finger and the ring finger, showing some deep-seated difficulty in relationships. There is a deeply curved Heart Line.

Conclusion This is a busy, active, energetic person who works with people in some way. He or she is warmhearted and emotional but has some relationship problem, possibly related to his work since he is psychologically stable in himself or herself.

Diagram 9.178 shows a Fire Hand, with whorls on the first and third fingers (individuality and art or creativity). There is a strong Fate Line from Luna. The Head Line curves down to Luna.

Conclusion Obviously this Fire person is imaginative, possibly creative, and public-oriented. It would be a good guess that he or she is a performer of some kind, and if you look at the "angles" of the thumb, you will see musical talent.

Diagram 9.179 shows the Water type. It has square tips, two whorls on the first fingers and a long index. The Head Line has a hook showing the ability to save money. Life and Head Lines are tied. There is a long, straight Fate Line.

Conclusion With his or her confidence, individuality, caution, attention to accuracy and method, and money-saving tendencies, this person seems set for a business career. The long clear Fate Line indicates that she commenced a life path of this sort quite early, and should continue in it.

Diagram 9.180 shows a Fire Hand with a predominance of arch fingerprints. The middle finger is short. The Heart and Head

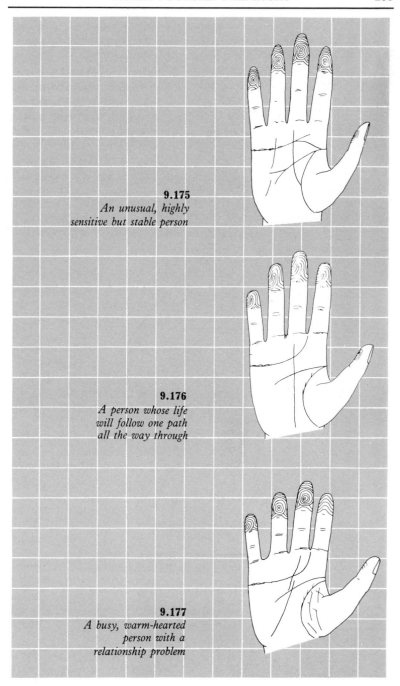

9.175
*An unusual, highly
sensitive but stable person*

9.176
*A person whose life
will follow one path
all the way through*

9.177
*A busy, warm-hearted
person with a
relationship problem*

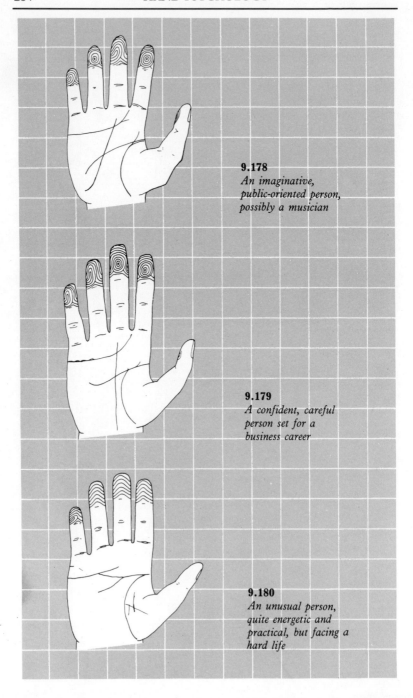

9.178
*An imaginative,
public-oriented person,
possibly a musician*

9.179
*A confident, careful
person set for a
business career*

9.180
*An unusual person,
quite energetic and
practical, but facing a
hard life*

Lines are short, with a Simian-type link between them. There is no Fate Line.

Conclusion The Simian pattern, arch prints, short Saturn and lack of Fate Line all point to someone who is not a typical citizen. However, the hand has no bad faults, and reveals some energy and practical skills. Within his or her limits, this person could play a worthwhile role but he will not have an easy time of it throughout life.

LESSON 9
MINOR LINES, MARKS AND SIGNS

THE GIRDLE OF VENUS

9.181
Simple Girdle of Venus

In its simplest form, this line runs in a curve above the Heart Line, below the second and third fingers (diag. 9.181). It is a sign of a sensitive personality, a person who reacts strongly to mental, emotional or spiritual stimulation. For this reason, it is common among poets and actors, and among highly strung people.

People with the line seldom have simple love lives. Oddities, ranging from sexual frigidity to a voracious or perverted sexual appetite often occur. The whole hand must be studied to determine what sort of oddity to expect.

A form of the line which runs *parallel to the Heart Line*, from the Saturn finger to the outer edge of the hand (diag. 9.182), suggests a person who needs stimulation in the love life. This

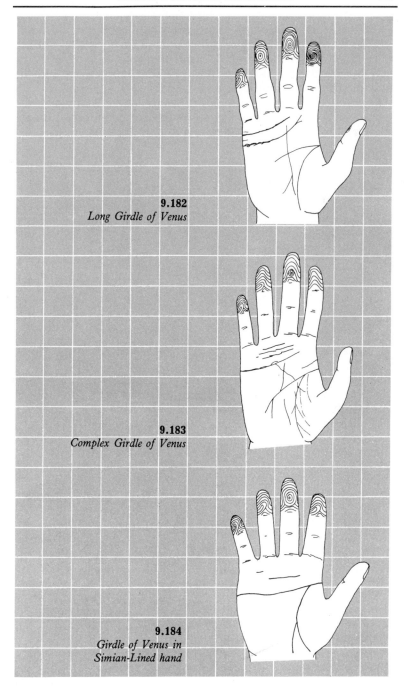

9.182
Long Girdle of Venus

9.183
Complex Girdle of Venus

9.184
*Girdle of Venus in
Simian-Lined hand*

leads to the person seeking many and varied romantic partners.

A Girdle of Venus made of *three or more* lines parallel to each other (diag. 9.183) indicates extreme qualities. A hand with the simple form usually belongs to a well-adjusted person, and the multiple form to neurotic or near-neurotic personalities.

A *partial* Girdle of Venus often occurs above a Simian Line (diag. 9.184). In such cases, it may be ignored completely. It does *not* have the usual significance in a Simian Line hand.

THE SUN LINE
(LINE OF APOLLO)

9.185
Sun line

The Sun Line is a vertical line running towards the ring finger (Apollo) (diag. 9.185). When present, it is usually quite short, and only rarely does it run from the base of the hand up to the finger. The meaning of the line is uncertain, but it appears to relate to happiness or creativity.

The line has less significance in a multi-lined hand than in a fairly bare one. In diagram 9.186A, the Sun Line would hardly warrant your attention. In diagram 9.186B the Sun Line is far more conspicuous and important.

The most common form of the line is a short bar above the Heart Line (diag. 9.187). People with this line are fairly friendly and cheerful. About 50 per cent of all hands show this line. Dr Eugene Scheimann claims that people with this line are capable of enjoying their retirement while those who lack it find early retirement empty and, consequently, die at an earlier age.

A rare form of the line *runs in a curve from the edge of the palm, high up, to the ring finger* (diag. 9.188). This shows an interest in self-development and metaphysics, e.g. yoga, meditation or mind development.

Unusually long lines, no matter where they start, are found on some highly creative people and, occasionally, on rich folk. The

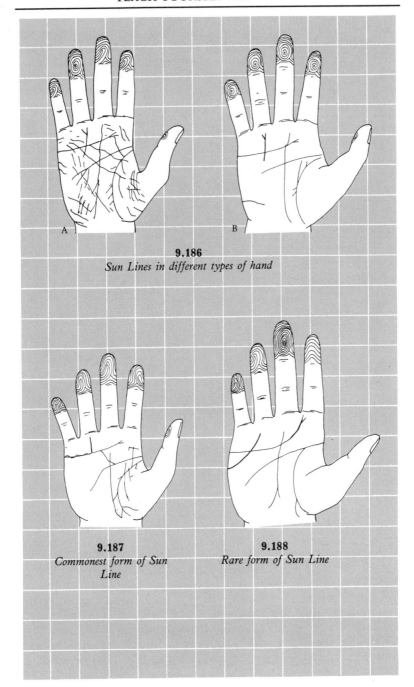

9.186
Sun Lines in different types of hand

9.187
Commonest form of Sun Line

9.188
Rare form of Sun Line

line therefore supports whatever signs of talent or interest are shown in the hand. Artists of all types are prone to showing the line. Because many rich and successful people have no Sun Line, it is foolish to draw any conclusion from its absence. However, people with this line do seem to *enjoy* what they do, while successful people with no Sun Line seem to get little pleasure out of their success.

The Sun Line is prone to *growing downwards* in the palm at any time when the person is pursuing a path which will lead to success, or at times when the person feels happy and successful.

THE HEALTH LINE

9.189
Health Line

This line runs diagonally from the base of the little finger to the base of the hand, usually either touching the Life Line or running close (diag. 9.189).

It relates partly to health, and partly to the subconscious mind. The line can come and go very easily, and of all the lines in the palm the Health Line is the most likely to appear or disappear in a matter of days.

Any strong form of the line, either a *long, slim, clear line* or *several parallel lines* running together, suggests some psychic or mediumistic ability. The long clear line particularly is associated with spiritualists and clairaudients.

A Health Line made of *many broken pieces* or fragments (diag. 9.190) indicates digestive problems.

A period of steady concentration or meditation can cause the line to develop in the hand.

There is a rare, *curved form* of the line (diag. 9.191) which is called the Line of Clairvoyance. It is found on some natural clairvoyants and some people of a highly mystical or spiritual nature.

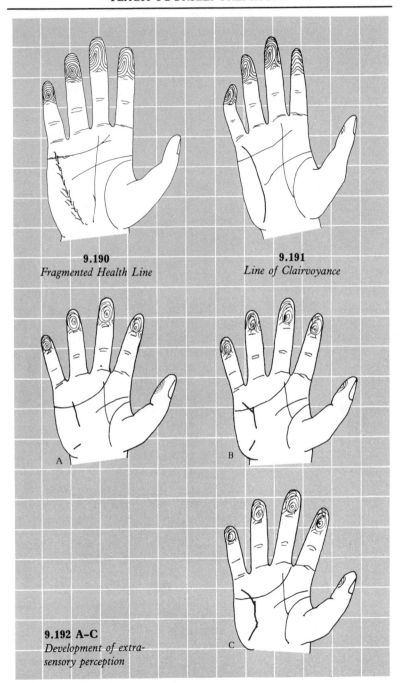

9.190
Fragmented Health Line

9.191
Line of Clairvoyance

A

B

9.192 A–C
Development of extra-sensory perception

C

Some people consciously develop clairvoyance and their hands reflect this through a sort of imitation Clairvoyant Line, made of *overlapping fragments* (diag. 9.192).

OTHER MARKS AND SIGNS

9.193
*The Ring of Solomon shows
a gift for understanding people*

The Ring of Solomon is a diagonal line under the base of the first finger (diag. 9.193). It shows a gift for understanding people. One could call this "psychological insight". It is not at all rare.

The Ring of Solomon sometimes appears *very well marked,* or *doubled-up* (diag. 9.194). These strong forms indicate real talent for psychology and tend to occur only in successful business-people or talented lawyers or psychologists. Such people are also prone to "playing hunches" and if they study astrology, ESP or kindred subjects, they invariably turn these studies to their own advantage.

A clear cross in between the Head and Heart Lines (diag. 9.195) is called the "Mystic Cross". It indicates an interest in the occult.

Two or three such crosses (diag. 9.196) indicate a strong belief in superstition or a very deep involvement in the occult arts.

A pattern of little vertical lines under the Mercury finger (diag. 9.197) reveals a gift for helping others, usually in a medical sense. Doctors, nurses, dentists and social workers often have these marks. It is usually known as the "Medical Stigmata" but some writers refer to it as "Samaritan Marks".

A bar line on the Mount of Luna (diag. 9.198) indicates strong reactions to chemicals and drugs. This can lead to medical difficulties. The bar line is known as the "Poison Line" or the "Hypothenar Bar". See Chapter VI for a full description.

An extension of this bar line (diag. 9.199) indicates craving for excitement or stimulation, in addition to the other effects. There

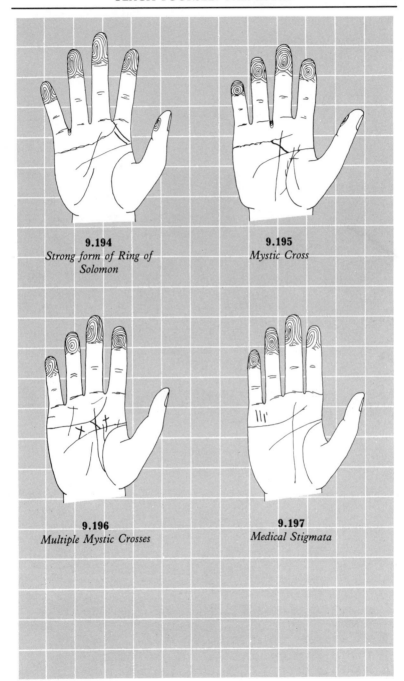

9.194
Strong form of Ring of Solomon

9.195
Mystic Cross

9.196
Multiple Mystic Crosses

9.197
Medical Stigmata

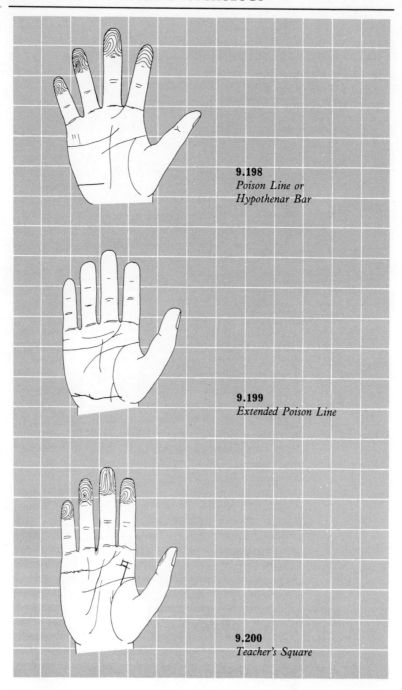

9.198
*Poison Line or
Hypothenar Bar*

9.199
Extended Poison Line

9.200
Teacher's Square

is a real danger of drug abuse or misuse with people who have this line.

A square formed by little lines on the Mount of Jupiter and attached to a rising line from the Life Line (diag. 9.200), indicates a talent for teaching or instructing other people. This is called the "Teacher's Square".

LESSON 10
SKIN-RIDGE PATTERNS

There are a number of patterns which can occur in the skin ridges of the palm. We have already studied the fingerprint patterns and the Loops of Seriousness and Humour. To complete our study of hands, you need to know the meaning of the less common patterns.

Besides the loops between the second and third fingers and the third and fourth fingers, there is sometimes a loop between the Jupiter and Saturn fingers (diag. 9.201). This is called the Raja Loop, because it is quite common among people who can trace their ancestry back to royalty or nobility. It is a sign of charisma, that subtle quality of personality which makes people notice and remember you. For this reason, there is a definite tendency for those with this mark to rise to the top of their field or profession.

Under each finger, there is a tiny triangular pattern formed by three skin ridges coming together (diag. 9.202). This pattern is called the tri-radius, and the exact position where each tri-radius falls tells something about the person concerned. Of all the tri-radii, the most important one, and the only one we shall consider here, is the tri-radius under the first, or Jupiter, finger.

The Jupiter tri-radius may appear in any one of three positions.
1. *Under the centre of the first finger*, which is the ordinary position (diag. 9.203).
2. Misplaced *towards the outside of the hand* (diag. 9.204), which indicates that the person is likely to be adventurous or unpredictable in some way. This pattern is found on people whose actions surprise or startle those around them.

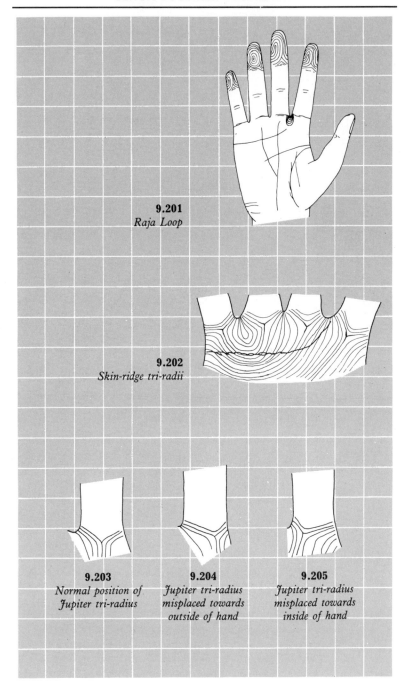

9.201
Raja Loop

9.202
Skin-ridge tri-radii

9.203
Normal position of Jupiter tri-radius

9.204
Jupiter tri-radius misplaced towards outside of hand

9.205
Jupiter tri-radius misplaced towards inside of hand

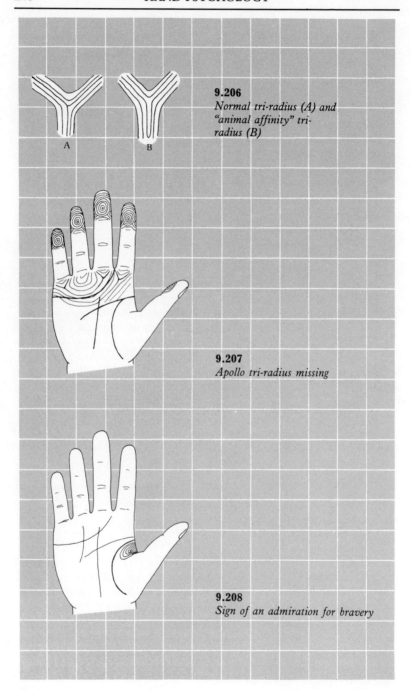

9.206
Normal tri-radius (A) and "animal affinity" tri-radius (B)

9.207
Apollo tri-radius missing

9.208
Sign of an admiration for bravery

3. Misplaced *towards the second finger* (diag. 9.205). The
   person with this pattern is cautious, making sure of
   everything before being committed.

The tri-radius *under the ring finger* (Apollo) is sometimes
formed in an unusual manner (diag. 9.206), which indicates an
affinity with animals. People with this mark can attract and
handle animals of all types and commonly are fond of four-footed
creatures. People with this mark who do not like animals still
have the animal affinity and when in a room with dogs or cats,
the pet will be attracted to the person!

Occasionally, the tri-radius under Apollo is completely *missing*
and the skin ridges simply curve around the base of the finger
(diag. 9.207). This indicates a lack of cheerfulness. People with
this mark find it difficult to enjoy life. If you know someone
with this pattern, encourage him or her to get more in touch with
his feelings. When he is doing something enjoyable, get him to
pause a moment to experience his own emotions. Help him to
become more aware of the happy moments in life. With this sort
of encouragement, his outlook on life may brighten. He may even
start to grow a Sun Line (page 238) across the Mount of Apollo.

A loop starting beside the thumb and running over the Mount
of Venus (diag. 9.208) indicates an admiration for bravery.

A loop starting at the edge of the hand, where the bottom of the
thumb merges into the wrist (diag. 9.209), indicates an
appreciation of brass-band music.

A little patch of skin ridges enclosed in a tiny oval on the
Mount of Venus (diag. 9.210), indicates a love of stringed-
instrument music.

There is a very rare loop starting at the base of the hand and
running upwards (diag. 9.211). It shows the ability to become
inspired. People with this loop have the ability to obtain
inspiration from "higher consciousness". Very sensitive,
creative people sometimes have this marking.

A loop entering the hand from the ulnar side, down on the
Mount of Luna (diag. 9.212), shows a gift for sensing
"vibrations" of places and objects.

A whorl on the Mount of Luna (diag. 9.213) shows a special gift
of imagination, which is the ability to visualise things so vividly
that they almost appear to be real. Such people "identify"
themselves with their daydreams.

An "S" bend print in this position (diag. 9.214) shows
"masculine" qualities when found in a woman's hand, i.e.
competitiveness, confidence and aggressiveness, and in a male
hand it indicates "feminine" qualities such as gentleness and
appreciation of artistic pleasures.

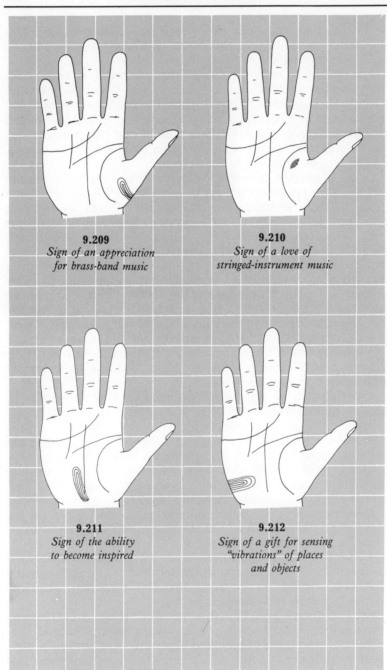

9.209
*Sign of an appreciation
for brass-band music*

9.210
*Sign of a love of
stringed-instrument music*

9.211
*Sign of the ability
to become inspired*

9.212
*Sign of a gift for sensing
"vibrations" of places
and objects*

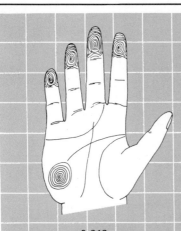

9.213
*Sign of a special gift
of imagination*

9.214
*Sign of "masculine" qualities
when found in a woman's
and of "feminine"
qualities in a man's hand*

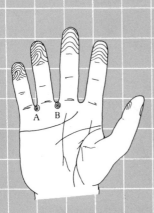

9.215
*Signs of humorous
sarcasm (A) and sarcasm
used as a weapon of
attack or defence (B)*

9.216
*Sign of a little
telepathic ability*

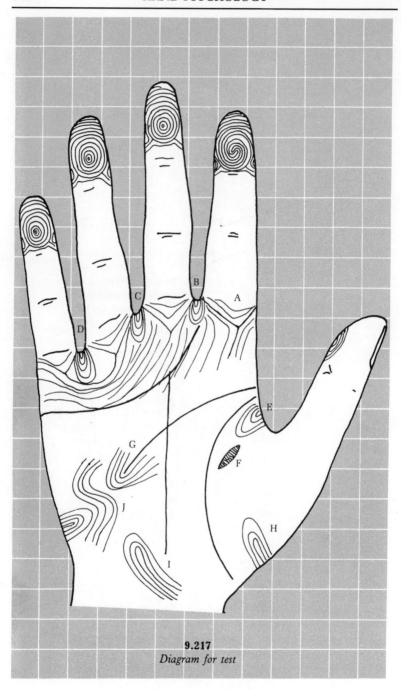

9.217
Diagram for test

Whorls occur very, very rarely in the positions where the Loop of Humour and the Loop of Seriousness are found (diag. 9.215). Only about one hand in a thousand would bear a whorl in these spots. But when found, they indicate humorous sarcasm when found in the humour position and the presence of sarcasm as a weapon of attack or defence when found in the seriousness position.

There is quite a common loop in the middle of the hand (diag. 9.216) which shows a little telepathic ability, usually a gift for sensing the moods of one's close relatives. This capacity is strongest when the Head Line runs downwards into this loop and particularly if there is a little pad of raised flesh exactly at that point.

Test yourself on this section by answering the following questions about diagram 9.217.

Questions

1. Identify the 11 patterns.

2. Which of the known patterns are *not* illustrated?

Answers

1. A. *Apex (tri-radius) misplaced to side of hand shows unpredictability or unreliability.*
B. *Presence of charisma; possibly royal blood.*
C. *Loop of Seriousness.*
D. *Loop of Humour.*
E. *Admiration for courage.*
F. *Liking for stringed-instrument music.*
G. *Telepathy with family members.*
H. *Love of brass music.*
I. *Inspiration.*
J. *"Masculine" qualities in female; "feminine" traits in male hand.*
K. *Gift for sensing "vibrations".*

2. *The sarcasm whorls; whorl on Luna, indicating vivid imagination; Jupiter apex leaning towards Saturn, indicating caution; animal affinity mark.*

3. What type of hand is
this?

3. *Fire hand.*

4. What psychological problem is revealed by this
hand?

4. *Low-set little finger reveals a parent problem.*

SOME TYPICAL HANDPRINTS

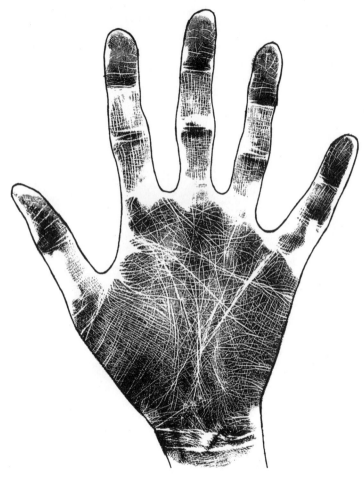

9.218

Diag. 9.218: THE FINE LINES OF A WATER HAND
This is an excellent example of a nervous hand covered with
thousands of fine lines. However, apart from this excessive
nervousness, the lines and marks in the hand are quite well-
balanced. The fingers are widely spaced and the fingerprints are
whorls.

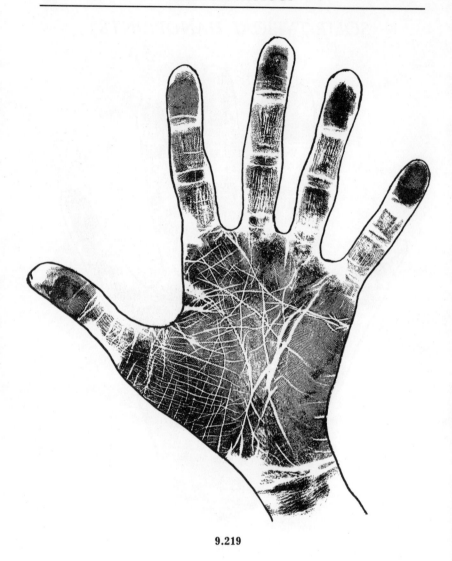

9.219

Diag. 9.219 HAND OF A SUPER-EXTROVERT

This is the hand of someone with boundless energy and innumerable interests. Note the widely spread fingers and thumb, and the many strong lines. The prints are all very clear whorls and there is a Loop of Seriousness as well as a Loop of Humour.

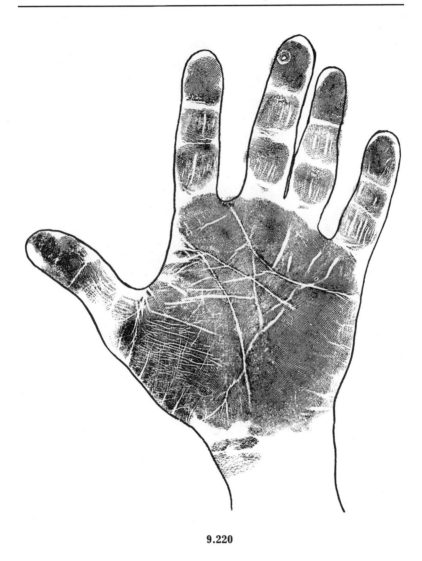

9.220

Diag. 9.220: AN EARTH HAND

This is a typical Earth Hand, except that the lines are rather finer than usual, indicating good intelligence. It belongs to the manager of a car sales yard, situated in the countryside outside a major city. Note the widely spaced index finger (showing his managerial ability) and his strong Loop of Seriousness.

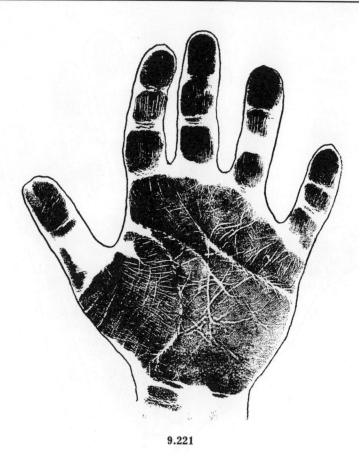

9.221

Diag. 9.221: THE HAND OF A TWO-YEAR-OLD BOY
This child's hand shows an excellent example of a low-set little
finger and a curved index finger. All the lines are clear and fine,
indicating a sensitive nature. He grew up under difficult
circumstances, losing both his parents. At 2 years of age, he
shows acute anxiety with associated psychological problems.

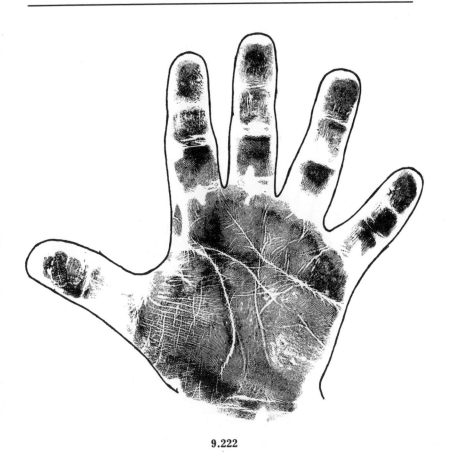

9.222

Diag. 9.222: HAND OF THE SAME BOY AT AGE SEVEN
See how this hand has dramatically improved. The index finger is
now straight and strong. The little finger is no longer low-set.
Several fine lines have vanished, while the remainder have
deepened and strengthened. Under the care of a loving relative,
this boy has overcome all his problems. He is now self-confident,
cheerful, full of energy — a pleasant, fun-loving youngster. Note
his strong Loop of Humour, visible both in this print and the
earlier one.

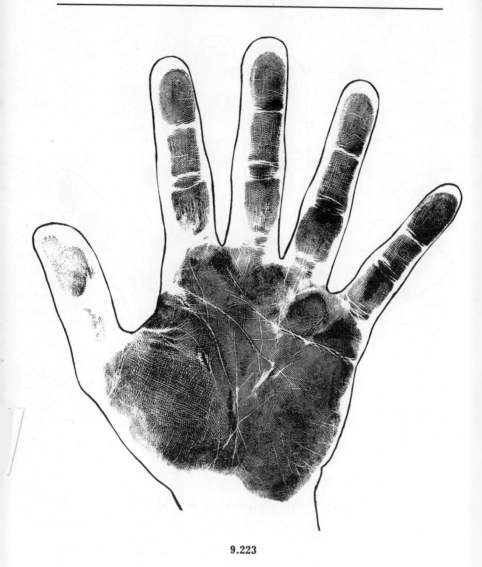

9.223

Diag. 9.224: THE HAND OF A PALMIST

This is an Air Hand, and from its widely spread fingers it obviously belongs to an extrovert. It belongs to the famous London palmist Mr Jackson Smith, who has pursued his work all over the world. Note the clear whorls on the first and fourth fingers.

BIBLIOGRAPHY

Many of the best books on scientific palmistry are out of print but some have been reprinted by an Indian Company, Sagar Publications, of Box 553, New Delhi, India. Libraries and used book stores may help you to find others.

THE BEST BOOKS AVAILABLE

Benham, W. G. *The Laws of Scientific Hand Reading*. 1900. G. P. Putnam's Sons, New York
Gettings, F. *Palmistry Made Easy*. 1973. Wilshire Book Co., Hollywood, USA
Hutchinson, B. *Your Life in Your Hands*. 1967. Sphere, Falmouth, UK
Jaquin, N. *The Hand of Man*. 1967. Sagar Publications, New Delhi
St Hill, K. *The Book of the Hand*. 1978. Sagar Publications, New Delhi

OTHER INTERESTING MODERN BOOKS

Altman, N. *The Palmistry Workbook*. 1984. Aquarian Press, Wellingborough, UK
Brenner, E. *The Hand Book*. 1979. Celestial Arts, Millbrae, USA
Hipskind, J. *Palmistry, The Whole View*. 1977. Llewelyn, St Paul, USA

SOME EXCELLENT OUT-OF-PRINT BOOKS

Gettings, F. *The Book of the Hand*. 1965. Paul Hamlyn, London
MacKenzie, N. *Palmistry for Women*. 1973. Warner, New York
Robinson, Mrs *The Graven Palm*. 1911. Herbert Jenkins, London
Scheimann, Dr E. *A Doctor's Guide to Better Health Through Palmistry*. 1969. Parker, West Nyack, USA

A complete bibliography of all palmistry books in the English language was privately published by Andrew Fitzherbert in 1979. It will be republished in 1986 as part of a larger text, *Recent Advances in Palmistry*, edited by Dr Geoff Dean and published by Recent Advances, Box 466, Subiaco, Western Australia 6008.